On the Far Side of Liglig Mountain

On the Far Side of Liglig Mountain

The Adventures of an American Family in Nepal

Thomas Hale

the author of Don't Let the Goats Eat the Loquat Trees

Zondervan Books
Zondervan Publishing House
Grand Rapids, Michigan

ON THE FAR SIDE OF LIGLIG MOUNTAIN:
ADVENTURES OF AN AMERICAN FAMILY IN NEPAL
Copyright © 1989 by Thomas Hale

Zondervan Books are published by
Zondervan Publishing House
1415 Lake Drive, S.E.
Grand Rapids, MI 49506

Library of Congress Cataloging-in-Publication Data

Hale, Thomas, 1937–
    On the far side of Liglig Mountain : adventures of an American family in Nepal / by
Thomas Hale.
    p.   cm.
    ISBN 0-310-21671-0
    1. Nepal—Description and travel. 2. Medical care—Nepal. 3. Hale, Thomas,
1937—   —Journeys—Nepal. 4. Missionaries, Medical—United States—Biography.
5. Missionaries, Medical—Nepal—Biography. I. Title.
    DS493.53.H35   1989
    610.69'5'092–dc20   89-31287
[B]   CIP

Unless otherwise noted, all Scripture references are taken from the *Holy Bible: New
International Version* (North American Edition), copyright © 1973, 1978, 1984 by the
International Bible Society. Used by permission of Zondervan Bible Publishers.

All rights reserved. No part of this publication may be reproduced, stored in a retrieval
system, or transmitted in any form or by any means—electronic, mechanical,
photocopy, recording, or any other—except for brief quotations in printed reviews,
without the prior permission of the publisher.

Edited by Linda Vanderzalm

Printed in the United States of America

89 90 91 92 93 94 / PP / 10 9 8 7 6 5 4 3 2 1

CONTENTS

THE COST OF DISCIPLESHIP

INTRODUCTION

"NEW MEDICAL WORK begins in remote and forbidden Himalayan kingdom. Christian physicians and nurses urgently needed."

So read the front leaf of a little pamphlet I picked up in 1954, during my junior year at Phillips Academy in Andover, Massachusetts. The pamphlet went on to describe the opening of a new mission work in the far-off kingdom of Nepal, a kingdom which until recently had been completely closed to the outside world. I was sixteen. Only three days earlier, I had vividly experienced the presence of God for the first time, and had told God that I would give my life to Him. Now as I read this pamphlet, I concluded that God must be telling me to go to Nepal as a medical missionary; and so I said yes. The transaction was as simple as that. I had little notion of what I was getting into.

My friends and teachers smiled at my decision. My parents wondered how many months it would take for me to grow out of it. But as for me, looking back, I can't recall a time since that decision when I planned to be anything else but a medical missionary to Nepal.

Through the rest of high school and college, God bombarded me with books and articles about Nepal and about missionary life in general. However, I wouldn't want to give the impression that my mind was always focused on the goal. I spent more time during my three years at the University of Arizona climbing mountains than I did studying. At the end of the three years I entered medical college in Albany, New York, where on the first day of classes I met my future wife, Cynthia—across a cadaver in the anatomy lab. We were lab partners.

Cynthia had also gone into medicine with the idea of becoming a medical missionary. She, too, had given her life to Christ in high school. Though a gifted piano player, she turned down a full scholarship to the Julliard School of Music in order to pursue pre-medical studies at the University of Rochester. She chose to turn her back on a career as a concert pianist, rather than disobey God's call to become a medical missionary.

She expected, however, to go to the mission field single, as she was sure that she'd find no eligible male in her hometown of Albany, New York. That was, until she was introduced to me, courtesy of the silent, formalin-filled figure lying on the anatomy table between us.

Things moved right along after that. Having met in Anatomy, we married in Pathology—second year of medical school.

After finishing our specialty training—Cynthia in pediatrics and I in general surgery—we spent two years in the Army, during one year of which I was stationed in Vietnam. Then in 1970 we went off to Nepal with two little boys, along with ten crates and twenty-nine drums of household goods and medical supplies. It had been sixteen years from the time of our original call to be missionaries until our plane touched down in Kathmandu, Nepal. Now our Nepal adventure was to begin.

Nepal today, as it was then, is one of the poorest countries in the world. The Tennessee-sized kingdom lies between India and Tibet, straddling the highest section of the Himalayan mountain range. Eight of the ten highest mountains in the world rise within her borders. Eighty-five percent of Nepal's land area is not arable; that leaves the remaining fifteen percent to support a population of eighteen million people.

Until 1951, Nepal had remained a hermit kingdom, virtually isolated from the rest of the world. Nepal's isolation was partly the result of geography, and partly the result of the policies of her rulers, who desired to keep out any foreign influence which might threaten their hold on the country. A bloodless revolution in 1951 restored the ancient and legitimate line of kings to power, after which Nepal opened her doors to the outside world and invited the industrialized nations to assist in the development of the country. Not only did the governments of developed nations start programs to assist Nepal, but many non-government agencies joined in the effort as well. Among these were a number of Christian mission organizations, the largest of which was the mission to which we belong, the United Mission to Nepal.

The United Mission now has about four hundred missionaries in Nepal, working in the fields of health, education, agriculture, and rural development. Among its various projects, the United Mission runs four hospitals. One of these hospitals, the one to which Cynthia and I were assigned, was located way out in the foothills seventy miles northwest of Kathmandu (as a crow flies), near the top of a 4,700-foot mountain called Liglig Mountain. The hospital had just opened when we arrived in 1970. It was, in the beginning, the only modern medical facility for a population of half a million people spread over an area the size of Rhode Island. There was another interesting thing about this hospital: You had to walk fifteen miles to get to it. The last half of the trail took you up the slopes of Liglig Mountain, and then around its far side to the village of Amp Pipal, where the hospital was located.

The hospital came into being through the vision of a pioneer missionary from Canada, Dr. Helen Huston, who had started working in Amp Pipal long before we arrived. It has been our privilege to work closely with Dr. Helen over many years. A more Godly women we have never known.

Because of the centuries of isolation, Nepal virtually has been catapulted into the twentieth century. Even after three decades of foreign aid, the rural areas remain much as they have been for generations. The first wheel that many of the hill people ever saw was the wheel of an airplane. Since the early 1950s, a tremendous social upheaval has been taking place, as young Nepalis, newly exposed to the age of technology, strive to become educated and thus escape the drudgery of subsistence farming. But there is still much resistance to change. And one of the major areas of such resistance is religion.

Nepal is a Hindu theocracy. Over eighty percent of the people are Hindu, the remainder being mostly Buddhist. The people consider their king to be an incarnation of the Hindu god Vishnu. The law forbids Nepalis to change their religion, and those who do so are liable to a one-year jail sentence. A pastor who is caught baptizing a new convert can receive a six-year sentence. Even if Nepal Christians escape going to jail, they invariable are ostracized by their families, friends, and neighbors. Nepali Christians pay a high price to follow Christ. Yet, in spite of that price, the church in Nepal today is growing rapidly. Forty years ago, there was not a single Christian in the country; today there are many thousands.

It is understandable that the government of Nepal regards missionaries with mixed feelings. Nepali leaders value our professional and technical help, but they want it without our religion. Thus we are invited to work in the country as long as we agree not to "proselytize," which we interpret to mean public and aggressive evangelism. But we are free to practice our own religion, which of course includes witnessing discreetly to our own faith and participating in the life of the Nepali church. Foreign missionaries have never planted churches or baptized new believers. The church in Nepal is truly an indigenous church, self-governing and self-propagating.

We have been greatly privileged to work together with Nepali leaders to alleviate the suffering of their people. These leaders are highly trained and motivated; they are also fully competent to lead their nation in the years ahead. But the years ahead will be difficult. Nepal's population is doubling every thirty years, and already the Nepalis have run out of land. In the past fifteen years alone, Nepal has lost one third of its forests to the woodman's axe. These major issues, together with many others, threaten the success of development programs. Although great strides have been made in these past three decades, the obstacles to further improving the people's lives are enormous. Nepal needs help today as much as it ever has.

Not only have we been privileged to work with Nepal's leaders, but we have also been blessed and inspired by our fellowship with the Nepali Christians, most of whom have sacrificed much more for their Lord than we have. It has been a joy to stand with them as they seek to spread the light of the Gospel throughout their land.

This book describes some of our experiences living among the Nepali people on the far side of Liglig Mountain. In the book *Don't Let the Goats Eat the Loquat Trees* (Zondervan, 1986), I have described some of my adventures as a surgeon working in the Amp Pipal Hospital. In what follows, we relate a broader range of experiences, not only as doctors but also as a family and as fellow believers with our Nepali brothers and sisters in Christ. It is to these Nepali believers that this book is dedicated.

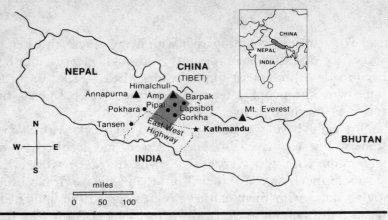

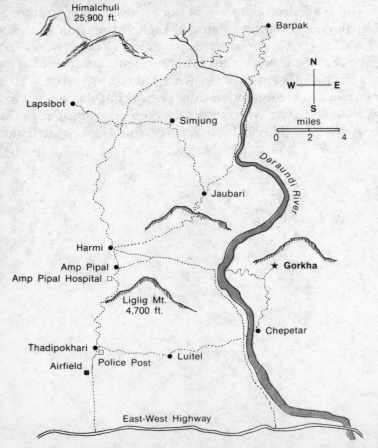

Life on Liglig Mountain

The FPO

*W*HEN CYNTHIA, the boys, and I first went to Nepal in 1970, we stayed for several months in the capital city, Kathmandu, learning the language and adjusting to the culture in preparation for our move to Liglig Mountain, where we had been assigned to do medical work. We got some of our first lessons in cultural adjustment in a most unexpected place— Kathmandu's Foreign Post Office, otherwise known as the FPO.

The FPO is a department of His Majesty's government, originally established to control the importing of goods through the parcel post. Housed in a large, modern building, it can be easily identified by the words "Foreign Post Office" in bold red letters across its front. At first glance, foreigners are reassured just to see this post office as they go down the main street of Kathmandu; they get the impression that they've been singled out for special consideration in the delivery of their parcels. And indeed they have.

My first visit to the FPO took place in October, 1970. A friend told me he'd seen a package there for the Hales, this friend having chanced upon it while searching for one of his own packages, about which yet another friend had told him. I arrived on a hot day. Having found no one to help me, I began wandering down the long corridors into offices and sorting rooms, most of which were strewn with packages in various stages of disruption, some of them partially opened. Then I entered a large room in the back, where hundreds of parcels lay in heaps all over the floor or on shelves. Around the periphery of the room were desks at which young men sat chatting, reading magazines, or just relaxing. I mumbled something about my having a package here, and they waved me on, indicating that I could look for it if I liked. It was evidently self-service.

I looked. For about forty minutes. It became a challenge not to be given up lightly. I was learning a great deal about the FPO, even on this first visit. Finally, as I was on the verge of quitting, I caught the name "Hale" on a tiny package the size of a cake of soap. I grabbed for it, only to discover that it was addressed to another Hale, who also happened to be living in Kathmandu. That was a disappointment. I left the FPO forty-five minutes after I'd arrived, with all the clerks still sitting in the same places I'd seen them at first. That was to be my most benign and uneventful visit to the FPO.

Soon after this, another friend told me I had a package in the FPO. I smiled, thanked him, and told him I knew about the package, but it was for a different Hale. But he persisted that it was for me. So with some hesitation, and my wife's encouragement, I went again to the FPO.

This day was hotter than the first, and unfortunately I had a tight schedule. Two mistakes already. Everything looked the same, the same clerks sitting in the same places. I was allowed into the Great Package Room again, and as before, I benefited from the same assistance in locating my parcel.

I had no idea what I was looking for. I didn't know what the package contained or who had sent it. In fact, we had instructed our family and friends not to mail us packages. At that time we weren't permitted to receive more than two parcels per person per year, and we wanted, therefore, to be sure that those two parcels contained items that were really crucial. The clerks at the FPO kept track of how many parcels each person received by marking the person's passport and entering the person's name in a Great Package Book. When I found my package, I would have to decide whether to have my passport marked or simply not to accept the package. I hoped to get a clue to its contents by looking at the green customs label that is always affixed to every international parcel.

After searching for fifty-five minutes—I'd allowed myself one hour—I actually found the package. It was from my mother.

During my search, none of the six clerks in the package room had left his seat except one who twice had to prevent me from going into small side rooms that were also filled with interesting-looking parcels. He informed me that the parcels belonged to people that either had died in Nepal or couldn't be located. That explanation stimulated my imagination because I had distinctly seen in one of these rooms a package addressed to Dr. Bethel Fleming, one of the founders of the United Mission, who was at that time very much alive and living in Kathmandu. Nearly everyone of importance in Kathmandu knew Bethel and her husband, who was the secretary of the Kathmandu Rotary International. If she could be "dead and unlocatable" in the eyes of the FPO, what about the rest of us? I reassured myself that perhaps the package had just been thrown there by accident. I later learned, however, that other people also had seen in the "dead and unlocatable" section parcels for various active mission personnel.

In any event I held on securely to my diminutive package and walked out to the customs room. The seven clerks I'd seen at the customs counter on my way in were now in a frenzy of activity. Apparently, while I was hunting for my parcel, some man had found a large package that contained Christmas presents for himself and his family. As the clerks inspected the man's package, they found it contained fifteen or twenty smaller packages, all nicely gift-wrapped in attractive Christmas paper.

I watched as these clerks descended on the large carton like birds of prey: two ripped open the small packages, a third inspected their contents, two more tried to reconstruct the opened parcels, while a sixth tied them up with string from other packages that lay in fragments about the room. (I suspect these package fragments had belonged to people who decided the packages weren't worth accepting as one of the year's two allotted packages.) A seventh clerk busily recorded the contents of each parcel on a separate 2′ by 3′ sheet of paper and then rushed off to what must have been the customs evaluation room. There five men leafed through huge books of interminable lists, computing the duty they would inflict on this man's Christmas presents.

Looking at that distraught victim standing powerless as his family's packages were dismantled, I gained perspective about my own difficulties and began to calm down. I figured that, for me, the worst of the business was already over. This man's plight unsettled me a little, but then I had only one small package. My package wouldn't take long.

I still had to decide whether or not to accept the package. But my decision was complicated by two facts: The package was from my mother, and she hadn't specified on the customs slip what it contained. After thinking about it, I decided to accept it. After all, no one else would be sending us packages, and I couldn't risk offending my mother by refusing to take it. So I stepped up to the counter.

Thirty minutes later, having finally disposed of Mr. Merry Christmas, the clerks were ready for me. They opened my package. A peculiar expression passed over their faces and then upon mine. From a distance I couldn't quite make out what my mother had sent me, but drawing closer, I saw that it was a set of homemade Christmas-tree decorations: tiny little angels or elves with golden hair and with bodies made from gold-painted pine cones. Well, that was touching—six of them—and exquisitely done. They were far nicer than an old plastic ball or bell or store-made Santa Claus—really a delightfully appropriate gift, especially since Christmas-tree decorations weren't available in Kathmandu. In fact, that was the problem: Christmas-tree decorations, it turned out, weren't included in the Great Customs Book of the Foreign Post Office.

The customs clerks rose to the challenge. There was much discussion and argument. I told them the elves were Christmas-tree decorations—homemade at that—but that didn't help the clerks. In fact, it didn't help them at all. The officials in the customs appraisal room pored over their lists. They carried the little elves all over the post office so that other clerks could try to identify and evaluate them. Other clerks came out of their offices to discover the cause of the commotion. At one time as many as twenty people had congregated in heated debate over how to classify the smiling objects.

After another half hour they settled on something that everyone could agree on, though I didn't catch the particulars. In the end I was asked to pay a duty of one rupee (eight cents) on the elves, a small gain for their effort, I thought. One thing I had discovered for sure: There were more clerks in the FPO than first met the eye.

As I reached in my pocket to get out a rupee, a clerk handed me a slip stating I owed three rupees. The other two rupees were for duty on the *postage* of the package. It was interesting to pay more duty on the postage than on the contents. It was interesting to pay duty on the postage at all. It was interesting just being in the Foreign Post Office. I got out two more rupees.

But I couldn't pay in that room. I forget how many more offices I had to go to and how many clerks had to stamp or sign the many forms before I paid my money and got out. As I stepped into the street, I vowed I'd never darken the door of the Foreign Post Office again as long as I lived.

I was hardly outside, however, when I suddenly remembered that the package hadn't been marked on my passport. Now I'm not a compulsive stickler for rules, and the thought that I may have put something over on the FPO by escaping the passport marking didn't particularly prick my conscience. But I was seized with an irresistible curiosity to know whether they had overlooked doing it (perhaps disoriented by some special power of the elves) or whether perhaps it was no longer necessary. Maybe the two-parcel-per-year law had been changed.

Forgetting my newly made resolution, I went back in and inquired. To my amazement, I was told that the law had been changed that very week! Any foreigner could now receive an unlimited number of packages. What exciting news! There would be duty to pay, of course, but it was good news nonetheless for all our mission people, none of whom had yet heard about it.

Well, after that episode, the FPO faded from my mind. We wrote home, of course, asking for twenty items we wanted our friends and family to send us immediately and suggesting a few dozen more items they could send at their leisure—say, within the next week or so.

Soon the packages began to come. At least for six months. Then the government changed the law back again. We might have accepted it philosophically, except that we were expecting at least a dozen packages that were already en route. Naturally, everyone else was caught by surprise in the same way. It wasn't long before we heard that parcels were piled one-third of the way to the ceiling of the Great Package Room. The vision of those piles rising higher and higher even led some of us to hope that the law might be changed back again when the packages reached the ceiling.

We hoped in vain. The law didn't change. And our problem didn't change either. Packages addressed to us continued to arrive, among them packages that contained highly perishable and expensive rabies vaccine, an assortment of medical supplies, and a variety of other worthwhile items.

Having determined to spend no more time in the FPO, I let

Cynthia formulate a master scheme for extricating our goods. I was, of course, urged to go and see—just see—the mountains of packages extending by this time halfway to the ceiling. I wasn't interested.

But Cynthia's brother, Dicran, who along with Cynthia's mother was visiting at the time, was interested. He received a notice indicating that a package had arrived for him. Thinking it might be some special American medicine he was expecting, Dicran determined to go to the FPO. Since I was his host, I naturally felt obliged to go too. Besides, I was curious to see the Great Package Room again. I figured I might even enjoy the visit since I wouldn't be trying to get something out for myself this time.

When we arrived at the FPO, Dicran gave his little slip of paper to a man who said he would take care of it. While we were waiting, we noticed a somewhat agitated Westerner engaged in a slight altercation with another clerk. He had received an envelope with six or eight colored prints in it—developed pictures—and was required not only to have his passport marked but also to pay duty. He was getting more and more excited. We watched with a mixture of sympathy and amusement. Finally an English-speaking clerk, who was obviously of a higher station than the others, came out. He attempted to console the owner of the prints in a roundabout way by pointing out that it wasn't just prints that were being singled out—he couldn't receive tapes either, for example; even if he were blind and could get mail only in the form of tapes, he'd still be limited to two parcels a year. The implication, I guess, was that he should keep quiet and be thankful he wasn't blind.

We had no chance to assess the effectiveness of this approach, however, because just then our clerk appeared with Dicran's tiny package—I think no more than twenty minutes had passed. Unfortunately, it wasn't the medicine that Dicran had been counting on. Instead it was some developed slides.

Dicran was happy enough to see the slides, but he had a problem clearing them through customs. The clerks in the customs inspection room began to open the box for examination. When Dicran asked why the clearly marked box of slides needed to be inspected, he was told it was routine. He was also told there was no duty for developed film, which made us wonder why the other man with the prints had been charged duty. Possibly Dicran wasn't being charged duty because his pictures were so bad—they being the first he had taken with a new camera. The slides seemed to entertain the customs clerks immensely, however, and were distributed around for all to enjoy, producing snickers of laughter wherever they went.

Then the writing began. We had already meticulously filled out a number of forms just to get the film from the package room to the customs counter. The slides were duly registered in the large 2' by 3' ledger and then whisked off to the customs appraisal room where clerks filled out more forms to indicate why duty was not charged on this package. These forms had to be marked, signed, or stamped by several different clerks.

After finishing the forms exempting us from duty, we went to the duty-payment room where we filled out two more forms, making official the fact that the duty-receiving clerks didn't have to receive payment from us. We were given receipts for every transaction and nontransaction. Finally we reached the passport-marking room, where more clerks recorded all the pertinent details of Dicran's passport and then filled out another form certifying that they had indeed got one. I thought for a moment that someone might fill out a second form certifying that the first had been filled out, but that wasn't necessary. We were given a final receipt to add to the eight slips of paper we'd already accumulated, the duplicate and triplicate copies of which would soon be forever filed in the Great Filing Rooms of the FPO. Having learned what was required to recover a box of slides, I've been thankful ever since that our initial household shipment of twenty-nine drums hadn't come through the FPO.

However, we still faced the reality that not only had Dicran not received his medicine, but we also hadn't received the twenty parcels of our own that by this time had arrived in the FPO.

When she heard about our latest adventures, Cynthia decided to take on the project of retrieving our parcels. Prodded on by her mother, who proclaimed the situation to be an international outrage, Cynthia proceeded full speed ahead to demonstrate that where there's a will there's a way.

Surmising that forms were the "in thing" at the FPO, Cynthia began making out forms of her own, forms applying for special permission to import more than two packages a year. Well, you ask, why didn't we do this right off? Well, I reply, we needed a different form for every addressee, for every country of origin, and for different periods of shipment. The contents of each shipment had to be carefully itemized and valued, which wouldn't have been easy since we didn't even know the contents of many of the packages, much less their value. Then there was a fee for each form, of course. In spite of these difficulties, Cynthia eventually filled out seven such applications and sent them to our mission agent for processing. But six weeks later they were still sitting in the agent's file. The reason? Unless each package was worth over 200 rupees, the forms were invalid. Cynthia, typically, had undervalued everything in order to keep the duty down, and each package had come out with a value of less than 200 rupees.

Well, she explored other avenues. She tried to get special letters stating we had medical supplies for the Nepali people, but nothing worked. Undeterred, Cynthia launched a final assault. She had heard that several people had taken letters declaring that their packages were personal goods and not for import, and somehow they'd actually gotten their parcels out. So, having made the necessary preparations, Cynthia and her mother arrived at the FPO armed with medical letters, mission letters, and passports. At the very least she was going to get out two packages on her passport. She had forgotten to bring my passport with her and so missed the chance to retrieve four parcels instead of two.

I hardly need mention how the "official-form-approach" ended up. Cynthia and her mother had arrived at the FPO a little before noon, and within ten minutes every one of Cynthia's forms had been rejected on one pretext or another. But Cynthia still had her secret weapon, a special letter written by our mission executive secretary, asserting with forceful, if inscrutable, logic that Cynthia was entitled to obtain *all* of her twenty packages, supporting this contention with a variety of arguments designed to meet the different objections that might be raised at the FPO. It was a careful blend of bluster and special pleading.

Cynthia handed this letter to an eager-looking clerk, who promptly disappeared into the interior of the building and wasn't seen again for forty-five minutes. Eventually, the clerk reappeared, and packages began to be found. A half dozen were brought out from one or more of the inner rooms of the post office and placed on the customs counter. Then Cynthia was actually allowed into the Great Package Room (under close supervision) to look for others. After another hour and a half, they had found a total of sixteen packages. Two crucial packages, refrigerator parts and laboratory equipment, couldn't be located.

It was now 3:30, and the FPO would close promptly at 4:00. A clerk informed Cynthia that she'd better stop looking and start clearing or she'd end up with no parcels at all. So with the sixteen packages laid out on the customs counter, Cynthia announced that they should start clearing them at once because she was taking them *all*. How was she going to do that, they asked, since she was entitled to only two? I have a special letter, she answered. Where's the letter?

Yes, where was the letter? I gave it to *this* boy, says Cynthia. I gave it to *that* boy says this boy. I gave it to *her* (Cynthia's mother) says that boy. Well, mother couldn't remember having received the letter. She looked everywhere—the minutes ticking by—it was 3:40. She didn't have it. Yes, she must have it. No, she didn't. Why should she be hiding it when they so desperately needed it? And furthermore, she never remembered receiving it.

Considering the frame of mind in which the FPO places a person, poor mother could well have eaten the letter without knowing it—much less remembering it. In any event, the letter was nowhere to be found. Thus hope of clearing all sixteen packages suddenly vanished.

Never at a loss when it comes to getting what is hers, Cynthia next tried for at least six packages, two for her and two each for our two children. The customs clerk asked for her passport, and when she claimed she had gotten out no packages on her passport in a year and a half, he didn't believe her. The Great Passport Marking Book was fetched and the hundreds of names reviewed—no Cynthia. Cynthia took heart. Were the children's names written in the passport? Yes, said Cynthia, hastily writing their names on the front page of the passport where the addresses go. After consulting for several minutes, the clerks refused to assign any packages to the children's names.

Having gotten nowhere with the "official-form" and "special-letter" approaches, Cynthia tried the "I-want-to-see-the-post-master" approach. This might have worked except that the postmaster had gone home for the day. His deputy was there, however, a nice young man, sensitive and considerate. Cynthia immediately switched to the "dear-kind-and-sympathetic-sir-I'm-just-a-poor-lonely-girl" approach, an approach she had spent the last thirty years of her life perfecting. To my knowledge, it had never failed. Today it would meet its severest test.

The young deputy postmaster softened like an asparagus

shoot in hot water. He said he couldn't do anything without consulting the central customs department at Singha Durbar, the main government office building in another part of town, but he'd be only too happy to call over there and let her speak to the director of customs. Cynthia, feeling her old powers awakening, eagerly took the phone, only to discover that the director had also gone home for the day. But the deputy director of customs could speak with her. Ah, that was even better— deputies were right down her alley. With stone-melting eloquence, Cynthia delivered a five-minute, nonstop lamentation on her four hours in the FPO, weaving together with subtle artistry the "official-form," "special-letter," "I-want-to-see-the-postmaster," and "I'm-a-poor-lonely-girl" approaches. When she had finished, there was a long pause at the other end of the line. Had the fellow understood English?

Yes, he had. His first words were: "Now lady, you listen to me!" It's unlikely that Cynthia really absorbed his five-minute reply. Indisputable though her artistry was, equally indisputable had been its ineffectiveness. She vaguely recollects his mentioning something about more special application forms. It was 4:00.

Cynthia came down to collect her two packages. When the clerk asked for the special receipt, Cynthia didn't have it; a clerk was sent upstairs to get it, but returned saying the special receipt filler had gone home. Cynthia rushed back up to her friend, the deputy postmaster, who rushed off to find a way to get the receipt filled.

Meanwhile, mother guarded the packages. While Cynthia was upstairs this last time, the clerks began to take the sixteen packages back into the Great Package Room, including, of course, the two packages to which Cynthia was still entitled. Mother began to decompensate. If she could have decompensated in the Nepali language it might have been more effective. She was helpless. Cynthia rushed down again with the receipt.

There was a scene, I believe—the accounts are confused. Somehow, the customs clerks were delayed fifteen minutes and the two packages were actually obtained. It must have been one of those never-to-be-forgotten finales. I'm glad I wasn't there.

The story of the remaining packages still incarcerated in the recesses of the FPO will never be fully told, because none of the principals can talk about it without beginning to mutter incoherently, their memories disordered by the complexity of subsequent events. The packages themselves contained many intriguing items, such as tulip bulbs, which by the time they were liberated had sprouted and were growing out of their box. Since those early days, I'm happy to say, sweeping changes in the operation of the FPO have taken place, and I'm given to understand that today it's a fine and efficient institution. However, I've not personally verified these favorable reports, though when I'm in town I do pass by the FPO from time to time—on the opposite side of the street.

In the midst of these negotiations with the FPO, we left Kathmandu to take up our assignment at the mission hospital in Amp Pipal, a village a long day's journey to the northwest. It's here that our real story begins.

A Day in the Life of My Wife

*W*E HAD COME to Nepal to do medical work: I to do surgery and Cynthia to do pediatrics. But in those early years, Cynthia was busy as a full-time wife and mother. When I left for work each morning and trudged lightheartedly down the path into the world of medicine, I had little idea what I was missing. For when I stepped out the front door each day, it was not to enter the arena but to leave it. If you want to know what missionary life is really like and who the real missionary heroes are, then you need to spend a day at our house in Amp Pipal with my wife, Cynthia. Just one day ought to do; it's possibly all you could take.

Since any day will serve our purpose, I'll just select one—a day back in August 1972. It was in the middle of the rainy season. Our older son, Tommy, was six years old at the time, and his brother, Christopher, was three. We had been in Nepal two years.

This particular day had begun early for Cynthia. She had been aroused at 5:00 by a commotion in the boys' room. A dispute had arisen over a pet frog that Tommy was holding, tightly squeezed, in his fist.

"That's my frog!"

"No, it's not. You have your own frogs, Christopher. Go play with them."

"I don't know where they are."

Christopher didn't know where his frogs were because he had

let them out of their box the evening before; and since one frog in hand (Tommy's hand) was better than three of his own loose in the house, that was the one he wanted. However, before the frog in question was pulled to pieces, Cynthia appeared, cheerful and rested from the night's sleep. With the frog rescued and the dispute settled, the day began.

The first order of business was to light the wood cooking stove. Cynthia had enough difficulty in the rainy season getting paper to burn, let alone wood, so you can imagine the scene. To begin with, it was still dark. Then she found a large, potbellied spider with a three-inch leg span sitting on the handle of the burner. She killed it without flinching.

Cynthia put on her poncho and groped her way through the early morning mist to the outdoor woodshed, raking down with her face three new spider webs in the ten-foot journey. It was raining. It had rained most of the night. It would rain much of the day.

The wood was damp, as it had been for two months. Firewood wasn't available during the rains, so you were supposed to stock up in the dry season—which Cynthia thought she'd done. But now her supply was almost gone, and we faced nearly two more months of monsoons. One problem was that Cynthia's stove consumed prodigious amounts of wood. The heat didn't circulate properly, and most of it went up the chimney. It took a roaring blaze to get the oven hot enough to cook anything, and then whatever it was would get cooked on one side and not on the other. The second problem was that Cynthia hadn't bought enough wood in the first place. She hadn't been willing to pay as much for the wood as the other missionary wives had been paying, so the firewood sellers stopped coming to our house. By the time Cynthia found out her mistake, the rains had arrived, and no more wood could be purchased at any price.

Cynthia felt around and selected the least wet wood. She

carried it back through the rain, into the house. The next step was getting it to burn. No, the next step was getting the matches to burn. The matches were made in Nepal; match manufacturing was at that time one of the country's prize industries. But however prized the industry might have been, it didn't always produce prize matches—though, I must say in fairness, no country's matches would have done well in those monsoon rains. There were several difficulties, aside from the fact that the matches were damp and soggy. First, the sticks broke unless you held the match near the flammable end when you struck it, in which case you'd usually burn your fingers. Next, if you missed on the first strike, the head would fly off on the second—often into the milk you were getting ready to boil. The last difficulty was the friction surface on the match box. In the rainy season this surface took on the texture and abrasive quality of soft cheese, which at least had the advantage of sparing the match head if it didn't ignite it.

This particular morning Cynthia was fortunate and got the third match to light. But then she dropped it. She had better luck on the sixth match, and soon she had the paper in the burner blazing merrily. Tenderly she began placing bark shavings and wisps of straw into the flame, then little twigs, then slightly bigger twigs. They began to smoke, then glow—but the paper was burning out. There wasn't much time left—would it catch? Yes, there was hope; some of the sprigs were beginning to burn. However, at that moment Cynthia thought she heard water pouring out of the bathroom sink onto the floor; but she didn't dare leave the fire. Yes, it was water. Christopher was bathing two of his frogs. By this time, because of the slope of the bathroom floor, the water would be running into the living room. If only she could get the fire to catch. Suddenly she heard a loud thud, followed by even louder screaming. One of the frogs had escaped, and in an effort to recapture it, Christopher had slipped off his stool onto the cement floor. Tommy appeared in the kitchen to say Christopher's mouth was bleeding. The fire was in a precarious state; it needed blowing. Cynthia had a special bamboo tube just for that purpose. After spending a moment to locate it—it had rolled under the stove— she gingerly placed the end of the tube into the burner, drew her breath, and blew the remains of the fire up the chimney. At the same time, clouds of soot and ashes billowed out of the other portals of the stove into the kitchen.

While Cynthia was attending to Christopher, someone began coughing outside the kitchen door. This was the Nepali method of knocking, and whoever it was had already coughed himself hoarse by the time Cynthia got there, since he hadn't been heard over Christopher's screaming. It was the *nashpatti* man, who had come to sell *nashpattis,* a variety of pear. We'd been eating *nashpattis* for three weeks; it was *nashpatti* season. *Nashpattis* plain or with milk, *nashpatti* bread, *nashpatti* jam, *nashpatti* pie. But as no other fruit was available, Cynthia purchased some more. Besides, if she didn't, the word would get around and the *nashpatti* sellers would stop coming. And if they didn't bring them to the door, we'd have to do without because we couldn't get them anywhere else. There are no markets in our part of Nepal; whatever shopping we did depended on who coughed at our door.

The milk woman came with our two *manas* (one quart) of milk just as the *nashpatti* man was leaving, so Cynthia, having given up on the wood burner, lit the small one-pot kerosene stove she kept in reserve and put the milk on to boil. She generally tried not to use the little stove because of the expense and scarcity of kerosene, which, like all our other supplies, had to be carried up fifteen miles from the east-west highway. Not that using wood was all that preferable, of course: Wood was almost as expensive as kerosene, and getting more expensive by the month. Furthermore, we wanted as much as anyone to spare

Nepal's forests, which were literally disappearing before our eyes, ravaged by the woodcutter's axe.

Tommy by this time had gotten hungry for breakfast—"starved," he claimed—and asked his mother for some French toast. However, Cynthia had no eggs. She hadn't had any eggs, in fact, for the past two weeks, because somehow the last egg shipment from Kathmandu never arrived; eggs weren't available locally. Cynthia offered Tommy some *nashpatti* sauce instead, which was not well received. He settled in the end for "multimix," a homemade mixture of coarsely ground millet, corn, and soybeans. What it lacked in taste it made up for in nourishment, according to Cynthia. But I had trouble believing her: Nothing could have made up for that taste.

After breakfast Cynthia's day began in earnest. Didi (meaning "older sister"), our combination cook and housekeeper, arrived and needed supervision for the day. The gardener came and needed instructions. Soon after, the men showed up to move our kerosene refrigerator. It was rusting outside the house—where we had left it because we had no room for it inside. The four men struggled with the refrigerator for fifteen minutes and finally, with great difficulty, got it into the living room, ripping our new rug in two places and covering half the house with muddy footprints. Nepalis can carry enormous weights on their backs, but give them something to lift with their hands and you'd think it weighed a ton.

Well, no sooner was the refrigerator safely inside than a man came to the door selling a large quantity of "recently" butchered water buffalo meat. It was of questionable character and even less than questionable cleanliness. Cynthia remembered that we hadn't had meat for three weeks—but there was no room in the refrigerator, which was filled with tomatoes and squash from our garden, picked the day before because they were rotting outside in the rain. (No wonder the refrigerator was so heavy.) Cynthia bought the meat anyway, as this would be the only meat butchered for three weeks, and crammed it into every available corner, displacing tomatoes and squash in the process. We'd be having tomatoes and squash every meal for the rest of the week.

Today she had the usual odd jobs to do: cleaning up, reading the boys a story, paying a couple of bills, taking the kerosene pressure lantern down to the workshop to be fixed. Then she needed to check on the gardener, which took a lot of Cynthia's time. In the first place, she placed a high priority on feeding her children nutritious food, and in Amp Pipal that meant having her own garden. In the second place, our gardener's performance tended to be erratic, and unless closely watched, he often undid in a few minutes what had taken him hours and days to accomplish. Just the previous week, for example, while weeding the beet patch, he had "weeded" fully two-thirds of the beets. Beets weren't a vegetable familiar to Nepalis in general and to our gardener in particular. This had agitated Cynthia greatly because she liked beets; but remembering her position, she had smiled weakly and sent him off to do something else.

The rest of her morning passed uneventfully. The children played happily in the rain, collecting millipedes, slugs, land crabs, and more frogs. Cynthia had always been a little uneasy about the boys' zoological pursuits. Two days earlier Christopher had brought in a four-inch-long centipede to show her. Fortunately, he wasn't bitten. However, she made sure he knew never to pick one up again. Millipedes he could play with, she offered by way of consolation; at least they were harmless, and besides, they were more abundant. But somehow not nearly so interesting.

Just before lunch the week's supply of eggs arrived from Kathmandu, so now the boys would be able to have scrambled eggs, a great favorite. Cynthia called to them to get ready to eat. In they marched, covered with mud, bringing with them their recently collected species of animal life. Baths were in order, but much to Cynthia's dismay, there was no water. It was the middle of the monsoon rains; there was water running down the hillside, washing away topsoil and causing small landslides; water was cascading down footpaths, transforming them into muddy streams; there was water everywhere. Except in the faucet. For one of a half-dozen frequently recurring reasons, the tanks were empty. Christopher didn't want a bath anyway.

Cynthia always liked the scrambled eggs cooked at the last minute. I had just gotten home from the hospital, so we all sat down at the table, ready to eat. Didi had gotten the wood stove going and was heating the skillet. We heard an egg crack—there was a loud gasp, a howl rather, and Didi was out the door. Cynthia ran to the kitchen to see what had happened, but she needn't have bothered: Within two seconds all of us knew. The egg was rotten, utterly rotten. I'm convinced that no one should go through life without smelling at least one bad egg: All other smells will seem sweet after that. We got to smell more than one that day as Cynthia and Didi sorted through the rest of the eggs. We had gotten many old eggs before, but never ones like this. We later learned that these eggs belonged to *last* week's shipment, the one that never arrived. They'd finally come this week, with a vengeance. Cynthia found only a few really bad ones, and many others that were a little "off." Cynthia, loath as always to throw out anything that could possibly be used, was sure that a little cooking would improve the "off" ones and take the mustiness away. So Didi scrambled them up, and to our surprise they tasted almost normal.

As soon as lunch was over, the boys got up to go outside, hoping mother would forget to give them their respective medicines for intestinal parasites. No such luck. Tommy was taking his for giardia; Christopher was taking his for amoeba. Last month it was the other way around. The amoeba medicine, Flagyl, was particularly bitter, and it was no simple task coaxing

Christopher to take it. Today Cynthia tried mashing it up with a *nashpatti*.

She had much to do between lunch and supper time. We had invited two Nepali families for supper, which we tried to do at least twice a week. It had finally stopped raining, so Didi could take the clothes she had washed the day before out to the line to dry. There was bread to be baked. Most of the house needed cleaning again. An ill child was expected, whose father, a district official, had heard there was a pediatrician in Amp Pipal. The kids would need baths, and Cynthia would have to wash her hair—that is, if the water came back on.

I left for the hospital.

The bread was now ready to go into the oven. Didi had made a good fire, possibly a little hot for bread—but who could be sure? Having put the bread in, Didi began preparations for the rest of the meal. Cynthia was called out to buy some wood poles, for which she paid six times the proper price, she discovered later. Then another man came to the house selling the very finest *nashpattis,* but he was finally turned away after a long discussion. A brisk wind had sprung up in the meantime, blowing several articles of linen off the clothesline into the mud, including most of the napkins for the evening's supper. But before retrieving the napkins, Cynthia first had to go in to check the bread.

Back in the kitchen, Didi was struggling with a recent household acquisition, a secondhand cream separator, which Cynthia had obtained from one of our missionary colleagues. Whatever else this machine did, one of its cardinal effects was to reduce the person attempting to operate it to the state of a ranting lunatic—a process well under way in Didi's case on this particular afternoon. I'm not sure I ever understood the principle of this cream separator myself, but to casual observation it seemed that the idea was to separate one part of the cream into a pot and the rest onto the floor. But appearances can be deceiving.

At this point Tommy came running in to announce that some goats were eating the Chinese gooseberries. Someone had left the front gate open again. So Cynthia hurried out to repel the invaders, which led to an argument with a partially blind old woman who was ostensibly tending the goats. The old woman contended that she'd seen no plants, and if there were any, she hadn't seen her goats eat them. And furthermore, she didn't know anything about whose land this was, and she didn't care. She'd been bringing her goats here to eat for forty years, and she didn't see why she should stop now.

During the conversation the goats meandered off and began eating our avocado tree, which hadn't yet been adequately fenced off. Cynthia discovered the goats before much harm was done. This time her case was greatly strengthened since the old woman could see the tree—but as to whether her goats were actually eating it, she couldn't say, though she reckoned probably not. Spitting a few times, she shuffled off while Cynthia hurled stones at the lingering goats.

Suddenly Cynthia remembered the bread. But as luck would have it, the rain began again before she got back to the house, and the clothes were still on the line. The clothes hadn't dried for three days. The boys had hardly any dry clothes left, and one couldn't use wet napkins for guests. The rain was coming on fast, and she hadn't a moment to lose. She knew she'd find no room to hang the things inside the house if they got wet now; damp clothes already filled the bathroom and kitchen and the back of every chair.

Anyway, Cynthia frantically called Didi to help, and in a few minutes they had gathered the clothes and returned to the house, only to find the kitchen filled with the smoke of burning bread. Yes, it was too late. It turned out that Didi had jacked up the fire in order to boil the water for rice. But there was no use pausing for tears or more lectures now. Didi had already been lectured six times on the point, but it seemed that she couldn't think of more than one thing at a time. (I'm personally convinced her major problem was the cream separator.) The guests were due to arrive in half an hour. The children needed baths, the house needed cleaning, and the dessert still wasn't made.

Cynthia had decided to have pudding for dessert; it was quicker than *nashpatti* pie. Before the *nashpatti* season we'd been having pudding for dessert almost every day. When Cynthia first taught Didi to make it, Didi had had ample vanilla flavoring, and the pudding was quite tasty. Then we ran out of vanilla, and all we could procure was some disagreeable fruit flavoring. We ate this fruit pudding for about two months. Then some Indian-made vanilla became available, and Cynthia bought six bottles of it; she told Didi we'd go back to vanilla pudding, which the family liked better. The pudding never seemed to change flavor, however. When we pointed this out to Cynthia, she said the new vanilla probably wasn't much good. This satisfied us, because eating pudding had become sort of routine—like brushing your teeth: You don't pay much attention to the flavor of your toothpaste.

For tonight Cynthia had decided on chocolate pudding. What a treat! In Amp Pipal chocolate was like gold: Even if you could afford it, it was hard to come by. Cynthia showed Didi how much cocoa powder to add to the pudding and then dashed off to find the children, hoping they wouldn't be too dirty. There was still no water.

But before Cynthia got out the door, Didi suddenly exclaimed that the refrigerator had gone off, and the milk to make the pudding had spoiled. The burner had probably been off all day. The meat would have spoiled too—it hadn't been that good to start with. Children and guests were forgotten in the face of this latest crisis. Didi was sent off to see if one of the neighbors had enough milk to lend us, and Cynthia with difficulty relit the refrigerator in hopes of salvaging the meat.

Nepalis don't have problems like these, thought Cynthia. *Life would be simpler if we lived more like them.*

Just then Christopher breezed in for supper, covered, as feared, with mud and buffalo manure from the garden, where he had been "helping the gardener." Tommy the zookeeper arrived a minute later with a praying mantis and a brightly colored beetle and demanded they be fed and housed. Each of the boys had two leeches on him. Cynthia sprinkled the leeches with salt, and they fell off and writhed about on the floor for a moment before spewing up the blood they had consumed. Good thing our jute rug was red.

Somehow the guests were late, and the water came on. It was a rare day when everything went wrong. The children were bathed, the house was tidied, the food was cooked. Cynthia needed to do only one more thing: kill the flies. There were fifteen or more flies sitting on the dining-room table. Shortly these would all be smashed. I've always objected to swatting flies on the table, which seems unhygienic to me; but reason has never prevailed with my wife in this matter. In her mind, the only good fly is a dead fly. She reminds me a little of our former Scottish nursing supervisor at the hospital, who once during a delicate eye operation swatted a fly on my back with such force that my hands shook for the rest of the case. But then, perhaps it was I instead of the fly that had been the cause of her vigor.

Finally everything was ready. Tommy announced that he could see the guests coming down the path, still three or four minutes away. Where was Christopher? Cynthia feared the worst: often after a bath and clean clothes he escaped outside to do "gardening." No, he wasn't outside. At that moment he appeared saying, "Ants, Mommy, ants." Cynthia breathed a sigh of relief. What's an ant or two? They were a lot less trouble than a muddy child at supper time. Besides, we had ants around all the time. They weren't like flies. So what if a few of them got into the sugar or the cupboard and laid eggs. At least they were clean.

But then why would Christopher even mention ants? There was time to check. Yes, Christopher was right. Out of a crack in the living room wall the ants were coming, hundreds—no, thousands—of them. And they kept coming, now from more than one crevice. Christopher clapped his hands with glee. "See, Mommy, ants!" Mommy sees. What to do now? The guests were knocking at the door. DDT was the answer—we had only recently gotten some from Kathmandu, thank goodness. So Cynthia began to spray it on the columns of ants with energy and determination, while Christopher watched this new method of mass extermination with increasing delight. Having just arrived from the hospital, I began to show the guests our garden.

DDT has an interesting effect on Nepali ants—these were a large black variety. I suppose if you were to submerge one of these ants in pure DDT for a minute or two, it might expire. In usual doses, however, DDT is decidedly stimulative. At the first whiff, those ants took off in every direction. Hundreds more poured out of the wall to get air. The more DDT Cynthia sprayed, the more ants appeared and the faster they ran. In no time they were all over the living room—and still coming. Didi suggested boiling water as an alternative, and soon steaming water was being splashed and sprayed all around the room. This bothered a few ants, but it bothered our rug and our furniture considerably more. Before long the boiling water had run out, so Didi and Cynthia resorted to fly swatters, and for the next ten minutes they romped about the room swatting ants.

Seeing this phenomenal activity going on through a window, I began to show our guests the garden a second time, trying hard not to point out things I'd already shown them. They expressed the same polite interest they'd shown the first time around.

Finally the activity settled down inside and returned to an appearance of normalcy. The food was cold, dead and dying ants were lying everywhere, and the house stunk of DDT. With admirable composure and graciousness, Cynthia ushered in the guests as if nothing had happened. She couldn't resist, however, swatting a dozen new flies that had arrived during the commotion. The meal began.

From here on things went reasonably well. The food Didi had prepared was so hot with spices and peppers that the boys and I could hardly eat it; but the Nepali guests loved it, and that was the main thing, I kept telling myself. The bread had been burned so badly it couldn't be removed from the tin. Our consolation would be the chocolate pudding. That would make up for everything.

At last it was time for dessert. As the guests dipped into the chocolate pudding, a funny expression came over their faces. They tried to look as if they were enjoying the pudding, but it was obvious they were not. Perhaps they'd never tasted chocolate pudding before—they shouldn't be expected to like it. Besides, if they didn't, there'd be that much more left for the rest of us. They were already talking about how full they were after three spoonfuls. Christopher, Tommy, and I were each passed a large helping. I eagerly put in my spoon, ready to savor the chocolate—something I hadn't tasted in at least half a year.

Christopher beat me to it. He took one mouthful of pudding and spit it halfway across the room. Before Cynthia could reprimand him for his behavior, Tommy had also ejected his mouthful of pudding with a groan of disgust. The Nepali children looked at one another and snickered. I gave Tommy and Christopher one of my sternest looks; their manners were an embarrassment. But my sternness melted away as soon as I tasted the pudding myself. In a twinkling, the mystery of the pudding all these months was solved. Tonight the pudding was chocolate in color only. Its flavor—if I may use the word—was simply revolting, as if someone had dumped a can of cocoa powder into a bowl of slightly rancid raspberry syrup and mixed them together. It was inedible.

Didi confessed the next day that she'd added fruit flavoring to the chocolate pudding. Furthermore she'd been adding it to the pudding all these months, which explained why the pudding hadn't changed flavor after the six new bottles of vanilla had arrived. And there they were—six unopened bottles sitting in the cupboard. Why hadn't Didi used them as she'd been instructed? The tops were too hard to get off, and she figured we'd been satisfied with the fruit flavoring. And she had added three times the usual amount to last night's pudding because she thought it was special. It was.

We had no tea after supper. All the hot water had been used to kill ants, and we couldn't heat more because we were out of kerosene. (It had all gone into the refrigerator earlier.) And Cynthia wasn't about to light the wood stove.

At 9:30 the hospital generator was turned off, and the lights went out. The guests left, having had a good time singing and playing games.

The house was a mess. Nine children had eaten on the floor; the adults had eaten at the table. There was food everywhere. Many varieties of insect life were gathering. Already the legions of ants that had escaped the extermination proceedings were regrouping for the feast. But by 10:30 the house had somehow been cleared of at least the gross debris, and it was time for bed. Then, Cynthia suddenly remembered that tomorrow was mail day. She needed to write a few important letters and get them into the mail bag, or it would be another week before they got sent. So by the light of the kerosene lamp, she began to write, and as the cockroaches, moths, and great buzzing beetles gathered about the lamp, she thought of the poor pet frogs who hadn't been fed all day. So she fetched them and set them on the dining-room table around the lamp; and as she wrote, they fed heartily on the insects that had been attracted to the light. The frogs never had it so good. Cynthia, I could tell, was fond of frogs. They ate bugs.

Hard Times

M ANY COUPLES tell us they would think about being missionaries themselves if it weren't for their children. The prospect of raising children on the mission field seems to frighten people. What happens when the children need to go to school? What happens when they get sick? What about bears and tigers? And germs and bugs and poisonous snakes? Won't the children miss out on a lot? We faced these questions—and more.

Even before we left for Nepal, Cynthia had made up her mind that under no circumstances would our children go off to boarding school before age nine, at the earliest. The common missionary practice of sending children off at age five was in her opinion a relic of an unenlightened past. She was a modern mother and a pediatrician as well. She said she'd have no part of it.

And she kept her word, after a fashion. Tommy didn't leave for school at age five; he left at age six.

School was in Kathmandu, where Tommy stayed in a hostel with a dozen other missionary children. From the beginning he loved school, every aspect of it, and that was never to change. The hostel situation, however, changed a great deal; Tommy went through ten sets of hostel parents in eight years. That was the hardest part of being away from home—having no secure and permanent living arrangement. For a year the hostel actually closed for lack of children, and Tommy lived with a family. But by and large the people who took charge of him were loving and dedicated, and he gained something of value from each one.

Christopher's experience was altogether different. When he was old enough for kindergarten, Cynthia began teaching him at home. Although Cynthia felt that things were going well, I was not happy about it. I felt Christopher needed the stimulation and discipline of a regular school. And after all, Tommy had done all right; why shouldn't Christopher? Besides, it would be good for Christopher to get away; he seemed to be a little too attached to his parents. I was right about his being attached. But that was all.

I remember the September day when Cynthia took the boys off to the school in Kathmandu, Christopher for the first time. He was five, going into first grade, and not at all excited about going away to school. I couldn't make up my mind whether or not to make the three-hour walk with them down to the grass landing strip at the foot of our mountain; I had other things to do, and besides, I didn't like partings—especially one like this. Tommy had been different somehow; he had been ready to go away to school.

I decided in the end not to walk with them to the airfield. I watched them go down the trail, past the hospital, and along the steep side of Liglig Mountain. When they had reached the spring several hundred yards below the hospital, I was suddenly seized with the urge to go with them to the airfield, or at least say good-bye one last time. So down I ran after them. They were surprised to see me. We all walked on together, not saying much, and I began to think this was silly; my presence wasn't contributing much, and each step I took meant one more step to walk back. When the trail turned sharply around the side of Liglig, I gave each of them a big hug and said good-bye a final time.

I could see the trail ahead for a few hundred yards, and as I watched them get smaller in the distance I began to regret my decision. I wouldn't see Christopher for another three-and-a-half months. It might mean something special to him that I had gone with him to the airport on his first trip to school. So before they were completely out of sight, I decided to run after them again. I caught up with them in ten minutes. As before, they were surprised to see me. I didn't explain why I was having so much trouble making up my mind today and no one asked. We trudged along solemnly.

Again I began to think this was ridiculous; it didn't seem to make any difference to anyone whether or not I was along. After another fifteen minutes the trail began to descend in earnest. Again I decided I wouldn't go any further; from this point the walk back was still fairly level. So for the final time I said good-bye and stood watching them as they went along, dropping from terrace to terrace. I could see the airport at the bottom of the valley, about four miles away.

I made several resolutions to turn and go back, but I just stood there, even after they were out of sight. Five, ten, fifteen minutes passed, and I was still fixed to the spot. Never could I remember having had such a case of indecision. Finally, on an impulse, I set out down the mountain toward the airfield. It was half an hour before I caught up with them, and this time they didn't seem surprised at all. There was no turning back now. I made it all the way to the airport, and then, of course, I was glad I had come. We were two hours early and so had to wait for the plane. It was important to get to the airport well beforehand: More than once someone had gotten down to the airfield with time to spare, only to find that the plane had already come and gone. Today the plane was on schedule. After seeing my family on board, I retraced my steps up the mountain, part of me still wishing I hadn't come—the foot part, mainly.

A few days later when Cynthia left Kathmandu to return to Amp Pipal, her parting from the boys was far more traumatic. Christopher didn't like the school. He didn't like his teacher. He didn't like the hostel. He cried a great deal when his mother left him to go to the airport in Kathmandu to catch the plane back to Amp Pipal. The plane didn't fly that day because of heavy rain, and the parting had to be repeated the next day. And the next day. And the next. For one whole week the plane was rained out! It was still the monsoon season. Cynthia badly wanted to bring Christopher home with her, but she was afraid of what I would say—I'd been so certain he should go to school.

It was an unhappy time for Christopher, but it only lasted a term. Shortly thereafter we went home to the U.S. on furlough. While we were home, we met in our church a delightful young teacher named Carole Cothran. After hearing our story, Carole offered to come to Amp Pipal for a year and a half to teach Christopher as well as some other missionary children who had arrived in the meantime. It was a provision from God. And our gratitude to Carole remains undiminished to this day. I don't know what we would have done if she hadn't come.

After Carole left, Christopher eventually went back to school in Kathmandu. Aside from his early experience, we were generally at peace about the boys' being away at school. Nevertheless, they seemed a long way off—if not in miles, at least in time, especially once the air service was discontinued. A person can fly from one U.S. coast to the other and back again in less time than it took to get from Amp Pipal to Kathmandu, a distance of ninety road miles. Mail came once a week. If the school sent us something to be signed—a permission for a field trip, for instance—it would be three weeks before they got it back, often after the event had taken place. The hostel parents usually took care of such matters, of course, but we couldn't help feeling remote from our children, unavailable, not really involved in their lives.

Only once was this difficulty in communication a serious problem and that was toward the end of Tommy's first term at school. One mail day at about 8:00 P.M., we got a letter saying that Tommy, then six years old, was in the hospital with a severe headache, a fever of 104°F, and "cells" in his spinal fluid. As there were no more details, we concluded he had to have meningitis, an infection of the lining of the brain, one of the most dangerous diseases a child can get. Tommy had been admitted three days earlier! The hostel parents had tried to send a message to our district capital by "telegraph" (there was a government telephone line between Kathmandu and our district capital, mainly for police business), but since there was no delivery service, the message sat there—and still sits there today, for all we know.

Cynthia, taking Christopher with her, went into Kathmandu the next day—fortunately there was a plane—and found that Tommy was already out of the hospital and mostly recovered. It had been only viral meningitis, much less serious than the bacterial form.

I received the happy news four days later from another missionary returning from Kathmandu. Then, a week after that, on a Tuesday evening, I got a letter from Cynthia saying she was coming to Amp Pipal with the boys on Wednesday, the very next day. Since the school term was almost over, she had decided to bring Tommy back early and let him recuperate at home. She also instructed me to send five porters—men we hire to carry goods and people up and down the mountainside—to meet the plane: one for Tommy, one for Christopher, and three for all the loot that Cynthia invariably acquired whenever she went into Kathmandu.

On such short notice, it wasn't easy to find one porter, let alone five; but with Didi's help, I located four men the next morning and sent them off to the airstrip in time to meet the plane at noon. Since I had no surgery that day, I decided I'd go down too and meet the family. I got to the airfield a few minutes before twelve. It was a glorious, sunny day, and the snow-covered mountains were sharp and clear against the sky; they would have had a lovely view from the plane. Except the plane didn't come. I waited until 5:00. Still no plane. The four porters decided to spend the night at the airport; I chose to return up the mountain. I had a vasectomy camp to attend the next day in a village three to four hours from Amp Pipal. In fact, I could see the village from the airfield. I could have gone directly to the village from the airfield, but I had to return to Amp Pipal to get my instruments.

At 2:30 the next morning a patient with an intestinal obstruction arrived, who needed emergency surgery. By the time I finished the surgery and got on the trail, I was several hours late. As I walked along, I could see the airstrip off to the west. I had no intention of trying to go via the airfield today; besides, Cynthia and the boys might not have gotten tickets for today's flight—if there even was a flight. Our airport was not a priority stop.

On the way, I passed through a village where a Finnish missionary nurse was living, and stopped to examine six or eight patients for her. I told her I'd be back that way the same evening. Shortly after I left her, she came down with a severe case of diarrhea and vomiting. They, along with the nurse, at least had the consolation of knowing I'd be dropping by on my way home that day and would be able to give them some medical advice.

A half hour later I stopped for tea at the house of an Australian teacher at the mission high school at Luitel. An hour after I left, his wife and son also developed acute cases of diarrhea and vomiting.

When I arrived in the village where the vasectomy camp was to be held, I discovered no one knew anything about it. Of the forty camps I went to, this was the only time that the government family planners got their dates mixed.

Finding time on my hands, I spent the next three hours having tea and chatting with the National Assembly representative for our district, who happened to live in that village. I was still pretty shaky with the language at that point, and I was gratified to be able to carry on such a long conversation—even if I only managed to get in one word to his ten.

I left his house at 4:00, with a three-hour walk ahead of me. I wanted to get home before dark, especially since I hadn't brought a flashlight. But he insisted I have tea and something to eat before I left. While that was being prepared, he asked me to examine his wife and one of his children. Then the secretary of the *panchayat* (local government) came to be examined and then the headmaster of the local school—and I was on the tenth patient at 4:45, when suddenly I saw the Kathmandu-Gorkha plane overhead on its way to the airfield. It had never come this late. The porters waiting for Cynthia and the boys would certainly have left and would be on their way back to Amp Pipal by now. There'd be no one at the airstrip to meet them. They'd have to spend the night in one of those miserable teashop "hotels," Cynthia would be in a fit—and at that moment I made up my mind to run down to the airport instead of returning to Amp Pipal the way I had come.

I took leave of my surprised host and set out running at full speed through the village. People stopped what they were doing to watch me go by. No one runs in Nepal—except children.

Beyond the village the trail began to descend. I ran faster. I was afraid Cynthia might start out somewhere and then I wouldn't know where she'd gotten to. From the assemblyman's house it had looked as if the airfield were only twenty minutes away at a run, but the trail wasn't heading in the right direction. Rather, it led tangentially down the ridge, at first even *away* from the airfield. I ran for an hour and arrived at the airstrip in a state of total exhaustion, only to discover that my family hadn't been on the plane anyway. It was a long walk up the mountain to Amp Pipal in the moonlight.

The next morning the missionary colleagues I had deserted

with diarrhea and vomiting each sent a runner asking for medicine and whatever advice I had to give them. I felt even worse about my dash to the airport when I heard of the plight I had left them in. Happily they recovered, as they had recovered from similar bouts in the past. For most missionaries, dysentery more or less goes with the job.

I knew that the plane made a scheduled flight the next day, and I figured Cynthia and the boys would be on it. I had the afternoon off, so I decided to go down partway and meet them on the trail. There had been heavy rain all morning, but by noon the sun was out and the countryside was bright and green and fresh.

I was about halfway down the mountain when to my delight I saw the plane flying up the valley toward the airfield. The landing strip itself was just out of sight behind a low tree-covered ridge. I watched the plane descend and disappear below the level of the trees. I stopped and said a short prayer for a safe landing. Just as I finished, the plane suddenly reappeared from behind the trees, flying in the same direction up the valley. *Maybe some buffalos on the runway,* I thought. *He'll turn around and land the other way.* But the plane, a small two-engine "Twin Otter," kept flying off to the west. Only when it was almost out of sight and I had given up hope did it finally circle around and come back. Phew! I was getting tired of these fruitless trips to the airfield. The plane again descended beneath the treetops, and again I stopped and said a short prayer. But then as I was starting out again, at a faster pace, I saw the plane flying off down the valley toward Kathmandu. This time it didn't come back, and I had the pleasure of a return trip up the mountain by myself—the last half hour in pouring rain.

For the third night in a row, Didi had prepared supper for four. I was still eating the extra food from the first night. I later learned that Cynthia and the boys had been on that plane. The plane hadn't been able to land because the field was soaked from the rain that had fallen that morning. It would've been hard to say who was the more frustrated, they or I.

The next day was Saturday, our day off. I debated whether to go down to the airfield once more; maybe if I stayed away, they'd be more likely to come. I compromised and went down halfway. I sat and waited. I hadn't seen a plane on my way down, and none came while I waited. At 4:00 I was trying to make up my mind whether to wait any longer, when suddenly there they were, right on the trail a few yards away! The plane had come earlier, but I hadn't seen it. It was a joyful reunion, at last.

The three extra porters trudged into view, loaded with boxes and suitcases. On top of one fellow's load was a nice, new-looking carton I didn't recognize. It was a slide projector. Another man was carrying the screen. For the mission, I thought. But no, it was for us. Like a typical American missionary, Cynthia had gone and acquired another gadget (purchased secondhand from another typical American missionary); it was just what we needed to go with our refrigerator, washing machine, and piano. As usual, however, Cynthia turned out to be more farseeing than I; we were able to put that projector to good use. Over the years it has provided more than a hundred evenings of entertainment to Nepalis who've come for supper, most frequently small groups from the hospital staff. And it's working fine still.

For Tommy, the whole affair brought an unexpected blessing. During the course of his illness, he had accepted Jesus into his heart. It was a childlike act of faith, but it was to be the beginning of a commitment that would grow and mature over the years. Here was one more illustration of the old truth that it's not the difficulty that counts but the way one responds to it. Tommy can look back now and say that this hard time was one of the most important experiences of his life.

Thinking about Tommy's meningitis, his only serious illness, serves to remind us how gracious God has been in preserving our health during our time in Nepal. Cynthia and I never missed a day of work in twelve years at Amp Pipal. Only twice did we have a real scare, both times with Christopher, both times with the same illness: croup.

Missionaries take a risk when they go into undeveloped areas to work, and not all missionary families escape tragedy. But with Christopher we experienced for ourselves not only the reality of the risk but also the reality of God's protection over us.

The first of Christopher's two serious attacks of croup came on Christmas Eve, our first Christmas in Nepal, only two weeks after we had moved into our house at Amp Pipal. I'd gone to bed at 9:30 with the generator, and Cynthia stayed up to wrap some last-minute presents. Christopher, who had been hoarse most of the day, now began to have trouble breathing. He became rapidly worse, and Cynthia immediately recognized the telltale signs of croup. She had treated many cases of croup during her training; usually the disease was self-limited and responded to steam inhalation. We had no vaporizer, of course, and the amount of steam that could be gotten out of the spout of our teakettle seemed too little to fuss with. So Cynthia just sat by Christopher's bed and waited for the attack to pass.

It didn't pass. With each minute Christopher grew worse, straining harder and harder to draw in his breath. His breathing became a succession of long, raspy croaks. He was tiring rapidly; he didn't have the breath to cry. He just stared at his mother with pleading, frightened eyes. Cynthia was too petrified even to call me. There would have been nothing I could have done at that point anyway. Things had happened so fast. Such children needed tracheotomies long before they reached that stage. And once that bad, they rarely recovered by themselves. Convinced that Christopher was about to die, Cynthia started to pray, asking God to spare her child. Within thirty seconds Christopher was over the attack and was breathing quietly.

That was a special Christmas for us the next day. God had given us an unmistakable sign of his presence with us; he had sent us to Amp Pipal, and he was going to look out for us in the bargain.

My turn to wait and pray came a year later. I'd never fully realized from Cynthia's account what a close call Christopher had had that first Christmas Eve. Cynthia tends to look at the dark side of things, and I must have filtered out the worst part of her story. So I was totally unprepared for Christopher's second attack of croup.

Cynthia was out at a prayer meeting, and the house to which she'd gone had no phone. Again the illness came on suddenly; Christopher merely had a slight cold at the time.

As I watched him, I grew more and more worried. I didn't like croup. As a surgeon I'd seen only the cases that needed tracheotomies, and a tracheotomy in a small child was a difficult business. I'd seen a couple of Vietnamese children Christopher's age die of croup during the time I was stationed in Vietnam.

As Christopher became worse, my alarm grew into a paralysis of mind and will. I just sat there watching him get paler, then bluer. Air was hardly moving in and out of his lungs, in spite of his straining efforts to breathe. Then his efforts decreased, and he lost consciousness.

It all happened in a quarter of an hour, and still I sat there, convinced that I was watching Christopher breathe his last. I didn't even dare go to the phone; I wouldn't have known who to call, as everyone was at the same meeting twenty minutes away. The hospital was empty except for an assistant nurse and a sweeper. They could have sent for Cynthia or Dr. Helen Huston, my colleague and founder of the hospital at Amp Pipal, but by the time they came, it would be too late. The fact is, I was immobilized—not even able to call for help, much less perform a tracheotomy, which was what Christopher needed. I could hardly pray. I just said "God do something" over and over.

For many minutes Christopher hung between life and death. He was limp and motionless except for his short, choppy breathing. But he held on. And as the age-long minutes passed, I thought I could detect a slight improvement in his breathing. It was becoming easier and less noisy. Gradually his color improved. And by the time Cynthia returned from her meeting, Christopher was sleeping peacefully, and I was lost in thought.

Having assured ourselves that Christopher was going to be all right, we got ready for bed. We were barely asleep when the phone rang. The call was from the hospital. It was about a three-year-old girl I'd admitted that afternoon with an upper-respiratory infection. The child's condition especially concerned me because she was the niece of our x-ray technician. He had brought her himself and had stayed on at the hospital that night. The assistant nurse had called to say that the child was not doing well and that I should come to see her.

When I got to the hospital, I found the little girl very much worse than when I had admitted her a few hours earlier. This child, too, had croup, a bad case, though not nearly as bad as Christopher's had been. But it got worse through the early morning hours, and by 7:00 the child's condition was serious. I knew that I couldn't put off doing a tracheotomy any longer.

I wasn't happy about operating. No one on our staff was skilled in children's anesthesia, so I'd have to do the operation under local anesthesia. That was never easy in a struggling child. Moreover, this would be the first tracheotomy ever done at Amp Pipal. The idea of slitting somebody's throat and putting a tube in the windpipe horrified the girl's family. Most of our Nepali staff were highly skeptical and advised against it. To my surprise, the x-ray technician came to the rescue. Although generally a negative and somewhat hostile man, he strongly urged the family to let me operate as the only means of saving the child's life. Because he was a staff leader and a forceful speaker, he soon prevailed. Without further delay we took the girl to the operating room and prepared her for surgery.

As I began the operation, I couldn't shake the thought that Christopher had gotten better and this girl had gotten worse—same time, same disease. Croup was not common in Nepal; this was the first case I'd ever seen in a Nepali. Was there any meaning to it, or was it just a coincidence? In my mind was a picture of Christ healing the demon-possessed man and then sending the demons into a herd of pigs. It had been a great loss to the owners of the pigs, but then, a man's life had been spared. But here it was different; both were human lives. God surely couldn't have meant to spare Christopher at the expense of this little girl.

In spite of a vague thought that I was interfering in something I didn't understand, I went ahead and did the tracheotomy. It went well, and within an hour the girl was back on the ward breathing quietly through her little tube. I was elated. The family was grateful. The hospital staff was impressed. As for the x-ray technician, he was mainly relieved that I hadn't let him down and caused him to lose face before all those people. That case more than anything else won for me his grudging allegiance and respect, which in later years I would have occasion to draw on many times. And beyond the hospital, the case became known over a wide area and did much to increase people's faith in modern medicine. Did it increase people's faith in God, too? That was the big question. I know it increased mine.

four

Good Times

*I*F OUR SONS were to talk to couples who have doubts about missionary life, they would tell them children are no reason for parents not to be missionaries. After twelve years of growing up in Nepal, they would say without hesitation that the advantages of their upbringing have far, far outweighed the disadvantages.

Our kids took to Nepal like ants to sugar. And in many ways the boys were better missionaries than we were. For one thing, they picked up the language without effort. Tommy, at five, was my unofficial interpreter for our first year in Amp Pipal, after which he went off to school, and I had to shift for myself. I can't say I enjoyed being outtalked by a five-year-old. One time the gardener was excitedly trying to tell me something, and I couldn't make out a word he was saying. I knew the Nepali expression for "repeat it slowly"—I used it more than any other—but even when he had repeated his message several times, I still couldn't understand it. Just then Tommy ran out the door to play, and the exasperated gardener stopped him and repeated what he'd been trying to tell me. Tommy understood it at once and told me. Before I could think up a reply in English, let alone Nepali, Tommy had answered the question and had run off to play. Without casting so much as a glance my way, the gardener set about his business. He'd know who to ask next time.

Many people think that missionary children are in some way

deprived—deprived of "necessary" things like Mister Rogers, the Muppets, E.T., roller skating, tennis, video games, good food, ice cream. Many missionary parents themselves worry lest their children suffer some sort of adverse reaction and end up hating everything connected with missionary work. No doubt that has often happened, but it's almost always due to another kind of deprivation—deprivation of parental attention. And the mission field has no monopoly on that. But let us also add that sending children away to boarding school does not preclude giving them adequate attention, as long as their separation from parents is made up for when they're home for the holidays.

School holidays were always our most joyful times of the year. We were usually able to put the children first during those periods, before the demands of work; either it was slow at the hospital or someone came to relieve us. The unmarried missionaries also cooperated graciously, adjusting their schedules to accommodate ours. We spent most of our holidays right in Amp Pipal. That was home for all of us, and no one cared to go off somewhere else. We always had plenty to do: mountainsides to dig in, wildlife to catch, tree houses to build. We even cut into the hillside below our house to make a small playground (about the size of a volleyball court) that served as soccer field, baseball diamond, and later on, a place for church meetings.

Far from being deprived, most missionary children gain much more than they give up. Their education is usually better than the education they would get in their home countries, often markedly so. They go to school with classmates from interesting and varied backgrounds. They are exposed to different cultures and have a chance to learn firsthand how people outside the West actually live. Missionary children in Nepal trek through the Himalayas in fifth grade and tour India in the sixth. They're hardly losers.

Take pets, for example. Our kids have had a profusion of odd pets during their years in Amp Pipal. How many American kids have ever owned a pet monkey? Of course, what the kids gained in pets, I lost in peace of mind. I didn't mind the snails or the land crabs with their big bulbous eyes. Or even the frogs, who used to sit in the chinks between the stones in the wall. If you got the sensation when you walked into our house that frog faces were peering at you out of the walls, you weren't going nuts. The frogs were there, five and six at a time.

But the cat was another matter. The cat was the first real pet, and the worst. Cynthia liked cats, and having convinced Tommy and Christopher that they liked cats too, she went out and got one from somewhere and brought it home.

It was a boy cat, so they named it "Tom," which merely added insult to injury. Tom took an immediate liking to me, which was odd because the feeling was in no way reciprocated. He would greet me enthusiastically each morning at 4:00—I'd be groping around for the matches and candles—by leaping onto my back from the top of the refrigerator or bookcase. Sometimes he'd wait until I had just poured my tea and had raised the cup to my lips. Once when he landed on me, he was soaking wet: He'd been in the toilet bowl. I couldn't keep the thing away from me; it rarely went to Cynthia and the boys. Its favorite snoozing place, when it wasn't on my lap, was a large flowerpot in which I was trying to sprout an Egyptian date palm.

The cat didn't catch one rat, to anyone's knowledge, though it never lacked for opportunities. It did catch a bird once. Only one time in twelve years did a bird ever fly down our chimney, and it had to be during the two weeks we had that cat. The fireplace happened to be filled with ashes, and the bird landed in the middle of them. When it emerged, it looked like a snow owl. Tom was into the fireplace in a second, and soon ashes were flying all over the living room. After a minute of that, the bird fluttered out of the fireplace with the cat in pursuit. Finally Tom pounced and got the bird in his teeth. Opening the kitchen door, I invited him to take it outside—we didn't need feathers all over the house too. The bird looked dead, or I'd have attempted to retrieve it: I liked birds a lot better than cats. Tom looked pleased with himself as he took it outside. He proudly strutted around the yard with the bird in his mouth and then came back and laid it on the kitchen stoop. The bird promptly flew off. Was Tom mad! He ran round and round in a frenzy of anger and humiliation, while the bird looked down on him from a nearby tree and dusted its feathers.

Tom's last caper took place on a night we had invited one of our mission executives and another guest to supper. For the main dish, Cynthia had prepared some roast water buffalo, a lump about the size of a small trout. I lovingly carved out half of it and set the rest on a stool beside me for second helpings. We had meat only on special occasions, and tonight it was especially tasty, even tender. We were just finishing our first helpings when I caught a flash out of the corner of my eye. The cat had leaped onto the stool, seized the meat, and dragged it off into the bathroom, where it sat glowering over it, as if daring anyone to take it away from him.

I rescued the meat and gave it to Cynthia, who washed it off, put it in the oven a moment, and then brought it out again to the table. The guests declined seconds, but the boys and I finished it off happily—almost as though we had planned it that way.

The cat was gone the next morning. Even Cynthia had had enough!

Tommy and Christopher didn't care for cats that much anyway; what they really wanted was a dog. But I had refused to have a dog. In the first place I felt uneasy about keeping a dog and feeding it when we were surrounded by hungry neighbors. In the second place there was the problem of rabies.

Rabies was the one disease I dreaded above all others. The hospital didn't have vaccine for dogs; we didn't even keep it for humans. The rabies antiserum available to us went out of date in six months, which is just how long it took for it to be sent to us. And even if we could have inoculated our own dog, we couldn't have done anything about the dogs that would have come to visit. Hundreds of scraggly dogs roamed the villages near us, and I didn't care to provide them with an excuse to come to our house. I even tried to dissuade others at the hospital from having dogs too, though without much success. At least we could do without one ourselves.

Even having a cat in Nepal was risky enough. One day a missionary doctor friend who lived near us was bitten by his pet cat. The doctor thought nothing of it until the cat suddenly died eight days later. The doctor was quite sure the cat died from eating a neighbor's rat poison, but he also could have died of rabies—and passed on the disease to the doctor. The possibility was remote, but it was there. If I had been bitten, I would have done nothing, but I found it difficult to give that advice to somebody else—especially a fellow physician and colleague.

We decided to send the cat's brain into Kathmandu to have it examined, which was the only way to prove whether or not the cat died of rabies. We weren't even sure if they could do the examination in Kathmandu.

The clinical pathology textbook we consulted said that the brain would need to be "preserved in the frozen state." The only way we could get the cat's brain into Kathmandu "in the frozen state" was to take it out of the skull, freeze it overnight, and send it in a thermos bottle first thing in the morning. We decided to send the mail runner on this special errand, and at the same time have him bring back a new, safer kind of rabies antiserum that had recently become available in Kathmandu. We couldn't afford to delay treatment until after we knew the examination result. That might take weeks.

Bhakta, my operating-room assistant, spent an hour getting the brain out of the cat's skull. One of our nurses, a young woman from New Zealand, offered her refrigerator to freeze it in, notwithstanding her qualms about having a rabid cat brain in among her ice cubes.

Early the next morning, the mail runner came by with the doctor's thermos bottle, but the brain, which had fit in nicely before it was frozen, wouldn't go through the neck of the thermos. I'm not sure how they solved the problem in the end—perhaps with a hammer—but without too much delay the runner was off to Kathmandu. When he arrived there, the cat's brain was mush: The thermos had broken en route.

The runner returned two days later with the requested antiserum—at $144 a course, an astronomical sum by our standards. We never could have recommended it for a Nepali. The runner also brought back word that we shouldn't have frozen the brain in the first place; newer techniques required that the brain be fixed in formalin.

Surely it was easier not to have pets to begin with than to go through all this—unless, of course, they could be confined to the house.

With cats and dogs ruled out, then, the next pets at our house were a succession of birds. They seemed safe enough and not too much trouble. Nepali children from the neighborhood, friends of Tommy and Christopher, kept the boys provided with a steady supply. Most of the birds died after a few days in our house, but one survived a whole year—a Scops owl, about eight inches high. The family quickly became attached to it, all except for Didi, our cook. Didi's sweeping bothered the owl somehow; whenever she came near it, even without her broom, the owl would spread its wings and hiss and glare at her, hopping about angrily all the while. We thought it was funny, but Didi didn't. But then, she didn't have much of a sense of humor.

The owl had several perches—the fireplace, the woodpile under the kitchen counter, the top of the bookcase. Gradually however, it began spending most of its time on a narrow ledge over the dining-room window. It liked the height, I suppose. It kept its perch clean; whenever it had business to do, it simply faced around, presented its backside to the room, and let drop into Cynthia's African violets lined up on the windowsill below. It fell short at times, streaking the dark-stained window frames with white—which we never bothered to remove, even after the owl's demise.

The owl was always hungry and ate almost any living object we gave it: praying mantises, rhinoceros beetles, locusts, frogs. Sometimes we went on family grasshopper-collecting excursions, but no matter how many we came home with, they were never enough. Once we brought the owl an eight-inch-long lizard with a bright red head. The owl swallowed it whole—except for four inches of tail, which it couldn't get down. The owl was distressed by this and began to prance around and flap its wings in an agitated manner. Having no better idea, I cut off the lizard's tail with a pair of scissors, following which the owl extended its neck in a curious fashion and with one final gulp got the lizard inside. The owl didn't eat again for two days.

We set about catching lizards after that; they satisfied longer.

The owl had many endearing peculiarities. It would screw its head around 180° so that you always had to look twice to see which way it was facing, an important consideration if you happened to be anywhere under it—which we often were; the dining-room table was right under its ledge. The owl would periodically regurgitate the indigestible parts of its meals, often during our supper hour; there would be some contorting and twisting on the ledge above, and then suddenly a golf-ball-size bolus of grasshopper legs, frog bones, and beetle backs would come bouncing down into the African violets. Occasionally the owl would fly into the kitchen to pester Didi, once dropping a bomb in the water pitcher as it passed.

We had the owl a year. Then, one time both Cynthia and I had to go somewhere for four days, and we left Didi in charge of the house. The owl was dead when we returned, thrown unceremoniously onto the compost pile. The mode of disposal bothered Christopher most of all; he felt Owl should have had a proper burial.

Sometime after that a man came to the house and tried to sell us a great Himalayan horned owl—that's what he said it was, anyway. It looked more like a vulture. It was the size of a full-grown chicken, with a wingspread of nearly a yard, and it was only two weeks old! We knew it would be too much for Didi— and probably for the African violets as well—so we turned it down. A fellow doctor from Elko, Nevada, who was with us a short time, decided to take it back with him to Kathmandu, where he was working. I couldn't help smiling to myself as he went off to Kathmandu with his owl stuffed into a tiny bamboo cage meant more for a hummingbird. What was he going to do when it grew up?

Our next pet was a myna bird, named Oliver, who belonged to Tommy in particular. It used to sit for hours on Tommy's shoulder and go with him wherever he went. It loved to peck at Tommy's teeth and pull at his hair. The myna liked company in general and would chatter away happily with anyone who gave it the time. It never once tried to fly off, evidently preferring the entertainment humans afforded to the company of other birds in the woods.

While Oliver was still with us, we got our monkey. It was a mistake, actually. A Nepali friend had offered to get the boys a pet and asked what I thought they'd like. I had jokingly said a monkey, knowing he couldn't get one anyway; but my friend replied seriously, "Oh, that's no problem. I'll send one around next week."

I couldn't very well back out at that point, not without insulting him. His offer had been genuine, and my response had been flippant. "Oh well," I thought, "nothing will come of it."

A few days later, true to his word, my friend sent someone around with a baby monkey about three weeks old. Its mother had been killed by a dog, and for the first day or so it was with us we thought it might die of depression. But it quickly learned to make do with Cynthia, latching onto her leg with all fours and traveling about with her wherever she went. It looked at first glance like a hairy growth on her leg. We named the monkey Bilbo, after the Hobbit. Tommy and Christopher spent one summer vacation getting it through the acute stages of infancy; then they went blithely off to school, leaving us to take care of Bilbo until they returned for the Christmas holiday.

Bilbo was lovable enough, but he had an intestinal problem. It's not easy to toilet train any monkey, they say, let alone one with intractable diarrhea. We used to hold him for minutes at a time over a little wooden box constructed for the purpose, but he remained determined to go anywhere but there. It was a job just trying to hold him. He'd struggle and shriek and shoot off like a loose fire hose, nailing whoever happened to be in the way. We gave up after a couple of weeks. We laid down a large plastic sheet in front of the fireplace, and chained him there with a short chain. We couldn't keep him outside for fear of the dogs.

Despite the trouble he was, Bilbo won our affection, especially Didi's. They got along famously. She took care of him, fed him, entertained him, and kept the plastic sheet fairly clean. Bilbo hated to be alone. Whenever we went out the door, he'd berate us angrily for deserting him. He had a little blanket (an old washcloth) that was his constant comfort. He didn't hold it to his ear (as Linus does) but drew it over his head like a monk's cowl. Then he'd sit and rock back and forth for hours on end. And just try to get that blanket away, which Didi had to do once or twice a week in order to clean it. One never would have thought such a small creature could scream so loudly or so long.

Among other things, we learned where the expression "monkey business" comes from. When Bilbo wasn't moping under his blanket, he'd be getting into mischief of one sort or another. Anything he could lay hands on he'd bend, crumple, chew, or pull to pieces. He'd climb the stone wall of the fireplace and yank the fur out of the llama rug that hung there. He'd throw his food about and delight in spilling his milk, like any two-year-old human. And he had to be in the center of everything. I'd be reading *The Count of Monte Cristo* to the family and there he'd be, turning the pages—backwards, to be sure, and twelve at a time—very much part of the action. When he thought I'd read long enough, he'd try to cover my mouth.

When Tommy and Christopher went off to school in the fall, Bilbo was sorry to see them go. But when they returned three-and-a-half months later at Christmas, he wasn't at all happy to see them. They were usurpers, taking his place in the household. He grew used to it though, and ultimately benefited from the extra attention he got from them. He also got a suit of clothes for Christmas, courtesy of Cynthia, which he must have taken for a game—something to be gotten out of as quickly as possible. All in all, it was a grand holiday, thanks in part to the monkey. But when the boys went back to school this time, we gave Bilbo to Didi. Enough was enough.

After that we noticed more people began accepting our invitations to dinner.

Monkeys thoroughly deserve most of the disparaging epithets they have received, except one: dumb. Monkeys are not dumb. Once a distinguished surgeon from Calgary came to Kathmandu to fill in for a furloughing doctor in one of the mission hospitals. He went off one day to visit a famous temple, known for its innumerable monkeys. I warned him that the monkeys would steal his lunch if he wasn't careful. He looked at me as if I had insulted his intelligence—did I take him for an inexperienced tourist?—and walked off, camera in one hand and lunch in the other. At supper that night we asked him how he had enjoyed his outing, but he didn't want to talk about it. It turned out that two monkeys had come up behind him, one on either side, just as he sat down to eat. One had reached for his camera, and as the good doctor swung around to shoo him off, the other had grabbed his lunch bag and made off with it—as slick an operation as you could ask for. The pair climbed onto a nearby roof, ate the lunch, and tossed down the empty bag. I thought the doctor might at least have taken their picture: He still had his camera.

We could have had many other pets: a flying squirrel, a baby leopard, a Himalayan bear. The leopard and bear tempted me terribly—here were pets worth having—but reason prevailed in the form of my wife. The bear was eventually bought by one of my wealthy patients, who took it home and tied it to his shed. The next morning he found the shed pulled down and the bear gone. And it was only a cub.

Our last pets were a pair of pigeons, named Napoleon and Josephine, who had the run of Christopher's room. Christopher wanted to watch their babies hatch—pigeons produce offspring every four weeks—but this pair could only produce eggs, no chicks. They produced more than eggs, of course; by the end of the six weeks the green jute rug in Christopher's room looked like a two-toned carpet. When Christopher returned to school, we gave Napoleon and Josephine to our cook, who took them home and ate them.

Solving the Food Problem by the Bunch

*I*N NEPAL we live in the midst of such immense and seemingly insoluble problems that frequently we feel the need to escape into more frivolous pursuits—pursuits that serve either to preserve our sanity or to demonstrate its absence. Aside from our mission's deadly serious efforts to seek solutions for the general problem of hunger, we've also been elaborating some curious solutions of our own. In the course of growing a variety of fruit and vegetables on the quarter-acre plot surrounding our house, we've inadvertently become specialists in raising bananas, a circumstance brought about more by necessity than by any fondness for eating them.

Banana raising is unique. The trees grow anywhere—like weeds. You can't stop them. You can chop them down; you can lop their leaves off to feed your goats; but whatever you do, they keep growing. And then come the bananas, all in a bunch—a hundred, two hundred, or more at a time. So you watch them, pinch them, wait until they're just about right, and then pick them. It all sounds easy. Why not raise bananas? In fact, why raise anything else? Bananas are a complete diet in themselves.

We really shouldn't count our first bunch. That tree blew down in a windstorm in early March before picking time, and the bananas didn't ripen properly: they petrified. No matter what we did, they wouldn't ripen. We sunned them, buried them, packed them in sawdust, hung them up, warmed them, cooled them—did everything except paint them yellow—but they merely solidified. Then they were eaten by insects. So we won't count that bunch.

The second tree had over a hundred bananas on it. Incidentally, have you ever lifted a hundred bananas? Have you ever lifted a hundred bananas while climbing down a banana tree? In fact, have you ever climbed a banana tree? On the edge of a terrace? With the bananas hanging out over the raspberry patch? Well, you get the picture.

Somehow we got the bunch down without calamity to man, banana, or raspberries. The undertaking was additionally complicated by some large bees that were feeding on two or three overripe bananas. There I was, perched precariously out over the raspberries, holding on to sixty pounds of bananas, with the gardener all set to sever the bunch from the tree (or my arm from my shoulder if I didn't stay out of the way of his sickle), when suddenly the bees got excited. Rising out of the bunch, they swarmed around me and lit on unprotected areas. It was a tense time.

However, getting the bananas off the tree is the easy part. The real challenge comes in caring for the bananas once they're down. What do you do with them? Where do you put them? Do you heat them or cool them? How do you do either? Do you cover them or hang them? What do you cover them with? If you let them, these bananas will upset your entire domestic routine.

After the gardener and I lugged the bananas around to the kitchen door, they became Didi's responsibility. She had some definite ideas about what to do with bananas. She divided them into groups of six to ten, placed them in a duffel bag, and covered them with sawdust. Then she let them sit. And sit. And sit. Soon they were beginning to petrify too.

Our gardener said they should be indoors above the stove. So for several days the duffel bag was placed on the stove, elevated slightly by blocks of wood to keep the bananas from burning. Didi would put her hand in the bag from time to time and give the bananas a squeeze to see if they were softening. Of course she felt only the top ones; as they were still hard, she concluded that none of the others in the bag had ripened either. But the bananas were in her way on the stove, so after a few days she put them on a shelf high above the stove, where, out of sight, they quickly passed out of mind.

Then one day Didi pulled out a few bananas and announced they were ripe. The others still weren't ready, she said. The ones she'd selected were indeed ripe, their positive identification with the banana family being a matter to be taken more on faith than on evidence. As to color, they were various shades of black; as to texture, they were cracked and dry, like old leather. From either end oozed a sticky substance resembling automotive grease, in which an arresting assortment of insects were contentedly stuck. The bananas were a sight.

Ordinarily, Cynthia resolves such domestic vexations without letting them come to my attention; this time, unfortunately, I was in the house. The sight of the bananas excited me greatly, especially when I remembered the many months of watching them ripen on the tree and the harrowing experience of picking them. Now to see them going to rot in our kitchen was intolerable. I demanded to see the rest of the "unripe" bananas in the duffel. They too were well on their way, not to petrification, but to putrefaction—discolored, mushy, moldy, nauseating affairs that looked as if they might decompose before our eyes.

It turned out that Didi, like most other Nepalis, liked bananas really ripe. But she well knew we didn't. She had forgotten to check them. She also figured that one family couldn't eat all those bananas anyway. The Nepalis rush around quickly and sell their bananas to the neighbors, so she figured we'd do the same. She was very nonchalant, as if to say: "Well, what did you expect? Bananas get like that, you know."

Cynthia sent her out to sell the twenty-five most rotten

bananas as punishment for her forgetfulness and indifference, and she promptly sold all twenty-five to Dr. Helen's cook, Tata, who had been told by Helen never to pass up bananas. She didn't.

After giving another dozen to our gardener (who politely said, on inquiry the next day, that they'd been a little on the ripe side), and a dozen each to two next-door neighbors, we still had over fifty bananas on our hands. We were eager to dispose of them, not only because they were rotting, but also because a new bunch was ripening on another tree and would need cutting in a day or two.

So Cynthia began thinking of possible ways to use up bananas. She made six loaves of banana bread and twelve jars of banana jam flavored with passion fruit and falsa berries. We ate banana ice cream, banana milk shakes, banana pie, banana mush with cinnamon sugar. For two days we ate mainly bananas. Bananas for breakfast, bananas for snacks. Banana bread with banana jam for lunch. And for dessert after supper, banana pie or banana pudding. After two days of this, there were still bananas. We weren't that fond of bananas anyway.

To prevent such a fiasco from occurring again, I announced that from now on I'd take charge of the banana business. This would include picking, separating, packing, and inspecting. I was to handle every phase of the operation. No one else could be trusted, obviously.

The next bunch was ready for picking well before the first bunch had been consumed. Now here was my opportunity to demonstrate the proper banana-ripening technique to these Nepalis, who had been doing it all wrong for the past two thousand years.

This bunch, like its predecessor, was picked with great difficulty, the gardener helping. I carted it around to the kitchen door and got ready to split off the bananas—over 140 of them. The gardener offered the usual Nepali cutting device, the *kurpa,* a small sickle. I disdained to use such a clumsy instrument and got out my old college hunting knife, sharp enough to open any airmail envelope. The knife wouldn't even cut through the skin of the few rotten bananas I tried to remove first, much less the stems of the healthy ones. Maintaining my composure (what a surgeon didn't know about cutting wasn't worth knowing), I remembered the new jackknife Cynthia had given me and started in with that. It was sharper, to be sure, but it kept springing shut unexpectedly. It also wasn't big enough. After cutting my left hand twice, I switched to a kitchen knife, with indifferent results, all the time lecturing the gardener on the delicate art of handling bananas, while he was quietly showing me where to cut. It occurred to me that perhaps I had hurt his feelings by not using his *kurpa;* so after struggling for some time without making discernible progress, I decided, for his sake, to try his method. It would enhance his self-image and sense of self-worth. As I reached for his *kurpa,* I could tell by his smile and sort of chuckle that my psychological instincts had not proved me wrong.

The work proceeded more quickly now, but unluckily it began to rain, so I had to bring the bananas inside. Cynthia was not too happy about this: The bunch was home for dozens of cockroaches, ants, and other insects, who dispersed angrily throughout the house as the demolition of their residence progressed. Cynthia pointed out with some passion that we already had enough remnants of previous bananas lying around or being transported here and there by regiments of ants. Why did we need more?

The job was finally completed. This time I packed the bananas in old copies of the *Rising Nepal* that had been shredded for the purpose. No more of that messy sawdust Didi had used the first time. It had stuck to the bananas and ended up in the jam and the pudding and maybe the banana bread too, though there it wasn't so noticeable.

When the packing was completed, I put the boxes of bananas on the shelf over the stove, this time not directly above the stove as Didi had done, but at the far end, below which Cynthia kept a seldom-used, two-burner, kerosene pressure stove. That was on a Thursday afternoon. On Friday afternoon I checked the bananas; they were hard as rocks. On Saturday, I didn't check; I figured I'd look Sunday morning. Unknown to me, however, Cynthia canned pumpkins all day Saturday, using the two-burner stove, right there under the bananas.

Sunday morning, on opening the first box, I was greeted with a peculiar aroma, rich and sweet and altogether disheartening. It was followed by a new generation of cockroaches and other creatures, who once they'd seen daylight couldn't seem to get out of the box fast enough. The bananas, however, looked beautiful. Not black, greasy, and moldy. Neither had they petrified. Far from it. My fears were confirmed when I poked them; they felt like they were filled with whipped cream. The bananas had liquified inside their skins! We'd have trouble just getting them out of the boxes.

Thanks to Cynthia's pumpkin canning, my banana-ripening technique had been accelerated fourfold. We were in a much worse mess than with Didi's system. Here were over 140 bananas that would be fermenting within twenty-four hours. I wanted to dispose of them before Didi and the gardener showed up for work, but there was no time—they were due to arrive any minute. I took the "ripest" and gave them to Cynthia, who then spent the rest of the day making great quantities of banana jam, bread, pudding, and pie. The "least ripe" I took around and distributed gingerly to neighbors and hospital patients, whose gratitude seemed to lessen when they actually got the bananas into their hands. Then we all embarked on another two-day banana-eating marathon, consuming an even greater number than on the first time around. We found the easiest way to get the bananas out of their peels was to squeeze. In the end we used up, in one way or another, every last banana; the compost pile claimed not a one.

The next bunch to ripen—about 180 bananas—was from a tall variety of tree. Since a banana tree bears only once and then dies, the best method of picking the bunch, especially one high up, is to chop the tree down. Of course, this must be done carefully so that the bunch descends slowly, lest the bananas be injured. It's really quite simple if you do it right; it certainly beats climbing the tree.

The tree in question was located on the middle one of three terraces in front of our house. On the upper terrace I stationed our gardener, Purna, who was to hold on securely to a length of clothesline I had managed, with great difficulty, to loop around the top of the tree. By applying some counter-traction on this rope, I reasoned, he'd be able to control the rate of the tree's fall. I would stand near the foot of the tree on the middle terrace and actually receive the bananas. But since the barrel-sized bunch was suspended ominously twenty feet in the air, directly above where I'd be standing, I felt it would add an element of safety to the procedure if, during the initial stages of the tree's descent, I were to support it with a long forked stick. In this way I could help ease the bunch down slowly. With Purna in position holding on to his rope, I would first cut *partway* through the main trunk, just far enough through for the tree to begin bending over. Then, as soon as it began to bend, I would run below and take up my position under the bunch with my forked stick.

It was a good plan. Only two things went wrong. First, if you cut the banana tree on the side *away* from the bunch (which we did), the trunk doesn't bend—it snaps. But we didn't discover that fact until the other thing had gone wrong. The long pole I was using had been selected as a summer home by a colony of termites. Everything was going exactly as planned, and the trunk was just starting to bend over, when, without warning, one prong of my forked stick broke off flush, leaving in my hands nothing but a straight pole. Once that happened, things moved quickly. It takes little imagination to guess how well Purna and his rope were going to hold up that tree once the main trunk snapped and my stick had only one prong. In fact, the last thing I remembered was the sight of Purna being jerked off the edge of the terrace where he'd been standing, placidly thinking, no doubt, that I was the one with the worst end of the job.

Which was true. I was trapped in a two-and-a-half-foot-square space with a banana tree in front, an exuberant rose vine to the right with eager long thorns, three newly planted papaya trees on my left, and the edge of the terrace dropping off behind me. I undoubtedly tried all of these directions momentarily, ruling out each one as an avenue of escape, until my anxiety was ended by the entire eighty pounds of bananas landing full on my head, accompanied by crashing banana leaves and, a split second later, the gardener, still clutching his rope in a catatonic grip. I immediately inquired what he thought he was doing forsaking his post like that and letting those bananas nearly finish me off (I hadn't yet realized what had happened), and he in turn wanted to know why I had neglected *my* end, causing both his arms to be wrenched from their sockets and nearly breaking his neck. As for the bananas, they were fine.

Our problems weren't solved by getting this bunch down: Cynthia refused to make any more banana jam. She claimed that the storeroom was full, that she had already moved out such nonessentials as soap and toothpaste to make room for the jam from the previous bunch. To add to our troubles, that very next week the bananas on three more trees ripened unexpectedly; at one time, before our distribution system was functioning at full efficiency, we had 500 bananas sitting in our house.

At least they weren't pumpkins.

six

A Garden on a Hillside

*T*HERE'S MORE to gardening than bananas.
No garden came with our house. The little mud-and-stone dwelling to which we had been assigned sat perched on a scrubby mountainside surrounded by heaps of rocks interspersed with tangled weeds. The newly constructed mission hospital lay a few hundred yards below on a small knoll jutting out from the hillside, while 2,500 feet further down the mountain a broad valley stretched out to the west, beyond which rose layer upon layer of hills culminating in the perpetually snow-mantled Annapurna Range, over 26,000 feet high. The nearest village, hidden around a shoulder of the hillside, was Rip Gaun, a fifteen-minute walk up the mountain from the hospital; and the closest bazaar—where one could "shop" for items like matches, candles, cheap fabrics, and a few staple grains—was in Amp Pipal, still further up, at the top of the ridge, half an hour away.

Finding herself plunked down on an uninhabited and undeveloped stretch of Himalayan foothill without access to fruit or vegetables, Cynthia at once determined to start her own garden. It was a courageous undertaking for someone who had never gardened before. A scraggly jumble of underbrush was all she started with, the soil half-stone, half-clay. But with the help of a few Nepali workmen, she cleared some land around the house, terraced it, and got rid of the bigger stones. She even had twenty baskets full of rich topsoil carried in from the nearby jungle. And then, when all was ready, she hired a gardener. Her garden was launched.

I doubt if Cynthia had much more than peas, beans, carrots, lettuce, and a few tomatoes in mind when she began. But one thing led to another, and Cynthia soon had her hands full of cabbages and cauliflower, broccoli, eggplant, spinach, and squash—not to mention pumpkins and cucumbers. We were on to our second gardener by this time, the first having lasted only a few weeks. Cynthia was rapidly becoming proficient in the art and science of gardening and was actually enjoying it.

At about the time we arrived in Amp Pipal, someone gave us a large number of fruit-tree seedlings, which we planted in our yard. Soon we had a dozen different varieties growing here and there around the house. Cynthia asked me to take charge of the fruit-raising end of the operation; she didn't have enough time, she said, to manage the vegetables and look after the fruit trees too. I agreed, unenthusiastically (I had no interest in horticulture). Cynthia took me around and showed me what trees had been planted so far. First, outside the kitchen door was a little fig tree a foot high. I'd never seen a fig tree before, and I'd never eaten a fresh fig. Next to it was a little litchi tree; that was a new fruit for me—I'd hardly heard of it. Then a mulberry tree. That was new to me too: I'd thought it was only for silkworms. A little way off, on a higher level, was a mango, another first. And a guava. And a lime. And before I knew it, I was hooked on fruit growing. We ended up with over forty varieties of fruit before we were through, from jackfruit to passion fruit, and persimmons to pomegranates. We had temperate fruits: apples, pears, peaches, plums, even a quince. And citrus fruits: tangerines, kumquats, and grapefruits; sweet lemons and sour lemons; sweet limes, sour limes; sweet oranges, sour oranges; also a citron. All this in a quarter acre of steep hillside.

Only half the fruit trees we planted did at all well, mainly those that were native to the Himalayas, like the citrus fruit, the banana, the papaya, the guava. We learned soon enough that the Nepali foothills were basically hostile to fruit growers. For one thing, rainfall was seasonal: most of it came during four months in the summer; then for the next four months there'd be hardly a drop. Plants drowned one season, dried up the next. For another thing, fierce winds whipped the hillside in the springtime, breaking branches and blowing off blossoms and immature fruit. Hailstorms also came in the spring; what fruit the hailstones didn't knock off they bruised, so that the fruit ripened on the top side while the bottom was still green and hard.

Another factor to contend with was Nepal's fauna—bees, bugs, and worms. Well, they had to eat too, we found out, and fruit and vegetables turned out to be their main staples. The bees ate our grapes; hornets ate the pears; and worms ate the pomegranates. When there was no fruit to eat, the trees themselves were eaten: caterpillars chewed the bark; grubs bored holes in the trunk; and everyone enjoyed the leaves.

The citrus fruits seemed the only ones immune to all this activity, but eventually even they proved to be vulnerable. One year I noticed some large, pentagonal stinkbugs sunning themselves on the maturing tangerines of our big tangerine tree. The fruit was nearly full sized, but still green—too early to be a temptation for insects. But I'd gotten wary over the years. A bug doesn't sit around doing nothing—especially when it's sitting on fruit—so I looked at these stinkbugs pretty closely. And they sat and looked back at me. They didn't even fly away when I shook their seats. I saw no holes in the tangerines, no wounds, nothing. The bugs weren't even moving. They were just sunning themselves after all.

As the weeks passed, I began seeing more and more of these stinkbugs, two and three to a tangerine. With a thousand tangerines on the tree, that added up to quite a few bugs. I kept an eye on them, but never once did I see them do anything. The gardener wasn't happy, though: the fruit was ripening earlier than usual, he thought, and the tangerines weren't as big as they should be. So I took another look. The bugs looked fat. I squeezed one, and out came orange juice. That increased my suspicions. Finally I saw what I'd missed all these weeks: an almost invisible hairlike proboscis, half an inch long, through which these dratted insects had been sucking out the juice of every one of those tangerines. A thousand tangerines sucked dry! It never happened again; when the bugs came back the next year, they got sprayed.

More irritating than bugs was a family of fruit-eating martens (weasel-like animals) that lived off our garden each summer. They prowled at night and could sniff out unerringly all the fruit we were planning to pick the next day. If we began picking the fruit a day early, they began eating it a day early. We could never keep ahead of them—unless we picked the fruit so early that it wouldn't ripen, in which case no one ended up eating it.

The martens exhibited a preference for guavas, persimmons, passion fruit, figs, and pineapple. One animal could eat two whole pineapples in a night. They chewed some of the fruit merely to get the juice. We'd come by in the morning and there by the passion fruit vine would be a dozen freshly chewed passion fruit lying on the ground. Or a dozen well-chewed tree tomatoes under the tree-tomato tree.

We ordered two traps from Kathmandu and set them out near whatever fruit happened to be ripening, but the traps weren't strong enough. The animals would spring the traps and then pull their feet out. We did finally catch one near the pineapple patch, a young fellow, not full size—but certainly full of pineapple. Cynthia cooked him for dinner, mostly in vengeance, I think—though she loves meat too; it doesn't matter what kind. The animal gave off as gamy a scent as any tiger could ask for, but it was too strong for me. I didn't care for the meat either; it tasted of overripe pineapple.

Encouraged by our success, we faithfully set the traps for the next couple of months, but except for tufts of fur, we caught nothing. Worse, the animals' fruit consumption didn't decrease in the slightest. We had caught only a baby; our traps weren't a match for the real villains.

I finally wrote my father, asking him to send us a wolf trap. That may have been overdoing it, but I was concerned lest he get one too small. You know how salespeople are: they'll assure you their little trap will catch elephants.

A fine wolf trap arrived from the States six months later, just in time for the marten season. With great anticipation we set it out and sure enough, within a week we'd caught a huge fellow almost four feet long, half of him tail. He was three full meals for Cynthia, with enough left over for soup.

But still the fruit was being eaten; at least one other marten was left, perhaps the wife. Then one morning I went out to check the trap, and it was gone. The next animal had gotten caught, all right, but it had chewed through the four thicknesses of rope that secured the trap and had escaped. It was almost as good as catching the animal outright, however: the nightly visitations ended after that. The heavy trap locked to its paw must have put a crimp in its tree climbing.

Wild monkeys were the final nuisance. Their specialties were pumpkin and papaya. I recall chatting out back one day with Seppo, a Finnish builder, whose garden was up the hill from ours. He had raised about forty pumpkins and had recently cut them and piled them just inside his fence. As we talked, I noticed a face peering over the pumpkin pile. It was a buck monkey as big as a bulldog, sitting there munching Seppo's pumpkins and keeping an eye on us to make sure we didn't get too close. The instant the monkey's eyes met mine, it ducked down, and for a moment I wasn't sure if I'd been seeing things or not. I nudged Seppo, and we both watched the pumpkins. Sure enough, up came the head, and Seppo was over there in about ten leaps. The monkey was faster though. He loped easily over the fence and sat down and looked at us impudently, his mouth full of pumpkin. He and his cohorts had ruined ten of Seppo's biggest pumpkins.

Monkeys are brazen thieves. One day Cynthia was sitting outside reading, only a few yards away from our papaya tree. In plain view a big monkey jumped the fence, climbed the tree, picked the largest and ripest papaya, and made off with it. Cynthia, whose chair was actually facing this performance, didn't notice the monkey until it was safely over the fence. And we'd been watching that papaya ripen for weeks.

Our garden also served as a vacation spot. After the first two years in Amp Pipal, we never went away on a family holiday. There was no sacrifice in that: few holiday spots anywhere could have matched our garden for peace and beauty. The main reason we stayed in Amp Pipal was our children's need to be at home during their holidays. But beyond that, Cynthia and I ourselves had little incentive to go anywhere else. To begin with, we'd already had one unpleasant experience: on our first and only family vacation out of the country, our big suitcase had been stolen on the second day, leaving us to arrive in Madras with only the clothes on our backs, filthy from three days straight on an Indian train. But it wasn't only our own experience that discouraged us: we watched our colleagues go off to Afghanistan or India or Bangladesh and come back physically and emotionally drained as a result of their travels. Many would have dysentery; a few got hepatitis and were sick for weeks. It seemed hardly worth it. Even if the holiday place itself was pleasant and restful, getting there and back from Amp Pipal would cancel out much of the benefit.

Our garden not only served for our holidays; it was office and study as well. Most early mornings and many evenings, I'd bring the little folding table I used for a desk outside and sit down to work. "Work" might be language study, correspondence, hospital business, or the preparation of Bible lessons, all made more enjoyable by the beauty of the setting. I wouldn't have traded offices with Henry Ford.

Each season had its special graces. Spring began in the middle of January with the plum blossoms. Right through to July something was blossoming somewhere: after the plums the peaches, filling the backyard with pink; then the mango with its strange clusters of tiny flowers; then the *nashpatti* down near the gate, its branches erect and tall and splashed with white.

Then the flowering shrubs and vines would have their turn: in March, the azaleas and roses, and the two jasmine guarding the steps going down the front path; in April, the rhododendron, transplanted from high up on the face of Liglig; in May, the gardenia, loaded with hundreds of blossoms whose heavy fragrance on a still night could be detected fifty yards off; the camellia in June; and in July, the hydrangea, the myrtle at the front gate, and the morning glories climbing up the terrace banks around the dahlias and gladiolas.

The rainy season offered fewer blossoms but brought a green beauty of its own. And spectacular clouds. Clouds above and clouds below. Clouds pouring over the top of Liglig like a foaming cataract, or sweeping up the mountain in great gusty billows. One moment Liglig would be there, a dark green hulk looming 700 feet above the house; the next moment it would be gone, whited out in swirling fog. Sometimes the clouds would swell up from the valley below, obscuring everything from sight and you'd be floating in a fairy cloud garden. Sometimes it would even be cloudy indoors as the mist drifted in through open windows. Not good for Cynthia's piano, but you wanted the air; it was so muggy inside.

Toward October the rain usually stopped, and the clouds vanished. The waterfalls on Liglig dried up, and the busy brooks that had rushed down the hillside slowed to a trickle. A new season was beginning, the most magical of them all. Sun, blue sky, and glistening snow-cloaked Himalayas suddenly reappeared after months in hiding. The land emerged from the shadowy dampness, clean and richly colored. It was as if someone had changed the bulb in the projector; everything looked bright and new.

With the sunlight came fresh blossoms—sweet peas, marigolds, and zinnias. But more striking than these were the poinsettias standing twelve feet tall in a wide semicircle along the upper border of the garden. In November these became a wall of scarlet, a dazzling concentration of color that could be seen for miles. When Tommy and Christopher were home for their Christmas holiday, we spent the sunny days up in their "digging place" outside the garden, just above the poinsettias. The boys would build roads and dig tunnels, while Cynthia did the year's mending and I read aloud to the family from Tolkien or Sir Walter Scott. And as we sat there, we could look out over the bank of red to the snow-covered Annapurnas in the distance, sparkling white above, while beneath and all around was green, dotted with yellow marigolds.

But the best was still to come. Just as the poinsettias were reaching their prime, the great bougainvillea outside the kitchen door would burst into color, a blaze of magenta covering the whole side of the house and spreading like tongues of flame onto the tin roof. No matter that it clashed violently with the poinsettias: the scene, taken all together, had a breathtaking luxuriance. An even larger bougainvillea, with deep violet bracts, grew around the outer side of the house and over the far slope of the roof, but from the "digging place" it was hidden from view. It bloomed much later, anyway; and when it did, I took my folding table around to that side of the house and had my office there.

There were other sights besides flowers. Birds for one. Nepal is known for its birds. And our garden provided front-row seats for bird-watching the year round. No bird walks necessary. One only needed to sit there and the birds would come to the fruit trees and not even bother that someone was watching them. We had unwelcome visitors, of course, like crows and the squawking myna birds. But the great majority were a treat to eye and ear.

I had many favorites: the high-flying kites circling gracefully overhead; the swooping, dipping swallows, which more than once flew right under my seat (while I was in it!); the blue and orange *natilvas,* which perched for hours on the window ledges; the minivets, the male a brilliant scarlet, and the female an equally brilliant yellow. We saw exotic birds, too, like the multicolored Himalayan barbet; the little sunbird, bright red in its upper half, with a long, curved beak for sucking nectar from the stems of lilies; the racket-tailed drongo, sporting two absurdly long tail feathers splayed out at the tips. We had cuckoos, magpies, shrikes, babblers, pipets, and rollers.

Over a hundred different species of birds visited our garden each year. But the most curious of them all were the white-headed laughing thrushes. Their snowy white heads were fluffed up like a poodle's, and were much too big for their bodies. They traveled in groups of ten to twenty, searching for food, moving slowly from tree to tree. Every few minutes, in the midst of their pecking and scratching, one of the group would begin to chuckle, and in an instant the whole crew would erupt in a chorus of raucous cackling, like a bunch of old soldiers howling at a bawdy joke. Picturing those old men sitting out in the trees, I often found myself laughing right along with them.

When the birds weren't around, we watched the lizards, stretched out lazily on branches, waiting for bugs to come by. The male had a red head, which became even redder when a female lizard chanced by. Spurred to life, off he'd go in hot pursuit. There were other creatures, too, like the four-inch-long hairy caterpillars, whose hair contained a poison that could destroy one's eye; or the three-inch-long spotted grasshoppers;

or the butterflies. And all the other more ordinary friends that made a home in our garden.

Things went on outside the garden too. Early one morning, I looked over the fence and saw a leopard thirty yards off, sitting and looking at me. He eventually wandered away into the brush. Since there were no other houses anywhere around us, except for those down toward the hospital, wild animals often prowled nearby.

And then there were monkeys. One spring morning I looked out over a nearby cornfield and saw a band of two hundred monkeys pulling the ears off the stalks like so many hired hands. Before I could do anything, the farmer himself arrived, and the monkeys ran off—each with an ear of corn under its arm. After that, for several weeks the tranquillity of the early morning was shattered by the farmer's son, who stood in the field at dawn and for two hours banged on an empty biscuit tin to keep the monkeys away.

I appreciated the tranquillity of the garden more after that, but I never would have wanted it silent. The sounds of the hillside were as much a part of the atmosphere as the sights were. We could always hear the chirruping and trilling of birds. The call of the cuckoo (*kaaphal paakyo, kaaphal paakyo*) was my favorite, informing us all spring long that the *kaaphal* berries had ripened. We could hear crickets galore and the *jhankri kiraa,* which sounded like someone winding a clock, only louder and longer.

In addition to animal sounds, the tin roof popped when the sun came out; the banana leaves flapped in the wind; and the bamboo creaked near the jackfruit tree. In the distance we could hear the pastoral sounds of woodchopping, of men calling to their animals, of boys blowing on "harmonicas" made from leaves. From the top of Liglig, in the evenings or on special holy days, we would hear the long eery notes of the temple horns. And on special occasions, like the day of the King's coronation, we would hear the crier, who stood on the summit of Liglig and shouted the glad tidings to the entire countryside—for the benefit, I suppose, of those who didn't own radios. And that would mean nearly everyone.

A Trek to Everest

*A*FTER WE'D BEEN in Nepal a year, we took our first vacation, which coincided with the arrival of Cynthia's mother and her brother Dicran. We decided that for part of the vacation Dicran and I, together with another missionary friend named Juhani, would take the trek to Everest, acclaimed by all who have gone on it to be one of life's greatest experiences. Ordinarily, missionaries didn't go on the grandest and most costly of the treks so early in their careers. It was considered more fitting if they waited until they had a certain number of years of service under their belts, otherwise they would be open to the suspicion that they had come to Nepal only to climb mountains. It was different in my case, of course. I felt obliged to serve as escort and translator for my brother-in-law—especially since he was paying my way. It would have been unthinkable to let him down.

We'd planned the expedition for mid-November, when the weather was usually clear, although very chilly at the altitude to which we'd be ascending. Dicran and I left Amp Pipal a day early and went into Kathmandu by plane to complete the arrangements for our trek. Our traveling companion, Juhani, a teacher at one of the mission schools, was to come in by road the next day, when the regular school holiday began. When Juhani didn't arrive in Kathmandu that next evening as expected, Dicran and I were a bit worried; we all had to leave for Everest by plane at 7:00 the following morning.

Juhani later told us that he'd walked the eight hours to the road and caught a taxi, which should have delivered him to Kathmandu by supper time. On the way, however, one of the vehicle's tires blew out. The spare wasn't much use either because it had a large tear in it. Juhani then noticed the driver busily occupied in gathering grass, twigs, and brambles and placing them in a pile by the flat tire. The driver motioned to Juhani to start making himself useful by collecting sticks and grass too. When they had gathered a substantial pile, the driver began to stuff the material into the tire through the blown-out opening. When he had stuffed the tire as firmly as he could, they were off again—for about two miles. By that time the stuffing had worked its way out through the same hole. They repeated the process several more times until the tire became so badly split that the driver gave up. He then told Juhani to wait in the car while he took the spare tire off to get it fixed; he would be back shortly. With tire in hand, he promptly boarded a passing truck and was gone.

Juhani wasn't long in deciding that the driver's chances of returning that night were nonexistent. It was almost dark, and few cars traveled on the road because it was under construction. Seeing a private car coming, he realized this would be his last chance to get into Kathmandu that night, so he waved it down. Luckily the driver stopped and picked him up. He arrived at midnight, in time to help us complete the last of our feverish preparations.

Our flight the next day was delayed three hours by the dense fog that enshrouds Kathmandu most mornings during the fall and winter months. By the time we departed, though, the weather was beautiful. As we flew eastward in our Royal Nepal Airlines "Twin Otter," we were treated to unparalleled views of the majestic Himalayan range, extending east and west for hundreds of miles. Looking below, we observed Nepal's countryside: the numerous small villages, their orange-colored houses gleaming in the sunlight; the intricate terracing, which had turned almost every available slope into farmland; and the scattered remnants of Nepal's once-great forests. On our left we could trace the origin of many of Nepal's rivers from their mountain sources. On our right we could see them meander onto the broad Ganges plain of northern India. And beneath and on all sides were the endless foothills, breaking up the land. At one glance we could appreciate why the hill people of Nepal had remained so isolated from the rest of the world and even from each other.

The terrain became more rugged as we progressed from west to east, and after an hour's flight covering approximately 120 miles, we began to descend into a narrow and extremely steep gorge. Looking ahead out the left-hand windows, we could see a high ridge coming up in front of the plane. Looking out the right-hand windows, we saw the same high ridge; the plane appeared to be heading into it. This didn't seem to concern our Nepali pilot nearly as much as it did his passengers. We had been told that he was a student pilot who was learning how to fly this new Twin Otter, which the Royal Nepal Airlines had recently purchased from Canada. With him was a Canadian instructor, who today for the first time had relinquished the controls and was letting his student fly the plane.

At the last exhilarating moment, the plane leaped upwards and shot through a small gap in the ridge directly in front of us and immediately plummeted into another chasm more precipitous than the last. On the opposite wall of this abyss we could make out a small, level strip, just about the right size for rolling marbles. As we approached the sheer wall in front of us, it became apparent that our marbles were going to roll here—or nowhere. Happily, distance and altitude had conspired to confuse our senses, for when we landed, we found ourselves on a perfectly adequate airfield halfway up the side of a deep valley.

The first order of business was to hire some Sherpa porters to carry our eleven-day supply of food and other equipment. We were fortunate to find four agreeable and experienced young men, who would prove indispensable many times over. The three of us intended to carry packs as well; I didn't feel comfortable traveling without a pack and letting someone else carry everything. I considered that to be somehow the mark of an imperialist. It was a scruple not shared, however, by most upper-class Nepalis, who rarely carried anything if they could help it.

By early afternoon we were on the trail. We soon found ourselves switchbacking down a steep decline into the narrow gorge of the Dudh Kosi River, a descent of 1,000 feet. *Dudh* (the Nepali word for milk) was an apt name for this churning, foaming river. We passed through groves of tall evergreens, the trunks of which had been ringed by the local Sherpas to obtain the pitch that fueled the tiny lamps that lit their homes. The day was beautiful, with hardly a cloud to be seen, and as we walked along, we caught glimpses of snowcapped peaks, a foretaste of what was to come.

At dusk, the flapping of Buddhist prayer flags some distance ahead announced the proximity of a Sherpa homestead, and a few moments later we were standing before a substantial, medieval-looking stone structure that was to be our stopping place for the night. At one end of the large main room crackled a cheerful fire, around which the occupants of the house busily prepared the evening meal. A robust Sherpa woman with a baby at her breast selected potatoes and tossed them to her impassive husband to be peeled. A lovely, bright-eyed Sherpa girl observed us shyly, while her older sibling, obviously retarded, gaped absently into the fire, uttering from time to time a low, inarticulate grunt in response to some inner rumination. The family circle was completed by an old granny hunched up in a corner, supporting on her knees what appeared in the dim firelight to be a small flesh-colored pumpkin. But to our wonderment, when she stood up, we saw that the "pumpkin" was a goiter so heavy that it caused her to stoop as she shuffled along. We were to observe among the Sherpas many other huge and similarly neglected goiters, all of them resulting from a deficiency of iodine in the soil.

After a dinner of boiled potatoes (the staple of the Sherpa diet) flavored with a small tin of Peking duck, we all sat around the hearth trying to keep warm, an enterprise that would require increasing ingenuity the higher we proceeded in altitude. We got no help from the Sherpas, who were forever leaving windows and doors open. Just as we'd finally be getting thawed out, a glacial draft of November air would catch us on the backside, undoing the effect of half an hour by the fire.

However, as if to make up for the frigid atmosphere, our host and hostess for this first night turned out to be warm and convivial company. We passed the after-dinner hours in spirited conversation on a wide range of topics. During most of the evening the husband rhythmically twirled a small prayer wheel containing, he said, a scroll upon which was written over and over a single prayer: "Oh jewel in the heart of the lotus"—an expression of adoration directed to Buddha. He told us that each time the wheel revolved, all the prayers on the scroll would be repeated in heaven. By this means the consequences of one's sins could be minimized and the prospects of good fortune enhanced. The more prayers that ascended, therefore, the better. The next day we would encounter some efficient prayer wheels four feet high and three feet in diameter, containing countless repetitions of this same prayer and operating day and night—by water power. When we had first seen them in the stream, we thought they were mills.

The weather on the second day was again clear: a typical November day. The monsoon rains had ended, and the heavy banks of clouds that had obscured the mountains all summer and fall had disappeared with the rain, leaving in their place sensational panoramas of the Himalayas on every side. For sheer height and grandeur these mountains had no equal anywhere; even after months of living in Nepal, we still couldn't get used to them.

Our trail now followed north along the Dudh Kosi River for ten or twelve miles and then climbed steeply up to the famous Sherpa village of Namche Bazaar, elevation 11,500 feet, where we arrived in the middle of the second day. That same afternoon we moved on to Nepal's most beautiful monastery at Teng-boche, 13,000 feet, set in the midst of the highest and most astonishing peaks in the world, including Everest, Lhotse, and Ama Dablam.

The scenery at Tengboche defied comparison with anything in our experience. We tried in our imagination to transplant the Alps or Sierra Nevadas into the setting before us and visualize what they would look like here: at best they corresponded to the thinly snow-sprinkled hills and ridges that surrounded the base of the real Himalayas like peasant huts at the foot of a feudal castle. The Tengboche monastery itself was perched dramatically on a promontory overlooking the deep valley of the Dudh Kosi River. It commanded breathtaking views in all directions. The nearest peaks, Ama Dablam and Kangtega, both 23,000 feet, towered so near at hand that we had to crane our necks to see their summits. The monastery buildings, only fifty years old, resembled an American Indian pueblo and faced a handsome meadow bordered with large pine trees, the last stand before the tree line. Awestruck and exhausted, we retired for the night to a small frame tourist bungalow adjacent to the monastery. The best was still before us.

It was a chilling experience—that second night, in an unheated wooden shelter at 13,000 feet in the middle of November. It's likely we'd have been too numb to prepare the evening or morning meals had not our hardy Sherpa porters done most of the work. And in spite of being bundled up in six layers of clothing inside two sleeping bags, I never really warmed up. I spent much of the night doing isometric exercises just to keep my blood moving.

We were glad to see the sun the next day. The trail above Tengboche soon leveled out onto a broad moraine without trees or shrubs—or firewood. The way was dotted with low stone huts used by the Sherpas for shelter in the summer months when they brought their yaks up to graze in the high pastures. The weather was again perfect, and this made us all the more eager to reach the Everest base camp as quickly as possible in order to make the most of the clear skies. We were soon, however, to reap the consequences of our haste. We had been accustomed to living at an altitude of 4,000 feet in Amp Pipal, and now in two days we had reached 13,000 feet and were proceeding higher still. That third day, Juhani, in particular, was beginning to puff harder than usual, and I was feeling lightheaded myself. That night we stayed in an abandoned stone hut, and with the help of our Sherpas cooked up an enormous pot of stew, throwing into it many miscellaneous items of food that we hadn't the energy to prepare separately. You'd think we would be hungry, but only Dicran ate with enthusiasm, consuming two huge platefuls. I ate little and Juhani ate nothing.

The next morning Juhani seemed refreshed and had something to eat. Since it was a beautiful day, we decided to try to reach the shelter near the Everest base camp by that evening. It was only six miles further, with an ascent of less than 2,000 feet. We figured we could spend the following day taking it easy and enjoying the area around Everest. So we started off in good spirits.

It quickly became evident, however, that Juhani was not himself; he was complaining of a headache and was sick to his stomach. I think each of us knew inwardly that we should turn back, but our desire to reach our destination was so great that we didn't heed these early warnings of altitude sickness. Juhani insisted on going ahead, mainly because he didn't want to spoil the trip for the rest of us. We had previously agreed that if one had to go back, all would go back, and he simply couldn't bring himself to ask us to make that sacrifice.

On this, the fourth day of the trek, we entered that weird world of snow, ice, and rock—a world known only to mountain climbers. Not even grass grew here. We ascended sharply onto the leading edge of the Khumbu Glacier, which from there on would serve as our route all the way to base camp. Several tributary glaciers on our left led to passes over into forbidden Tibet, less than two miles away. We threaded our way slowly between strange formations of ice and rock and crossed glittering snowfields studded with huge boulders. Finally we approached the upper end of the Khumbu Glacier, where we would spend the night—at the foot of Everest itself. Nearby was the base camp established in the early fifties by Sir John Hunt and used since by most of the succeeding Everest expeditions.

At dusk we arrived at the final shelter, 17,000 feet, and Juhani lay down to rest. As usual, Dicran, who had never climbed seriously in his life before, was in good spirits and ate with a hearty appetite. I felt as if I was coming down with something, and who knows what Juhani felt like—he was hardly talking. We passed our coldest night with little sleep, expecting that somehow the morning would find us rejuvenated. Such was not to be the case. Juhani had not become acclimatized during the night as we had vaguely hoped, and he decided to spend the morning sleeping. Dicran and I set out to climb a small mountain called Kalapatar, 18,500 feet, from which we'd be able to obtain a good view of Everest. We thought we would whistle up in half an hour, spend a short while on top, and then go down and bring Juhani up so he too could see the view. Because of the altitude, however, it took us two hours to make the short ascent. After every few steps I had to take a long rest, while non-mountaineer Dicran, exuberantly extolling the glories of the

Himalayas, darted off here and there snapping pictures. The higher we got, the harder it was just to lift each foot. It was like trying to climb out of a vacuum into a high-pressure zone. The force of gravity seemed to have tripled. Finally, having barely dragged myself to the top and thinking my head was about to explode, I flopped down without so much as a glance at the scene around me and slept for over an hour.

When I opened my eyes and got up, I was looking straight across at Everest, its summit emerging in full view and dominating the entire region. We hadn't caught a glimpse of Everest since we'd left Tengboche; it had been obscured by the steep ridges running parallel to our trail. Now I was startled to see it so close at hand. As my eyes moved from Everest to take in the surrounding vista laid out before us, I knew I was standing in a place that has few equals anywhere on earth.

The mountain on which we stood rose 1,500 feet above the Everest base camp and was surrounded on all sides by towering, sharply etched, ice-clad peaks. To our left was a pass, on the other side of which lay the strange land of Tibet; to our right, the scene stretched out across tiers of mountains: Tamserku, Ama Dablam, and dozens of others whose names we didn't know. Below was the rocky Khumbu Glacier—our route up—winding away between the distant peaks. Directly before us and rising 9,000 feet straight up from the glacier floor was Nuptse, its face roughened by numerous ice falls. And up to our left, still 11,000 feet above us, black and snowless, stood Everest itself, 29,028 feet high. Apart from the intermittent rumble and clatter of falling ice, there was no sound, no breeze. This silence, together with our relatively anoxic condition, gave us the sensation that we'd left the ordinary world behind. I could have stayed up there all day and never moved.

Arriving back at the shelter, we found that Juhani was worse. We soon realized that there was no point in waiting until he felt better in the hopes of his climbing Kalapatar. In his state he didn't care whether or not he ever saw Everest. He was too weak to walk. So the strongest of our Sherpas volunteered to carry him bareback four miles down to a lower shelter, where we could spend the night. The rest of us had to share both the Sherpa's ordinary load and Juhani's pack. Thus heavily laden, we trudged slowly downwards, weaving our way in and out among the great boulders that made up a large portion of the glacier's surface.

Two hours down the trail we met a large trekking party of about forty men and women, most of them in their seventies, who had spent the previous three weeks hiking overland from Kathmandu. It was a wonderful sight to see these spry and energetic British people, the men sporting knickers, tweeds, and touring caps and the women wearing assorted smart outfits— the perfect picture of an English touring party. They had just pitched camp for the day and were busily preening themselves and photographing each other in various Hillary-type poses. They all looked as fit as fiddles, and I felt like an idiot dragging past as if I were about to die—to say nothing about how Juhani must have felt. He probably couldn't have cared less—it was hard to tell whether he only wanted to die or whether he thought he was going to—or both.

We stopped to rest for a few minutes some yards away from this jovial group and watched as several Sherpas constructed a tiny portable outhouse for the trekking party. After selecting a suitable spot, they precariously erected their installation on top of some large boulders on the other side of a little stream, in plain view of the entire camp. It didn't look large enough to accommodate even an average-size trekker, let alone some of the more rotund members of the party. One by one the men and women gingerly edged their way across the creek to try out the new facility, which looked like a miniature polling booth. Watching the outhouse quiver and heave as each person used it, we fully expected the thing to topple over at any moment. It was the one bright spot in an otherwise grim afternoon.

By the next day, our health and spirits had improved, and we were beginning to feel ourselves again. Having hurried on the way up, we now had leisure time on the way down. We detoured through the fascinating Sherpa villages of Pangboche, Khumjung, and Kunde. We became acquainted with the Sherpas, whom we found to be a genuinely open and friendly people—like Nepalis almost everywhere. Their houses were centers of hospitality for weary trekkers.

The trip was over much too soon. In spite of the unpleasant bout with altitude sickness, we all agreed that the Everest trek was one of the highlights of our lives. And it wasn't only the spectacular scenery and friendly Sherpa people that made it worthwhile; we also had spent many hours in profitable conversation with each other. I found some encounters with my brother-in-law particularly stimulating. We'd always had widely divergent views on most subjects, but this time we didn't rise up and shout at each other as we did in the old days—we kept seated. Some of our debates were triggered by our differing manners of dealing with the local people. In the true missionary tradition, I was firm in my dealings with the porters and wary of getting overcharged. In short, I was a mean and calculating penny pincher. At the other extreme was Dicran—benevolent, casual, uncritical. Able to calculate expenses only in terms of the American economy, he couldn't understand what was so important about a few rupees here or there. This difference in our attitudes highlighted for me just how much my way of thinking had changed after living in Asia for a year. When I saw myself through Dicran's eyes, I discovered that I'd become *too* acculturated. By the end of the trip we both had helped the other move closer to that ideal middle ground that lay elusively between us.

Armed Robbery

IT'S HARD to imagine a more tranquil place than Amp Pipal. Apart from the daily dramas occurring in the hospital, life for most of the inhabitants drifts lethargically on from season to season, enlivened only by the periodic festivals, the misadventures of certain missionaries, and an occasional minor robbery.

The Amp Pipal Hospital had been open about five years when into this placid setting came a new business manager, a phlegmatic and unassuming Mennonite from Ohio, named Stu Amstutz. His temperament suited his surroundings perfectly, and he and his wife, Loretta, quickly made themselves at home in a little stone cottage that also included the one-room project business office.

So peacefully had his first few months passed by that Stu registered little alarm one hot and sticky Saturday morning at 3:00 when he was awakened by a knock on the door. A young Nepali announced that he'd been sent with a message from Dag Amstadt, a Norwegian schoolteacher who lived an hour away in the village of Harmi. Since Stu was already expecting a visit from Dag that same day—though not quite so early—he assumed the message was simply to say that Dag would be unable to come. Suspecting nothing, Stu opened the door. Suddenly a well-built Nepali sprang out of the darkness. He was brandishing a long *kukri*, the Nepali sword made famous by the Gurkha regiments during the Second World War. If the mere sight of that sword was sufficient to strike fear into the hearts of the Nazis, it was no less disconcerting to Stu on that early May morning in Amp Pipal.

"If you make a sound, we'll kill you," said the sword wielder in a hoarse whisper.

"We want money," said his partner. "Open up the office."

Stu duly complied, and with one eye on the *kukri,* he opened up the locked cabinet where the money was kept and handed them the safe box, which contained $600 and about 18,000 Nepali rupees (approximately $1,600). The thieves put the money into a bag and backed slowly out of the office.

"If you make a sound or call for help, we'll kill you," said the one with the *kukri,* as if Stu hadn't been sufficiently impressed by the first threat. And with that, they turned and walked quickly out of the house.

Stu stood for a moment to recapture his thoughts, which had scattered like butterflies over a green meadow in springtime. It was a major robbery—that much he knew—probably the biggest heist ever pulled off in all of Gorkha District. As business manager he'd be held accountable for this loss of mission funds. Had he been careless, negligent in any way? Or just too timid?

It was utterly quiet. The little village was sound asleep. One butterfly that had gotten loose for good was the thought of waking up the villagers, sounding the alarm, and setting out in immediate pursuit. But it was hard enough rousing folks from their languor at high noon—let alone at 3:00 in the morning. Had he tried, he would have stirred up only the dogs.

Stu settled for stirring up me, as growly a dog as he could have asked for at this time of the morning. After discussing the matter, we gloomily concluded that the money was lost forever. It would be difficult even identifying the robbers, much less catching them. Apart from the *kukri,* Stu's impression of the men was indistinct. Hopeless though it seemed, we nevertheless felt obliged to report the robbery to the police; and Stu, happy to make even a token gesture toward regaining the stolen money, volunteered to go in person to the police station, taking with him his Nepali office assistant as an interpreter.

"Don't be upset if the police don't send anyone," I told Stu. "After all, it's Saturday. And they probably aren't going to do anything anyway."

The nearest police station was down at the foot of the mountain in the village of Thadipokhari, a two-hour walk away. We had no idea what they would do in a case like this, and beyond the routine filing of a report, we entertained little hope that aggressive action would be taken to bring the thieves to justice.

Imagine, then, my surprise and pleasure when Stu arrived back about eight hours later with two policemen in tow. Since a two-hour walk downhill in the cool of the morning easily translates into a four-hour walk back up in the heat of the midday sun, their enthusiasm for catching robbers had considerably slackened in favor of cool drinks and rest in the shade. It was over an hour before we were able to sit down with the two policemen and begin discussing what should be done. We invited one of the leaders of the Amp Pipal *panchayat*, Rudra Bahadur, a former *pradhan panch* (local mayor) and faithful friend of the hospital, to sit in with us. The current *pradhan panch* was out of town on business—conveniently so, as it turned out.

The policemen asked a lot of routine questions. No one had a clue about who the robbers were or how we should proceed to find out. After an hour, we had gotten nowhere.

Then Rudra Bahadur, as if trying to keep the conversation going, began to tell of an incident that had happened two weeks before—about some fellow named Top Bahadur, who had stolen a goat in one village and then had sold it to the brother of the owner in another village. It was a long and involved story, and we all grew impatient listening to it—especially as it seemed to have no bearing whatever on the matter at hand. Rudra concluded his tale by saying that the goat thief, Top Bahadur, lived near the school where Dag Amstadt taught. We recalled that at least one of the thieves had to have known Dag, since they had claimed to be bringing a message from him when they knocked on Stu's door. It was a flimsy thread to follow.

Dag had come up from Harmi that afternoon as planned and was staying at Stu's house. We invited him to join the meeting at this point, which he was eager to do since the 600 U.S. dollars that had been stolen happened to be his own money, which he urgently needed for his return to Norway on furlough the following week. It turned out that Dag knew Top Bahadur very well and had told him just the day before that he was coming up to Amp Pipal on Saturday. Dag also confirmed that Top's character was admirably suited to robbing missionaries, and that his physical description was compatible with Stu's recollection of the *kukri* wielder. Here suddenly was a lead worth acting on, and although it was still a long shot, it was sufficient to ignite our enthusiasm for the chase. The nagging thought that the thieves had probably already left town and were by now miles away on any one of five hundred different trails was, for the moment, forgotten.

I urged the group to set out at once to seize Top Bahadur at his home. Already the whole village was alive with talk about the robbery, and the prompt arrival of the police, especially on their day off, added to the excitement. Surely Top would hear about the police and be gone by the next morning; if we didn't act immediately, we might lose our only chance of catching him. But I was overruled. The police were tired and hungry. By this time it was 7:00 P.M., and they were reluctant to tangle with a *kukri* in the dark.

So we settled on a plan for the morning. Dag was to return at daybreak to his house in Harmi, an hour's walk down the north side of our mountain in the opposite direction from the police station. Immediately upon his arrival, Dag would send his water carrier to Top Bahadur's house, fifteen minutes away, to invite Top to his house for a farewell visit (since Dag was leaving on furlough) and to receive a parting gift. Half an hour after Dag's departure, Stu, the two policemen, and I were to set out for Harmi as if on casual business. To avoid attracting attention, the police decided to wear plainclothes instead of their uniforms.

The plan was that as soon as we neared the center of Harmi, where Dag's house was located, Stu and I were to separate from the police and proceed directly to Dag's house, where the unsuspecting Top Bahadur would be waiting to receive his "going-away" present. Stu would then identify him as one of the robbers (if indeed he was) and give me a nod, whereupon I would somehow signal to the police waiting outside. They would then quickly undress and put on their uniforms, because it's unlawful for Nepali police out of uniform to arrest anyone. While they were changing, Stu and I would hold Top Bahadur at bay, using our umbrellas for weapons, until the police got there for the final capture. It all seemed much more exciting than another routine day at the hospital, and filled with anticipation for what the morrow would bring, we concluded the meeting, congratulating one another on our cleverness.

The only thing that remained was to feed the police. In Nepal, whoever calls the police must be prepared to feed them or at least pay their bills. Since we were anxious that the police should remain content in mind and body while pursuing our business, we made no objection when they ordered a triple helping of meat and then washed it down with liberal quantities of *raksi*, the local brew. We also didn't object when the bill came to eighteen rupees ($1.50) apiece—four times the cost of an ordinary meal. We could only hope that the thieves would be rounded up expeditiously, before too many mealtimes had gone by.

We arrived at Dag's house the next morning, umbrellas in

hand, only to learn that our prey had just left home that very hour. His family knew nothing about why he had left or where he was headed. We saw this as additional evidence that Top Bahadur was, in fact, one of the thieves. Our initial disappointment at not finding him was quickly dispelled by the thought that he was at that very moment walking down the main trail from Harmi with all our money—and with less than an hour's head start.

We then called an impromptu meeting that included Dag, Stu, the two policemen, the Harmi *pradhan panch,* a couple of other *panchayat* members, a schoolteacher who was a good friend of Dag's, and me. A sense of urgency pervaded the meeting because we all knew that if Top Bahadur succeeded in reaching the main east-west highway, a seven-hour walk away, we'd never be able to track him down. But whenever it was proposed that one or more of us should actually get up and chase the thief, the sense of urgency would suddenly give way to calls for caution and circumspection.

Not one of us was eager to run after Top Badahur; in fact, some of us had superb reasons for not doing so. It was a sweltering day to begin with. Who could tell where the chase would end? From teashop to teashop it would be the same story: "He was just here an hour ago." That's if we could even keep on his trail—or keep up his pace. And then, supposing we caught him—and he wasn't the thief!

"It's no use," said one of the policemen, looking at his watch. It was almost time for the morning meal. "He's too far ahead. We'll never catch him."

"Besides," said the second policeman, "we're not even sure he's the thief. People are always leaving home to go somewhere; that's no big thing."

As Dag, Stu, and I exchanged glances, we realized that if there was to be any thief-chasing that day, one of us would have to go along. It couldn't be me; I couldn't just up and leave the hospital. In fact, my colleague, Dr. Helen, was supposed to have gone on holiday that very day, but she had reluctantly agreed to work until I got back from Harmi. Dag was leaving in two days to go on furlough. He was in the process of moving his family's belongings from their house in Harmi up to Amp Pipal for storage. He had packing to do. How could he take the time to go running after a thief for one or two days—even if it *was* his money? And Stu, poor fellow, wasn't used to walking; he had blisters on both feet from his journey down to the police station the day before. He hadn't brought his walking shoes. And he didn't know the language.

So the discussion went round and round, each participant extolling his neighbor's thief-chasing qualifications and eagerly devising a plan to send off anyone but himself in pursuit of Top Bahadur. The most enthusiastic member of the group was the Harmi *pradhan panch,* who in any case was in no danger of being enlisted himself. After ten minutes of dithering, Dag couldn't stand it any longer. Conscious that Top Bahadur was getting farther away with each passing minute, Dag announced to the group: "I'll go and take Dil Bahadur [Dag's water carrier] and one policeman. We'll leave immediately."

The proposal met with the hearty approval of almost everyone present. There followed a brief but animated discussion between the two policemen. Finally one of them stood up and said, "All right, I'll go." The entire group burst into applause. With this demonstration of our enthusiastic support and best wishes still ringing in their ears, the intrepid party quickly left the house and was soon out of sight down the trail.

Those of us who remained sat in silence for a while, some feeling a little bit sheepish, others a little bit smug, but all feeling immensely relieved not to be running at that moment down the mountainside. After about five more minutes of desultory conversation, Stu and I decided to return to Amp Pipal. Just as we got up to go, a young man ran into the room and announced that another man had unexpectedly left home that same morning—a notorious gambler and cheat, named Thakur, who also happened to be a nephew of the Amp Pipal *pradhan panch*. Thakur had taken with him his current wife (the fourth) and their new baby. The circumstances of his abrupt departure were suspicious, and the more we talked about this second fellow, the more we believed he might be Top Bahadur's accomplice. Each member of the group recalled some incident that suggested Thakur was well suited to committing armed robbery. His physical description also matched Stu's recollection. We decided he'd be fairly easy to catch. He'd left less than an hour before, and his wife and baby would slow him down. Even Stu with his blistered feet might be able to gain on him.

Stu could understand just enough Nepali to realize that he was being elected to chase Thakur. He tried various legitimate means to avoid it.

"I have only one pair of socks on," he said to me. "I can't possibly walk without two pairs." Without hesitation I offered him my socks.

"I've given my umbrella to Dag. I can't walk in this sun without an umbrella."

"You can take mine," I said. It wouldn't do to be less helpful to Stu than he had been to Dag.

"I have no boiled water for drinking," Stu said with a wry grin, knowing that I had generously given all my water to Dag. "That will be a little harder to fix up."

Unfortunately for Stu, it didn't prove to be so. We quickly discovered that Dag's gas stove was still working, and one of the Nepalis put some water on to boil. We didn't want Stu getting dysentery in mid-chase.

The final problem was Stu's need for an interpreter and everyone began looking at me. Actually I would have been happy to go at that point but for the fact that I had no water, no umbrella, and no socks. However, I suddenly noticed Ishwari, the schoolteacher, sitting quietly in a corner trying to look inconspicuous. I said, "Ishwari can speak English. Maybe he'd be willing to go."

The Harmi *pradhan panch* seconded the suggestion and urged Ishwari to go, eloquently citing the need to restore the honor of the Nepali people, which had been so besmirched by the robbery of these foreigners who had come to serve them. Everyone nodded in agreement and looked expectantly toward Ishwari. Having no excuse ready at hand, Ishwari agreed. Thus, within a few minutes a second party was formed, consisting of Stu, Ishwari, and the second policeman. The water having been boiled but hardly cooled, the three solemnly said good-bye and left by the same path that Party Number One had taken barely half an hour before.

Liglig Mountain, on which Amp Pipal is situated, is 4,700 feet in altitude and looks down over river valleys 3,000 feet below. Liglig has three main sides: a south side looking down to the Thadipokhari police station and beyond to the east-west highway; a north side facing Harmi; and an east side sloping down to the Daraundi River, which flows north to south. Across the Daraundi and up another mountain is the town of Gorkha, the district capital. The main trails leading east from Harmi and Amp Pipal join at the foot of Liglig to continue on to the Daraundi River four miles away. Here the main trail turns south along the river to the east-west highway.

When proceeding to the district capital, one needs to ford the river and then negotiate a steep 2,000-foot ascent up the ridge on the opposite side. Myriads of little side paths branch off in every direction, which to the inexperienced eye look no different from the main trail, inviting travelers to spend many hours wandering miles out of their way.

It was down the main trail leading east from Harmi that our two parties set out in pursuit of the thieves. After about two hours of walking, Party Number One stopped at a teashop and learned that Top Bahadur had been there an hour before. Heartened by this news, they sped on. Then at the main trail junction near the Daraundi River, they overtook Thakur, suspected Thief Number Two, with his wife and child, about whom, of course, they knew nothing at all. Thakur, however, knew very well what Dag and the policeman were doing there because he, indeed, was the second thief. No sooner had Dag and his friends disappeared into a nearby teashop than Thakur hastily passed to his wife his share of the stolen money and instructed her to go to his uncle's house in Gorkha. Realizing he hadn't been suspected, Thakur then followed Dag and the policeman into the teashop, with the hope of finding out whom they were chasing.

The robbery had already become the subject of a lively conversation among the occupants of the shop, and Thakur, feigning ignorance of the whole matter, joined in. "Who do you think did it?" he asked Dag.

"There were two robbers," said Dag. "One of them, we think, is named Top Bahadur."

"Top Bahadur?" exclaimed Thakur involuntarily. His heart sank. He thought to himself, *How have they found out?* Thakur knew all too well that having discovered the first thief, it wouldn't be long before they discovered the second.

"Yeah, Top Bahadur," said Dag. "You know him?"

"Well, ah—yes, I know him a little."

Thakur felt all the eyes in the shop turn his way. No one spoke. Thakur nervously scuffed the dirt floor with his sandals, averting his face from the others lest someone might suddenly identify him as a close friend of Top Bahadur. Then in an attempt to divert suspicion from himself, Thakur said, "It's a terrible thing that's been done, robbing the mission like that. Top Bahadur could have done it. He's that kind of person. I know of other things he's done like that. I hope you can catch him." Then before he had a chance to reflect on what he was saying, Thakur added, "In fact, I'll go with you now and help you catch him." Perhaps he thought to warn Top Bahadur or in some way help him escape.

"That's great," said Dag. "Let's get going; he's not getting any closer."

If Thakur had any second thoughts, he kept them to himself. Without another word he followed Dag and his companions out of the teashop. After making some inquiries, Dag learned that Top had taken the trail south toward the east-west highway and was about forty-five minutes ahead of them. So the party at once set out again in that direction—the tall Norwegian in the lead, followed by his water carrier, the policeman, and Thakur, Thief Number Two.

For four hours Party Number One raced along under the hot May sun, stopping at every wayside teashop for a quick drink and for any news of their prey. At about 3:00 in the afternoon Dag, tired and thirsty and far ahead of the others, arrived at a pleasant-looking little teashop. Walking in, he found himself face to face with Top Bahadur.

"Well, what are you doing here?" asked Dag in a friendly tone.

"I'm on business," said Top. "What are you doing here?"

"I'm on business too," replied Dag. "I was looking for you this morning to give you a going-away present, but you weren't home. But it's lucky I've met up with you, because now I'll have a chance to give it. Let me sit down with you, and we'll have some tea together."

"No, no, I've got to go now," said Top, eyeing Dag suspiciously. "I can't wait any longer, I'm already late." As Top got up to leave, Dag put his arm around him in a gesture of congeniality and drew him back down onto the bench, calling at the same time for two teas and some bananas.

"You can't just up and leave your friend like this," resumed Dag in a tone of gentle reproach, stalling for time until his companions should arrive. "I'm leaving on furlough in a couple of days. I may never get to see you again, you know."

At that moment the policeman appeared in the doorway, followed immediately by Thakur and the water carrier. The instant Top spotted Thakur, he started from his seat like a bolt. But he didn't rise an inch from the bench: Dag's arm lay across his shoulders like a steel girder.

A struggle ensued. Dag tried to get the attention of the policeman, who had become thoroughly absorbed in purchasing some choice bananas from the pretty proprietress of the teashop and remained oblivious to the increasing commotion behind him. Suddenly Thakur burst through the door and hurled himself at Dag. Retaining a grip on Top's collar, Dag tried to ward off this new assailant. Stunned, Dag was at first uncertain as to the object of Thakur's attack. For a brief interval it appeared that the thieves, having the upper hand, would break free and make their escape. But the big Norwegian was too much for them, and in a moment he had thrown them both to the floor. The cursing and grunting finally aroused the policeman, who turned around to discover both villains immobilized on their backs. Then with gravity and dignity, he stepped forward and pronounced them arrested.

"Aren't you going to put handcuffs on them?" asked Dag incredulously as the policeman turned back to the girl and began paying for his bananas.

"Nope. Can't do that; they're only suspects. Got to have proof. Got to have formal charges." It was incomprehensible to Dag why these two rogues should be treated with such delicacy, when he knew of other cases, even involving innocent people, that had been handled quite differently. But the policeman was adamant and wouldn't permit either thief even to be searched.

Dag consoled himself with the reflection that almost single-handedly he'd captured not just one thief but both of them. The people back at Amp Pipal wouldn't believe it! But all the same, he couldn't lay a hand on the stolen money, half of which was literally within arm's reach.

The policeman announced that they would proceed together to the Thadipokhari police station, where Stu had gone the day before to report the robbery. By walking briskly, they'd be able to reach their destination by sundown.

They set out again, but within a short time Dag became faint with hunger and thirst. He hadn't gotten to drink his tea at the previous stop or munch bananas with the policeman. So when he passed a basket of ripe tangerines at a small teashop, Dag stopped, and called to the policeman to wait for him. The policeman, however, kept going until the party had reached a point about fifty yards down the trail.

As Dag emerged from the teashop with his mouth and pockets stuffed with tangerines, he saw both thieves suddenly break away and run in opposite directions into the woods on either side of the path. The policeman and the water carrier quickly leaped after Thakur, tackling him before he'd gone ten steps. Dag, tearing the tangerines out of his pockets, raced down the trail and into the woods near the point where Top had disappeared. On breaking out into the open again, Dag caught sight of Top darting up a steep slope on the opposite side of a wide expanse of rice fields. Leaping over the terraces, Dag quickly reached the foot of the slope and began to climb. But the long day's journey without sufficient food and water had taken its toll. By the time he gained the top of the slope, Dag was winded. Seeing Top even farther ahead than before, he reluctantly gave up the chase.

When Dag reached his companions again, he noted with relief that Thakur was now handcuffed. The little party set out once more and reached the police station at dusk. When they arrived, however, they were crestfallen to discover that Thakur had on him only 500 rupees. Where was the rest of the money he had stolen? Thakur, seeing his chance, promptly denounced his captors and claimed to be innocent of the whole matter. The speechless policeman was roundly chastised for arresting the wrong person, and Dag was rebuked for meddling in the affairs of the police. Exhausted and discouraged by this unexpected turn of events, Dag barely managed to extract from the police inspector the promise to detain Thakur for twenty-four hours in order to give Stu a chance to come down to the station and identify him. If Stu didn't come within that time, the prisoner would be released.

Before dawn Dag was on his way up the mountain to Amp Pipal, and over breakfast he breathlessly related to us his tale. But when he came to the end and told us that Stu should leave immediately for the police station, we looked at each other in dismay: Stu and Party Number Two hadn't returned yet, and we had no idea where they'd gone or who they were chasing— much less when they'd be back.

A third policeman, who had accompanied Dag up to Amp Pipal that morning in order to question some other villagers about the robbery, advised us that if Stu wasn't back by noon, I should go down to the station to make formal charges or else the case would be dropped and the prisoner would go free. So when noon had come and gone with no sign of Stu, I set out on the two-hour jaunt down the mountain, having asked Dr. Helen to interrupt the second day of her holiday to help Cynthia at the hospital.

When I arrived at the police station, I stated my business to the guard, who ushered me into a large room and invited me to sit on a bench along the wall. Across the room stood the sub-inspector of police, a lean man, immaculately uniformed, with a finely curled moustache, over which extended a thin, pointed nose. I was so transfixed by his striking appearance that as I started across the room, I almost tripped over the legs of a man sitting on the floor. Losing my balance, I lurched forward into the center of the room. Amidst the roar of laughter from a dozen officers, I looked back at the rude fellow who hadn't even bothered to move his legs, and discovered that his ankles were fastened to the floor by steel rods shaped like croquet wickets. I immediately recognized him as the prisoner, Thakur, whom I'd treated several times at the hospital.

After I sat down, the sub-inspector eyed me skeptically, wondering how anyone who couldn't even walk into a room without stumbling could possibly be the medical director of a hospital. In the roadless hills of Nepal, a person's ability to walk is considered the basic measure of intelligence. To my relief, however, I was quickly forgotten, and for a full twenty minutes the policemen continued their joking and bantering, as if I had never arrived.

Finally the sub-inspector strode into the middle of the room, cleared his throat, and in a sharp, high-pitched voice began an extraordinary tirade about why on earth the doctor had come, he wasn't needed, how dumb that he had showed up, of what use could he be, it was the business manager that was wanted, why had they sent the wrong man, why had the doctor gone to all this trouble—a question I had begun asking myself—and he kept this up for ten minutes, half addressing me and half addressing everyone else.

The sub-inspector was extremely rude and I told him so, whereupon he quieted down slightly, chewed out the guard who had brought me, and told me to send Stu the minute he arrived. As I got up to go, the sub-inspector stood by the door and called me aside. In a manner at once ingratiating and smug, he said, "Please leave us twenty rupees to pay for the prisoner's food."

It was the custom. Mustering whatever pleasantness remained to me, I handed the sub-inspector two ten-rupee notes. As I turned to leave, I heard another voice call out: "*Namaste* [good-bye], doctor." It was Thakur, grinning at me from ear to ear.

I got back to Amp Pipal that evening to find a great buzz of excitement: Policeman Number Two had just arrived with our first news of Stu and his party. As he told it, they had followed thirty minutes behind Party Number One until they reached the Daraundi River. There they learned that Dag and company had turned south, hot on the trail of Top Bahadur. However, no one knew anything about a second thief. As they inquired from shop to shop, one shopkeeper told them, "I haven't seen any man and his wife such as you describe, but about twenty minutes ago a young woman bought an umbrella from me. She was in a big hurry and was throwing money around like I've never seen. She handed me a fifty-rupee note and told me to keep the change."

"Did she have a child with her?" asked Ishwari, the school-teacher.

"Yes, she did."

The party agreed that this could indeed be Thakur's wife, and since they had no better lead, they decided to follow her. They reasoned that Thakur might have gone on ahead and left his wife behind to follow along at her own pace. She had headed across the river in the direction of Gorkha, and our friends hoped to catch up with her quickly. However, Stu's feet had begun to revolt. The blisters acquired the day before had now turned to tender mounds of raw flesh, and each time Stu stepped on a pebble, a jolt of pain would shoot up his leg with such intensity as to buckle his knee. This slowed the party down. Crossing the knee-deep river, Stu slipped and fell, losing his container of boiled water.

As they neared Gorkha, they finally caught up with the young woman. They followed her into town and watched her enter a house just off the main thoroughfare. Then, while Ishwari stood guard, Stu and the policeman went to the Gorkha District police headquarters, reported the robbery in detail, and returned to the house, accompanied by a policeman who had orders to seize and search the young woman. Entering the building, they caught the young woman in the act of hiding a large wad of bills in a hole in the floor, whereupon she immediately broke down and confessed that she was Thakur's wife and that this was indeed her husband's share of the stolen money. She and all the residents of the house were hauled off to the Gorkha jail.

No one at the Gorkha District police headquarters, of course, knew that Thakur was at that very moment being conducted to the Thadipokhari police station south of Liglig. There was no telegraph or telephone communication between the two stations. Therefore, Policeman Number Two had been promptly dispatched via Amp Pipal to the Thadipokhari station with word that half of the money had been recovered and that the identity of the second thief had been confirmed.

So here was Policeman Number Two just arriving in Amp Pipal, with the Thadipokhari station still two hours away—while Thakur, having already been detained for the twenty-four-hour limit, was due to be released any minute. Even though we urged the policeman to go on to Thadipokhari immediately, he refused to walk a step farther that day. It was dusk, he was tired and hungry, and he figured he could get a better meal at our expense than he could expect from the cook at his quarters. So we were obliged to send our own runner with an official letter from the policeman stating that Thakur was the thief and requesting that he be held overnight and then escorted in the morning to the Gorkha District police headquarters, where Stu would be waiting to confirm his identity. We tried to conceal our feeling of futility as we sent the runner off, but the truth was that we had little hope that he'd reach the station in time to prevent Thakur's release. And once free, Thakur would waste no time reaching the east-west highway, using the cover of darkness to ensure his escape.

That night we were all gathered at Stu's house for a previously scheduled team meeting, when Ishwari, the schoolteacher, suddenly showed up. He had tired of waiting in Gorkha and had decided to return without Stu, whose feet were too sore to walk that day anyway. He informed us that Stu was planning to leave

Gorkha early the next morning and would be arriving in Amp Pipal in the early afternoon.

This was a fine fix. We had been counting on Ishwari and Stu being in Gorkha to see the case through to a satisfactory conclusion and, if possible, to bring the money back with them. With no one there, it seemed unlikely that Thakur would be brought to justice or that we would ever see our money again. We assumed that Stu would be needed to identify Thakur (provided that the runner had arrived in time to prevent his release from the Thadipokhari station!) and to press formal charges. So it was determined that someone should be sent at the crack of dawn to Gorkha in the hope of intercepting Stu before he had come too far. The "someone" chosen turned out to be me, and Dr. Helen, for the third day, agreed to delay her holiday.

I left early the next morning, but as it turned out, Stu had left equally early. We met midway at the Daraundi River, which runs at the bottom of the deep valley lying between Gorkha and Amp Pipal. Stu was not overjoyed at the prospect of retracing his steps back up the mountain to Gorkha, but with a willing spirit he turned around. As we walked back to Gorkha, he entertained me for two-and-a-half hours with a detailed account of his adventures, including two sleepless nights in Gorkha hotels—one night with cockroaches, the other with a bedful of bedbugs.

We passed the middle part of the day talking with the district police inspector and visiting other government officials. All were amazed to hear about the pursuit of the robbers and pleased that one had actually been caught. However, the pleasure was marred by the fear that Thakur had already been released. When we asked what could be done about it, we were informed with a shrug that we could only wait and see if Thakur showed up. The police felt they had the matter completely in hand, so we were told we could leave. The wife's testimony was sufficient to prove

Thakur's guilt. The police assured us we would get our money back after the trial—minus ten percent for court fees. Since it was 3:00 P.M., with a six-hour walk ahead of us, Stu and I decided to return to Amp Pipal without further delay. In spite of his sore feet, Stu had no heart to hazard another night in a Gorkha hotel.

An hour out of Gorkha we came to a place where the trail divided, the right fork leading west across the Daraundi River to Amp Pipal and the left fork leading toward the southwest in the direction of Thadipokhari. And just as we reached this junction, we saw coming up the left-hand trail a troop of nine policemen escorting a handcuffed prisoner. It was Thakur. He wasn't grinning today; he merely glanced at us sullenly and trudged ahead. We waited until the procession had passed, and then with lighter hearts we set out on the trail to Amp Pipal.

Stu had to return once more to Gorkha several weeks later in order to claim our money, which he obtained only after a two-day bureaucratic hassle with a plethora of minor officials. He was consoled, however, to find that Thakur and his wife had been safely imprisoned in the district jail. Thakur's efforts had earned him an eight-year sentence, a stiff but just penalty designed to deter other would-be robbers from attempting similar exploits in the future. In the end, it was as happy a conclusion as we could have hoped for.

Justice for Thakur, however, proved to be short-lived; he was set free within eight months. His wife followed several months later. As for Top Bahadur, justice never had her day; neither he nor his share of the money was ever seen again.

Medical Practice
in the Hills of Nepal

Occupational Hazards

N *O SELF-RESPECTING* accrediting commission would ever accredit the Amp Pipal Hospital. What would the officials say if, on their inspection tour, two scrawny chickens fluttered excitedly out from under a bed in the critical ward? (We'd say they were the patient's protein supplement.) What would they think of the mangy stray dogs wandering through the hospital, lapping up leftovers from the patients' plates—even, on occasion, food that a patient was getting ready to eat? Would they overlook the cobwebs that hang like lacy decorations from the rafters, undisturbed by the myopic exertions of our sweepers? Or the red streaks on the walls near the patients' beds, the squashed remains of bedbugs full of blood? And what about those two bedpans sitting out in the main corridor (we keep patients in the corridor too), one filled with partly digested *kaaphal* berries and the other filled with a hundred fat, pink roundworms, writhing in a knotted mass like the locks of Medusa?

From the patient's point of view, a few reminders of village life help lend warmth and intimacy to the otherwise bleak, unfamiliar, cement confines of the hospital. Our patients feel frightened and uncomfortable in tidy, sterile surroundings; a bit of dirt, a few cobwebs, some chicken droppings here and there all help to make them feel more at home. And these minor lapses in our hygienic standards aren't nearly so harmful as the blizzard of dust raised by the sweepers when they've been ordered on a periodic cleaning binge by our Norwegian nursing superintendent. Better to have the dirt on the floor than in the air, I've always maintained.

Being "unaccredited" has at least one important advantage: It allows us to operate the hospital on a shoestring and cut every conceivable corner—without seriously jeopardizing our patients. We can offer adequate treatment for many kinds of illnesses for less than one percent of what it costs in an American hospital. If some of our American friends were to have their gall bladders removed in the Amp Pipal Hospital, the money they'd save would pay for their trip three times over.

Running hospitals cheaply, however, doesn't come naturally to those trained in the West. Indeed, the greatest professional adjustment missionary doctors or nurses make is in dealing with money—or the lack of it. Financing a hospital is probably the last thing on the mind of a new medical missionary coming out to the field. "Nothing but the best for our patients" is the usual watchword, and only after years of struggle and frustration does the new doctor finally abandon it. He painfully discovers that almost every treatment regimen he's learned in training must be modified—often drastically—and, in many cases, completely discarded.

Most Nepalis are as concerned with the cost as they are with the cure, and often more so—especially when it comes to their wives and daughters. Both the cost and the duration of treatment are determined less by the doctor than by the patient, who will decide for himself how much he can pay and how long he'll stay. On every front, the doctor or nurse must compromise on the ideal treatment in order to render any treatment at all.

These economic realities extend right through the hospital and require not only lower standards of treatment and nursing care but also a reduction in the level of cleanliness (particularly hard on nurses), restraint in the utilization of expendable goods (dressings, tape, soap—even water in the dry season!), and many other unwelcome strictures on our medical lifestyles. The underlying imperative is always the same: Reduce the patient's bill. Missionary doctors and nurses need to keep their priorities straight, and the closer their priorities are to those of the people they're serving, the more service they'll be able to provide.

The patient and his family are correct, more often than not, in the assessment of their own priorities. The doctor and nurse are accustomed to consider only the medical aspects of the case, and therefore find themselves very often giving the wrong advice for the total situation. Rather, they need to see things from the patient's perspective, and this means thinking about who's taking care of the goats back home, what needs to be done in the fields, where porters can be found to carry the patient back and forth, when the next full moon comes, or the next religious festival—and, above all, how many days it takes to walk home from the hospital. Any of these factors is at least as important to the patients and their families as the little green pills the doctor is prescribing.

It's not only the patients who are poor; the hospital is poor too. We give charity when needed, but we don't give it indiscriminately. We must keep treatment to a minimum for all but the wealthy patients who can afford the frills. Determining what treatment is essential and what is a "frill" is an interesting exercise; but the longer medical people stay on the mission field, the wider becomes their definition of frill. We choose the cheapest drugs. We don't give them for nearly as long as our textbooks tell us to. We select the shortest and least complicated treatment regimens. We avoid injections when pills will do—except when a patient requests an injection and is willing to pay for it. Then it's a frill.

The most difficult dilemma for the missionary doctor is what to do with the patient who has only a small chance of recovery. Our natural inclination is to go all out. Well, that inclination should be put to rest as long as one remains on the mission field. Nepalis are very practical. They count the cost. If the patient has only a slight chance of cure, the family in most cases is simply not interested, and the doctor is unwise to urge further expensive treatment. Nothing is more distressing than finally to give up on a patient (or have the patient die) after running up a huge bill that neither the hospital nor the patient's family can begin to afford. Taken on the average, restraint on the part of the doctor in such cases will ultimately benefit many more people than it will harm. Besides, Nepalis have a much more wholesome attitude toward dying than we have in the West, where death is to be avoided at *any* cost. In this regard, we have much to learn from them.

You may be thinking, *Good grief, I hope I never get sick in Amp Pipal!* To the contrary, almost all of our patients—including the severely ill—get well; and for the types of illness we deal with, our recovery rates are comparable to those of most hospitals in the West. For example, our incidence of surgical complications is actually less than that found in most American hospitals. Out of 2,500 surgical cases done in a recent two-year period (more than 800 of them major operations), there were only two deaths resulting from surgery and two wound infections—one of the infections developed in a woman with an enormous pelvic abscess that had ruptured into her abdominal cavity sometime during her five-day journey to the hospital from near the Tibetan border.

Why are our recovery rates this high? Nepalis develop an extraordinary resistance to germs; if they don't, they die before they reach the age of five. Our low infection rate, however, is due not only to patient resistance but also to the competence of our staff. Other hospitals in Nepal reportedly have surgical infection rates as high as twenty and thirty percent.

Things have not always gone so smoothly, however, and in earlier years our record was not so good, largely because of the inexperience of the operating team, including myself. Having been the only surgeon at Amp Pipal during most of the hospital's first twelve years, I'm obliged to take credit for the bad along with the good. Even in more recent years, we've had our share of close calls, and the favorable end results shouldn't obscure the fact that we daily tread a mine field of potential disasters. The triple menace of poor equipment, inexperienced staff, and unpredictable patients, all brought together under one leaky tin roof, never fails to make each day a circus of surprises, where the acts are ever new—and always unrehearsed.

Bizarre tales are ordinary fare in Amp Pipal. The hospital is filled with a hodgepodge of outdated and incompatible equipment that peevishly goes out of order at inconvenient times: homemade intravenous sets come apart and crash to the floor just as you've finally gotten into a difficult vein; foley balloons don't deflate when you need to take out the catheter; ill-fitting needles and syringes pop apart during injections, spraying medicine all over the walls. And when you write to order spare parts, you learn several months later that none are available because the model in question went out of production ten years before.

It's the human element, however, that makes the practice of medicine so entertaining in Amp Pipal. To begin with, just speaking the language keeps you on your toes. It's quite easy, for instance, to ask a patient if he has pain in his umbrella—the words for "chest" and "umbrella" are similar in Nepali—to which the patient, to be agreeable, is likely to reply in the affirmative. It's less well received to ask a young lady impending miscarriage if she has passed the banana. Sometimes in a busy clinic, you even forget what you're saying. More than once I've placed my stethoscope on a patient's chest and said, "Hello, hello"—as if I were making a long-distance call—when I really meant to be saying, "take a deep breath."

It's not surprising that many patients don't follow our instructions—they often haven't understood them. Some patients don't even speak Nepali, especially women who come from northern tribal villages. Other patients, after getting their medicine and being told how to take it, wander around for hours clutching their handful of medicine packets and asking each staff member they happen to see, "Hey *baabu* [little boy], what am I supposed to do with these?" Try as we might to prevent it, our patients eat their suppositories, drink disinfectants, and confuse even the simplest instructions in numerous imaginative ways. One old woman with tuberculosis was quite negligent about taking her medicine, but she ate without fail the plastic bags the medicine came in. Other patients simply have minds of their own. Once two village women, on comparing their medicines, found they each had been given white pills and yellow pills. So the one traded her whites for the other's yellows, and they both walked off, each with one color, as happy as larks. Even if patients have everything clear in their minds when they leave the hospital, they still may lose their medicine fording a waist-high river, or they may find their pills have turned to soggy mush in a monsoon downpour. Merely prescribing the right medicine is the least of our problems.

Working in the outpatient clinic has special joys and challenges of its own. The hospital was originally built with only two offices for doctors and a waiting area barely sufficient to handle fifty patients a day. Soon we had to divide the original examining rooms in half to allow four doctors to work simultaneously. However, the "waiting room," a narrow corridor lined on either side by benches, has remained unchanged. In recent years it has had to accommodate an average of 150 patients a day (each accompanied by one or more friends or family members). The patients push and shove their way down this corridor, positioning themselves as close as possible to the doctors' offices for fear of missing their turn. Several diminutive female office assistants call out the patients' names one by one and somehow manage to usher them in and out of the examining rooms or the x-ray department or pharmacy, all the time bustling back and forth in a cramped little space the size of a Burger King restroom. Just to get out of the office to any other part of the hospital, one has to plow a way through this jostling crowd. The continuous uproar is, at the least, distracting, but during peak hours, the scene can only be described as bedlam. And the partial deafness of two of the office assistants doesn't help matters; it's hard enough to attract their attention as it is. All in all, it is not an ideal setup.

I've mused, on a busy day in our cramped and crowded clinic, on the extravagant use of space in public buildings in America. Visiting Valley Forge with our family a few years ago, my sharpest impression was of a Visitor Center three times the size of our entire fifty-bed hospital. Some weeks later, at the new billion-dollar mall in our home city of Albany, New York, we walked through a basement corridor into which I could easily have fit ten Amp Pipal Hospitals side by side with room to spare. Nepal is a different world.

Speed is essential in running a clinic like ours. In the first place, seeing patients quickly and sending them on their way is the only means we have of reducing the congestion, thereby making work possible at all. Second, our patients have two equally important objectives in coming to the hospital: to see the doctor and to get home before dark. Complete workups and prolonged counseling produce one happy patient and two angry ones. The doctor must adjust his style to meet the real needs of those he serves, or else, after a long and self-satisfying day of examining patients carefully and thoroughly, he'll discover that forty patients couldn't wait and walked the long road home without having even been seen.

Naturally we try to minimize unnecessary delays. We do so, however, with only limited success. Nepali clothing, for example, with its numerous tiny snaps and buttons and inaccessible knotted strings, is not designed for rapid removal. The women, in particular, put on their finest outfits for their visit to the doctor, the centerpiece of which is always a five-yard-long *patuka* wrapped round and round the waist, holding the skirts and petticoats in place. It must be a letdown when the doctor's only reaction to all this finery is to demand its prompt removal as soon as the patient sets foot inside the office. The women, of course, are reluctant and embarrassed; they stall and pretend they don't understand, hoping you'll change your mind and decide not to examine them after all. Finally the disrobing begins . . . slowly . . . deliberately . . . each article is folded carefully and laid aside. The *patuka* is unwound with a circular overhead motion, turn by tedious turn—and all the while the doctor paces up and down, listening to the shouts of the crowd outside the door.

"When is my turn coming? I've been here three hours."

"Me too. I can't wait all day. The friends I came with have already gotten their medicine and are about to leave."

"My x-ray's ready by now. When's the doctor going to look at it and tell me what's wrong with me?"

"I've lost my turn. You've put his file ahead of mine!"

"No, she hasn't. My file was there first. You're trying to butt in front of me!"

"Where am I supposed to take this stool specimen?"

"Not here! Not here! To the lab."

"Where's the lab?"

"Down the corridor," says a chorus of voices.

Meanwhile, you've finished examining that patient, and she's putting on her clothes—with equal slowness and deliberation. Soon she's ushered out the door, and another patient is ushered in—and the game repeats itself. The dressing and undressing isn't the only cause for delay, of course. Some of the young women refuse to lie still; they squiggle and squirm all over the table. You might as easily examine an eel.

Aside from the clothes and the generally low level of patient cooperation, there's another source of delay that particularly unsettles me. Something about meeting the doctor makes small children want to go to the bathroom. Just entering my office triggers some sort of reflex, and behold—before I can say "Jack Spratt"—little Ram or little Hari has deposited his stool specimen on the clean cement floor or on the examining table or on my chair. And why not? Children in Nepal grow up regarding the whole world as a toilet, and neither they nor their parents give it a second thought.

But I do. The problem in the doctor's office is aggravated by the unwillingness of our office assistants to clean up the messes of little children. A special cleaning woman—usually grumbly old Laxmi—has to be summoned, and it's frequently five to ten minutes before she is found, as often as not at the far end of the hospital, where she's gone to have a smoke. Meanwhile, all work in the office comes to a standstill.

The infant's mother, observing my distress, hastens to render the offending material less noticeable by smearing it over a wider area with a foul cloth that usually accompanies Nepali infants for such purposes. Over the years I've developed a special acuity (perhaps it's that look in the child's eye that says, "I'm going to get you") that enables me to anticipate at least half of such accidents and deftly get the baby positioned over the foul cloth.

One day—I remember it well—a Gurung tribesman came into my office carrying his infant son, who had been sick for many weeks with dysentery (a serious form of diarrhea). The father was a simple man who had never set foot in a hospital before. He himself had brought the child because the mother was ill and couldn't make the trip.

Unfortunately, the father had come without the special cloth. As I was examining the infant, I was suddenly warned by my special sense that an accident was about to occur all over my examining table. I began to gesticulate excitedly to the father, who, finally comprehending what it was all about, calmly removed his *topi* (cap), placed it under the child's buttocks until it was full, and carefully carried it out of my office. Passing through the crowd and down the corridor, he emptied it into the flower garden outside the operating room. Within one minute he was back in my office, with the *topi* on his head— unwashed; I could tell because it was dry on the outside. He looked at me sympathetically, as if I had some sort of problem, picked up his child who had been screaming the while, and taking the card on which I had written his medicine, walked slowly out of the office and down the corridor as if this were just one more day like any other.

You'd think I'd have gotten used to this sort of thing living in Nepal, but in fact, the reverse is true. On one busy clinic day a few years ago, I had just stepped outside my office to call one of our deaf assistants when I noticed something amiss in the throng of waiting patients who were pressing in toward the examining area. There, almost hidden from view in the midst of the tightly packed crowd, was a little girl squatting down right in the center of the main thoroughfare doing her business on an 8″ by 8″ piece of banana leaf. The reason she'd come to the doctor was plain to see: amoebic dysentery. But here was a public health calamity! How was one to keep a hundred barefooted people from stepping on that banana leaf in the next two minutes?

The situation, logistically, was desperate. The toilet was fifteen yards down the patient-packed corridor. No one else had noticed the girl. Even the girl's father was staring ahead abstractedly, with the air of a man contemplating a Jackson Pollock painting. I became agitated. I vigorously gestured to the office assistants, but I had difficulty making them understand what was the matter. Everyone, naturally, began to shove closer to see what the doctor was getting excited about and what he was pointing at. I waved them away, but it did no good. The little girl was almost crushed in the press. Finally, Sita, the brightest of our assistants, saw the problem, and with a serious expression behind which she was scarcely able to conceal her mirth, she somehow managed to push the crowd back and clear a way down the corridor to the bathroom. With the mystery revealed, a murmur spread through the spectators: "So, why all the fuss about that? What do they expect? That's what little girls do. Especially when they've got *ragat-maasi* [bloody dysentery]."

The father, meanwhile, became a study in helpfulness. With no more concern than if he were picking up a dropped handkerchief, he reached down and gathered up two opposite corners of the banana leaf with one hand and swung off down the corridor, losing two-thirds of his load before reaching the toilet. The little girl followed, and oblivious to the commotion, proceeded to finish her job just outside the bathroom door. I deny becoming unhinged, though I later overheard Sita saying as much to one of the other assistants. Laxmi, the special cleaning woman, might as well have been tending camels in the Sahara Desert for all the help she was going to be in wiping up those twelve puddles of stool in the next sixty seconds. And so it proved. When I looked a moment later, the twelve puddles had turned to twenty-four footprints . . . forty-eighty . . . ninety-six . . . and again the crowd had filled the corridor as before.

A missionary can't afford to be finicky, of course, much less impatient. I am a failure on both counts. However, God doesn't give up. He keeps arranging little lessons for me—no matter if it's the same lesson over and over. So I wasn't surprised three days later when another little lesson came my way. I usually have three patients in my office at one time: one being examined, the other dressing or undressing, while a third waits near my filing cabinet behind the door.

I'd been intent for some time on a patient with an unusual problem, and remembering an article I had saved on the subject, I walked over to get it from my files. As I was reaching to open the cabinet, Sita uttered a little squeal and blurted out, "Doctor, don't step—" It was too late. The third patient waiting, a child I hadn't even noticed, had relieved herself on the floor near the filing cabinet. Sita, not wanting to upset my equilibrium, had quietly escorted the child and her mother out and had sent for Laxmi, the cleaning woman. Sita's ploy, by any reasonable expectation, should have succeeded, since I hadn't been over to get anything out of these particular files for months. A pile of stool there wouldn't have held us up in the slightest—except that I had stepped in it. It was tenacious, like old glue. I quickly extracted my foot, but half the pile came with it, and there was no putting my foot down again. Containment, I reasoned, was the best policy. So there I froze, balanced on one foot in the unused corner of my office like a man whose leg had gone to sleep. I was unable to do anything constructive—not even get at my article.

The minutes ticked by, but Laxmi was nowhere to be found. No one had seen her. I sent the office assistants off in every direction to look for her, and when they came back without her, I sent them back again to look some more. Little did I know they were all down in the lab, doubled up, howling with laughter. It took exactly twelve minutes for dear old Laxmi to show up. She had never been so long. Throwing a contemptuous glance at Sita and then at my foot, she slowly cleaned the floor and my sneaker with her disinfectant solution, and then stalked out with an air as if to say: "What will they ask of me next?" Happily for everyone, we didn't have to call her again that day.

There is more than one way to "put your foot in it" while working in the clinic. Some of our patients come with the complaint that a "water worm" has gotten into their nose. Water worms are real worms between one and three inches long that live in springs and crawl up the noses of people who come to drink. There they remain, living on blood sucked from the mucous membranes lining the back of the nose. Children in particular suffer for months from these worms, which, unmolested, grow and grow until they fill the whole nasopharynx. The bigger the worm, the easier it is to remove; the smaller ones are more lively and quick, usually managing to elude the grasp of the doctor's forceps by slipping back out of reach into the posterior recesses of the nasal cavity.

One day a Christian Nepali from Barpak, a large village two days' walk to the north, arrived at the hospital with a worm in his nose. He said that God had sent the worm into his nose as an incentive for him to come down to Amp Pipal to attend the series of meetings our church was then holding. Now that he had come, he added, there was no further purpose to be served by the worm and he wanted it out so he could enjoy the meetings.

I was happy to oblige him. We have a number of stratagems to outwit these worms, but in this man's case nothing worked. Every time I reached in with my forceps the worm slithered out of sight into the back of the man's nose. Finally, after at least half an hour of this kind of cat-and-mouse game, frustration gave birth to a new and cunning idea. I put one hand in the patient's mouth and wiggled my fingers around in the back of his throat, hoping thereby to frighten the worm into moving to the front of the nose. With my fingers still wiggling, I passed the forceps into the patient's nostril with my free hand and began to grab blindly. (I usually do this under direct vision through an otoscope but with this new method my "otoscope" hand was still engaged in the back of the patient's throat.) To my astonishment it worked on the third grab, and out came a two-inch worm wriggling furiously at the end of my forceps. I had invented a new technique. The patient thanked God and went off to the meetings.

When a month later a seven-year-old boy came in with a worm in his nose, I was eager to try out my new method a second time. This young lad had been suffering for a month with frequent nose bleeds (one of the signs of a water worm) but had apparently not complained much about it. He'd been brought by his mother, a nervous, fussy woman—the kind whose every look and gesture conveys doubt that the doctor knows what he's doing—and a stuffy, pompous gentleman who proved to be the boy's maternal grandfather. Little Raja (meaning king), seemed well behaved. Sensing I'd get no help from the mother or grandfather, I proceeded to worm my way into the boy's confidence with soothing and reassuring words. Little Raja listened attentively when I told him how I proposed to get out that nasty old worm. "It won't hurt a bit—just a little tickle in the back of your throat and—poof!—we'll be done, and you'll be rid of that naughty worm and on your way home as happy as can be. . . ." After all, it takes time to build up a patient's confidence, and a doctor is foolish not to invest that time. It often means the difference between success and failure.

Now we were ready. Sita held the child's head. Aruni Gurung, another assistant, held a flashlight. The mother, without enthusiasm, held the child's legs, murmuring "Raja, Raja" over and over again as if I were about to amputate her son's nose—perhaps after the manner of Nepal's first king, who used to cut off the noses of his enemies. Then, very gently, I insinuated my longest finger into little Raja's mouth, back, back into the nasopharynx. Little Raja lay perfectly still, without a peep. Aruni Gurung held the light on the nose. With my free hand I slowly inserted the long forceps into the child's nostril, talking all the while in dulcet tones. Then, when all was in readiness, I wiggled my finger in the back of little Raja's throat, my other hand poised to clamp down on the outwitted worm with the jaws of my forceps.

I really don't fault the method for what happened next; given a chance, I'm sure it would have worked. But, alas, it was another set of jaws that clamped down at that delicate moment. On my finger. Little Raja bit my finger, and I mean to say he really bit hard and didn't let up. At least when your finger gets caught in a car door, someone opens the door. But not Raja. And he'd never said a word or given any indication of his intentions. I guess I had had it exactly backwards about who had wormed whose way into whose confidence.

I was transfixed. And like Raja, I was speechless. For a full minute neither of us made a sound or moved a muscle. No one else had a clue what had happened. Even when I began to holler, "Open your mouth! Open your mouth!" the others assumed it was merely part of the procedure. But then I started to call the boy a *badmash* (rascal) and began to slap his face—which only increased the tension in his jaw muscles. The mother and grandfather were obviously scandalized by this sudden and apparently unprovoked assault on their little boy, for they glared at me reproachfully and continued to do so even after I told them that Raja had bitten my finger—down to the bone, I was sure.

Sita, always ready with a cheerful smile in every predicament, handed me a metal tongue depressor with which I pried apart Raja's teeth and extracted my bloody finger. The worm was forgotten. The grandfather announced that it was time they went, that they would find another way to get the worm out, that they had come to this mission hospital instead of the government hospital in their own town because they'd heard how good it was. He was too courteous, in his stiff way, to verbalize the disappointment written all over his face. Only when I showed him my finger and assured him it was *my* blood, did he soften slightly and raise an eyebrow as if to say: "And what did you expect, putting your finger in a little boy's mouth like that?"

The mother gathered little Raja up in her arms and marched out of the office without a word, followed at a stately distance by the grandfather. As he went out the door, Sita whispered to me, "You know, don't you, that he's the second highest official in the district?"

Now she tells me.

Cynthia collecting her loot from the Foreign Post Office in Kathmandu (*photo by Dicran Berberian*)

Main palace square in Kathmandu

An incarnation of Shiva, the destroyer and creator god of the Hindu trinity

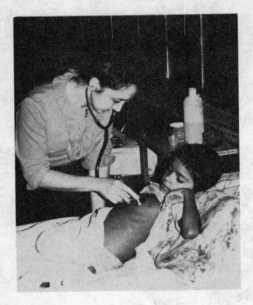

Cynthia examining a patient in the Amp Pipal Hospital (*photo by Dicran Berberian*)

Author performing minor surgery in the outpatient department (*photo by Dan Condit*)

Didi husking rice with the *diki*, while author's son Christopher (*center*) and friend look on (*photo by Cynthia Hale*)

Author finally catches the fruit-eating marten. But it is only a baby. The mother and father are still at large. (*Photo by Cynthia Hale*)

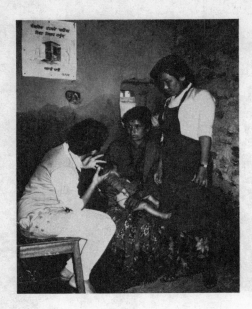

The Lapsibot clinic. Cynthia examines a sick child while Moti Maya (*right*) assists.

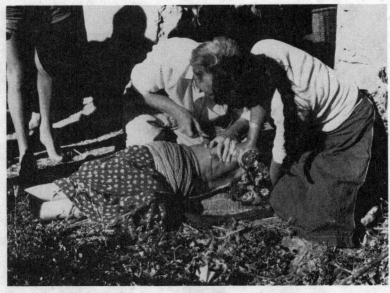

The Lapsibot clinic. Author performs minor surgery. (*Photo by Dicran Berberian*)

The site of the author's first vasectomy camp, the abandoned house about to fall into the river. Family planning workers are shown with the operating table they carried a day's journey from the district capital.

Two young men serve as oxen in a field near Barpak.

Himalayan "classroom." In the winter months it is too cold to conduct school.

Mount Everest, 29,028 feet

Mount Everest summit

The village of Amp Pipal, a day's walk from the nearest road, viewed from the top of Liglig mountain. The Ganesh Himal lie in the distance. No level country here!

The summits of the Himalayas generally remain above the clouds. Twenty miles from the author's home, a view of Himalchuli (25,900 feet).

Author with sons Tommy and Christopher, hunting for grasshoppers to feed Owl (Tommy is holding net).

The Hale Family—(*left to right*) Cynthia, Tom III, Dr. Tom, and Chris

Surgeon Beware

Y OU MAY ASK, with justification, how crazy one has to be before he tries doing major surgery in a primitive place like Amp Pipal. Without replying to the question directly, let me just say that surgery in Amp Pipal is strikingly different from that practiced in the West—not the actual operative technique so much, but everything else.

What surgeon at home, for instance, while performing a cystoscopy, has ever seen the bladder suddenly flooded with tea leaves? (Only in Amp Pipal do they make both the bladder-irrigating solution and the staff tea in the same kettle.) When has a surgeon in the States, in the midst of an abdominal operation, ever watched the operating room fill with soot from a malfunctioning kerosene stove (used to heat the pressure cookers in which our supplies are sterilized)? Or had two swallows fly into the operating room and be unable to fly back out? Or operated during a dust storm so thick that each instrument left its outline on the table?

But these are momentary distractions compared with the one-hour hailstorm that lasted through most of a vaginal hysterectomy. Aside from rattling our eardrums, the golf-ball-sized hailstones knocked loose the nails in the tin roof, and water poured in through a hundred nail holes. First it began to drip onto the instrument table, so we moved the table. Then it began dripping on the patient, and then on me, so we moved the operating table. Soon we had to move again and again. After a while there was no use moving. Rain was coming in everywhere—on the patient, the doctor, the instruments, the wound. We might as well have been outside. It would have been quieter. No sooner had the operation ended than the rain and hail stopped. The patient never turned a hair.

Most problems are merely diversionary—such as stomach tubes blocked with roundworms, dead rats in the scrub sink, and disagreeable buckets that leak underfoot when you're not expecting it. Other problems are recurring—such as running out of water in the middle of a busy day in the dry season. Or the proliferation of maggots in open wounds in the wet season. Actually, it's worth pointing out that these maggots are quite beneficial—contrary to popular sentiment. They live harmlessly in the dressings and feed on pus, thereby helping to keep the wound clean. Not surprisingly, Nepalis associate maggots with dead bodies, so despite my reassurances, they grow alarmed when they see the little worms crawling over their skin. We simply change the dressings more frequently in the maggot season—every three to four days, instead of five to six—and our patients remain perfectly happy. Well, almost. In the West, they'd have looked for another doctor—and another hospital.

Some problems, however, are more serious, especially those that arise because of errors in the pharmacy. Our pharmacy department consists of three young men, only one of whom has been formally trained as a pharmacy technician. Several years back, we hired a new pharmacy worker to replace one who was leaving. The new worker was an agreeable lad named Lal Bahadur, who had quit school after failing tenth grade. Although not brilliant, he was a steady plodder, whom we thought might keep his mind on his work and not be distracted by bursts of intellectual activity. Lal Bahadur was put in charge of making the intravenous solutions, a critical responsibility in any hospital. For the first several months he was closely supervised by the pharmacy technician.

Then one day the ward nurse called me to see a young man from whose kidney I had removed a large stone the previous day. He had just gone into shock, but I couldn't determine why. Then by chance I looked at the bottle of intravenous (IV) solution and was aghast to discover it was filled with a cloudy precipitate. We checked other bottles and found them to be the same. It turned out that the detergent used to wash the bottles had not been rinsed out; thus, carefully prepared and filtered intravenous solution had been poured into soapy bottles. The patient suffered no residual ill effect, but he would have been dead in ten minutes if we hadn't discovered the problem.

On another occasion, Lal Bahadur put a "distilled water" label on a bottle of atropine eye drops he had made up. The "distilled water" was used as the diluent for the day's penicillin injections, resulting in six cases of atropine poisoning—one of whom, a postoperative patient, died. Lal Bahadur accepted the news philosophically, explaining that he "must have gotten the labels mixed."

Some time after this, as we were anesthetizing a patient for surgery, one of the operating-room nurses noticed something floating in the IV bottle that had just been put up. It was an ant, just small enough to have passed through the 16-gauge needle into the patient's bloodstream. It was quite dead and quite sterile, but the idea was distasteful. I summoned all three pharmacy workers to the operating room. Swirling the contents of the bottle gently, I held it up for them to inspect.

"What do you see wrong with this IV?" I asked severely.

They squinted at the bottle for several moments but saw nothing.

"Don't you see anything in there?" I asked again, addressing in particular the IV maker and wondering whether he was blind as well as dull.

More squinting. They held the bottle themselves, looking at it from all directions. This went on for three or four minutes, at the end of which my patience was exhausted. The patient on the operating table was by this time fully anesthetized. I took the bottle and spun it one last time.

Finally, Lal Bahadur's eyes opened wide with amazement. "There's an ant in there!" he exclaimed, his gaze fixed on the insect orbiting gently round and round inside the glass. Then, with the wonder of a child watching a rabbit being pulled out of a hat, he said, "How ever did it get in there?"

"That's what I called to ask you," I said.

The hapless IV maker began to tremble, and in an unsteady voice he blurted out: "But what am I to do? There are ants everywhere!"

Yes, what was he to do? In our hospital potential disasters lurk at every corner. Yet when we consider the number and variety of mistakes that could have taken place but never did, we can only stand in awe of the unseen hand that has averted calamity so many times over the years. And should one have trouble believing in "unseen hands," he has only to work in the Amp Pipal Hospital for a while to see the extent to which God not only prevents accidents but also, when they occur, protects against their consequences.

As for the IV maker, he never made another mistake of significance. I couldn't have done as well myself. Our pharmacy workers are capable and conscientious. I question whether a fully qualified pharmacist could run things better than our pharmacy technician does. In fact all our Nepali staff, many with less than an eighth-grade education—some even fresh from the fields—perform their duties with signal competence. I would gladly trust myself in their hands—and, at times, have had to. Occasional lapses, yes. A few who have been negligent or dishonest, yes. These get weeded out. But on the whole I can't say enough for the work and attitude of these young Nepali men and women. I wouldn't trade them for anyone.

Many of our worst moments have come during the administration of anesthesia. For the first eight years at Amp Pipal, we had no proper anesthetist. I did most of the spinals myself, which was the anesthesia of necessity for anything below the diaphragm—except for Caesarean sections, which were done under local anesthesia. For thyroids I gave cervical blocks, and for hands, axillary blocks. We did anything to avoid ether, which no one was competent to administer. Even the spinals created problems sometimes. At one juncture several years back, the spinal anesthesia failed midway through three consecutive operations, leaving the patients to writhe in pain until they could be put to sleep. One of the three happened to be the wife of our Nepali purchasing officer. A great advertisement for our surgical department! The trouble was traced once more to the poor IV maker (this took place during his early days) whose job it was to make up the ten-percent dextrose we mix with the spinal anesthetic. Whatever it was he had made, it was not ten-percent dextrose: It was sour, not sweet, when we tasted it.

There are, of course, certain cases for which it is best not to use spinal anesthesia. I'll never forget a seventy-year-old man who arrived at the hospital with intestinal obstruction. He was critically ill and hadn't moved his bowels in ten days. Our two maintenance workers asked if they could watch the operation (surgery was a new thing in those days), and I readily agreed. I gave the spinal without any difficulty, but no one was available to watch the patient. An inexperienced assistant nurse from the ward was stationed at the head of the table to comfort the patient and put up new IV bottles when the old ones ran out. But she couldn't take a blood pressure. (Except for my surgical assistant, the regular staff had gone off for the weekend.) The spinal worked fine below the belly button, but whenever I reached my hand into the upper abdomen, the patient tried to climb off the operating table. I was grateful for the help of the two teenage maintenance lads, who managed to hold the old man down by brute force, while the assistant nurse tried to calm him with reassuring words. The patient's intestines were in bad shape, and it took me a while to remove the gangrenous segments and sew the ends together. Then all at once the old man stopped struggling and the maintenance lads, who were green in more ways than one, breathed sighs of relief. The patient was dead. The spinal had knocked out his blood pressure.

I can remember every calamity in the operating room as if it happened yesterday. One of the worst involved a young man who had fallen from a cliff near his home and was brought to the hospital late one Friday evening. The young man's lower back was broken and there were signs that his liver and intestine had ruptured. He needed emergency surgery. But because of his back, spinal anesthesia was contra-indicated; he would need ether.

However, the only person on the team capable of giving ether at the time, my colleague Dr. Helen Huston, had gone down the mountain to visit a friend for the weekend. So in spite of the man's broken back, I attempted to put in a spinal. Out of nearly a thousand spinals, there have been only two that I couldn't get in. This was one of them. I tried from midnight to 3:00 A.M. before I gave up. At dawn I sent one of the young man's relatives down the mountain with a note asking Helen to come back to the hospital as quickly as possible.

Helen arrived at noon, exhausted, and we began the operation at 1:00. Despite the fact that Helen gave ether only two or three times a year, she anesthetized the young man smoothly. On opening the abdomen, I found the small intestine ruptured in two places, but with surprisingly little contamination of the peritoneal cavity. The ruptures were easily repaired, and I began to close the abdomen. It had been a simple injury. The boy would do well. As for his back, it would heal by itself.

As I sutured the muscle layer, I distinctly remember thinking that this was one of those days when I was glad to be a surgeon. Out of the corner of my eye I saw Helen fussing with the blood-pressure cuff and thought she must be happy too. But she wasn't.

"The blood pressure is falling, and I don't know why," she muttered, half to herself.

That was odd. There was no reason for the blood pressure to fall at this point—I had begun closing the skin. The ether had been turned off five minutes earlier.

"Is the blood-pressure cuff loose?" I suggested.

No, it wasn't loose. We got another blood-pressure cuff, which gave the same reading. Then there was no reading at all. We watched in horror as the young man took a dozen final gasps of breath and died. Numbed, I finished closing the last inch of skin and pulled off the drapes. In an instant we saw the cause of his death: The endotracheal tube, through which the patient had been breathing, was kinked almost shut just as it left the mouth. The patient had slowly asphyxiated.

When I went out to tell the family what we had found and what had happened, they received the news calmly, expressing almost no surprise. In their experience it was foolish to expect anyone whose bowels had burst to survive. Helen went to her office, locked the door, and wept.

Dealing with death in the hills of Nepal has led us into some of our greatest clashes with the beliefs and practices of the local people. Even the "dead" part of the body—such as an organ removed at surgery or an amputated limb—has created interesting practical problems. For example, I can't seem to convince the staff that I really want to examine whatever I've removed at surgery. A dozen times I've fingered through a filthy bucket or a filthier trash pit looking for a specimen that had been too hastily discarded. Once I fished out of the incinerator a partially cooked uterus that I was extremely anxious to send to Kathmandu for pathologic evaluation. The report came back: "Unusual cellular abnormalities."

Our staff doesn't like to handle dead bodies or parts thereof. Usually the patient's relatives are enlisted to dispose of the remains. This disposing means different things to different people. One relative disposed of a leg, amputated at mid-thigh, by dumping it near the spring located along one of the three main trails leading to the hospital. Since the spring is the major source of water for miles around, a wide viewing was assured. Of course, there's a bright side to everything: Here in plain sight was a marker signaling the end of the journey for way-weary travelers coming to the doctor: "Welcome to the Amp Pipal Hospital!" I didn't learn of the leg until four days later, when several prominent local citizens suggested I'd better look into it.

Disposing of entire bodies creates even greater difficulties. When patients die, we put them at once into our rat-proof "dead-house" and then wait for the family to come to collect them. Patients dying in the hospital, however, often create a crisis of conscience for the surviving family members. They know that if they come to get the body, they'll have to pay an exorbitant sum of money just to hire carriers. (Carriers charge much more to carry a dead body than a living one: dead bodies are unclean.) On top of that, they'll have to pay a large hospital bill. (Relatives must settle their bill before they are allowed into the dead-house.) They know that if they abandon the body, they'll save money—a tempting but culturally unacceptable alternative.

Most families come to take the body, but some do not. And when they don't, we begin to have problems within a few days, especially in the hot season, and have to ask the *pradhan panch* for permission to bury the body before the smell gets unbearable. To a Hindu, burial is the ultimate degradation; in Nepal the accepted practice is cremation. Once, when we couldn't wait any longer, we buried a body, only to have the family arrive the next day and angrily demand we dig it up—which we did. Fortunately we've not yet had the unhappy experience of forgetting entirely that someone has died—as happened once at another United Mission Hospital, where for three days an overpowering smell enveloped the hospital compound before someone thought to look in the dead-house.

Getting a dead body expeditiously out of the hospital without attracting undue attention (a corpse isn't, after all, a hospital's best advertisement) can be a disconcerting experience even when relatives are on hand to take the body away. Some Nepalis treat death casually, like the man who put his mother's dead body, without even covering it, into a wicker basket and carried her all over the hospital looking for the cashier's office. Others regard death as a community event; the more people who know about it and share in the grief, the better they feel. Many a young mother, for example, has taken her dead child out under the big pipal tree near the main entrance to the hospital and wailed at the top of her lungs for an hour or more while the day's multitude of patients files past.

Still more disturbing, however, was the case of a thirty-five-year-old woman, Subadra Devkota. We had operated on Subadra early on a busy Tuesday morning: I had removed a simple ovarian cyst no bigger than a grapefruit, one of the easiest and least risky operations we do. The whole procedure was over in half an hour, and I had started on the next case, a vesico-vaginal fistula. Partway through the second operation they called from the ward to say that Subadra's blood pressure was dropping and that her pulse was fifty-two. That didn't make much sense, so I merely instructed them to speed up the IV and keep a close watch on the blood pressure. Ten minutes later an assistant nurse rushed up to say that the blood pressure had fallen to fifty and that the patient's condition was serious. I told her to call Dr. Helen, since I couldn't very well leave in the middle of an operation when there was another doctor available.

Thirty minutes passed, and I couldn't decide whether the long period without any news portended good or ill.

It was distressing enough to lose any patient, but I dreaded the thought of losing Subadra in particular. She was a member of a wealthy Brahmin family from a neighboring village. The family had insisted she go elsewhere for her surgery and had even taken her to the big mission hospitals in Tansen and Kathmandu. But in the end Subadra had refused to have her operation so far from home, saying she would have it done in Amp Pipal or not at all.

Even the previous evening she had been having second thoughts. "Is it a dangerous operation?" she had asked.

"No, it's not," I said. "We've removed seventy or eighty of these ovarian cysts—almost all of them much larger than yours, many, in fact, as big as this (here I indicated something the size of a large pumpkin)—and no one has had any ill effect."

"Am I strong enough for the operation?"

"Oh, yes," I assured her. "You are young and healthy, more healthy than most of the women we've operated on. Some of them have been over sixty."

"Will it take long?" she wanted to know.

"Under an hour," I said.

"Will I die?"

There is not a surgeon in the world who doesn't shudder at hearing that question. "No," I said.

It seemed as if I'd been operating long enough to have repaired half a dozen vesico-vaginal fistulas when Helen finally appeared with the dreaded news: Subadra was dead. Helen had no idea why she died. She and the nurses had attempted to resuscitate her, but to no avail. No sooner had they given up, she said, than a troop of relatives entered, led by a Hindu priest. The priest immediately stripped to his loin cloth and began to perform an elaborate ritual for the deceased. The family adamantly refused to have the body transferred to the dead-house. Helen left after being assured that they would take the body away as soon as they had completed the rites. Our rules didn't permit corpses to occupy hospital beds.

The rest of my morning passed drearily enough; there was a third operation to be done and a dozen surgical consults to be seen. At 1:00 I stopped for lunch. As I walked out of the hospital to go up to our house, there, to my horror, lay Subadra's body—right in front of the hospital! By this time it was surrounded by a crowd of curious onlookers.

The body had been lying there over two hours, the center of attraction. Not a person who came to the hospital that day failed to learn that she had died of an operation that very morning. As I walked past, I sensed all eyes shifting from the corpse to me. I felt like a murderer.

I ate my way through a tasteless lunch and returned to the hospital by a back entrance. The body was finally carried off in the late afternoon at the head of a long procession of family and friends, including two horn blowers dressed in white. Even after the procession had passed from view, the long plaintive notes of the horns could still be heard reverberating across the hillsides.

We never knew why she died.

Can anyone imagine a situation in which a surgeon would actually wish his patient to die during surgery? Such was the case one day when a young man in his thirties arrived at the hospital with severe breathing problems. He was beside himself with terror, clutching at whoever came near and begging them to "get this thing out of my throat." The "thing" was a huge thyroid gland, which instead of enlarging outwardly, as thyroids usually do, had extended downward into his chest and was exerting pressure on his trachea (windpipe). His plight was desperate. Unfortunately, another patient had already been anesthetized for surgery, and I was committed to performing that operation before turning my attention to anything else. In the meantime, I asked Robert Jonzon, our Swedish anesthetist, to be ready to pass an endotracheal tube in case the new patient's breathing should shut off completely.

When I finally was free to look after the young man with the obstructed trachea, I found him only partially conscious, his breathing even more labored than before. We had no choice but to perform an emergency thyroidectomy. We hoped the growth was a simple cyst or benign tumor into which there had been hemorrhage, which would have accounted for the patient's rapidly deteriorating condition. If this were so, it would be an easy matter to shell out the thyroid, relieving the obstruction and curing the patient at the same time.

Robert skillfully inserted an endotracheal tube through the compressed trachea, and soon the patient was anesthetized and ready for surgery. It proved not to be the simple case we had hoped for: it was thyroid cancer. The thyroid was adherent to the surrounding tissues of the neck and thorax, and only with great difficulty could it be freed. As I was severing its final attachments, I suddenly found I had cut two-thirds of the way through the trachea itself. I could see the tumor had invaded and replaced the anterior wall of the trachea for a distance of two inches. The patient's disease was incurable. To remove the tumor I would have had to cut out part of the trachea. This in turn would have required reconstructive surgery that in Amp Pipal was impossible, and which even for specialists in Western medical centers was a complex and formidable undertaking. It was futile to proceed any further.

We pushed the tumor back where it had been, quickly sutured the skin, turned off the ether, and pulled out the endotracheal tube—hoping the patient would die before he awoke from the anesthesia and thus be spared the agony of a slow death from strangulation. Then I called in the father and explained that his son could not survive more than a few minutes, and that he should be prepared to carry him home as soon as he had stopped breathing.

The father broke into tears at the news. It was his only son, he said. His wife had just died, and he was an old man. How would he get another son now? I was upset that he seemed so concerned for himself, until I remembered that nothing in the world is more important to a Hindu man than having a son to carry on his line and to perform the proper funeral rites for him. The old man's hope of salvation lay dying there before his eyes.

We all stood around the stretcher in the small room adjoining the main operating theater, waiting for the end. I didn't have faith to pray for his recovery—only for his death. I tried praying silently for the father, but that wasn't much easier. The patient, meanwhile, went on breathing—effortlessly, in fact—and showed no sign of stopping. We could shut off his airway by turning his head to one side or the other, but his head would always fall back by itself to a position that allowed him to breathe. To have held his head to the side would have been tantamount to murder, so we did nothing. At the same time we genuinely wanted him to die quickly, so that he wouldn't have to relive the terror of being choked by the "thing" in his throat.

An hour passed; the effect of the ether had begun to wear off. I'm not sure with what motivation it was that I rather abruptly urged the father to take his son home just as he was. Perhaps I didn't want to see the son wake up and to have to tell him what we found and then watch his final agony. Perhaps I was concerned about the many other patients that must have been piling up by that time and about the day's work that was being left undone while we were standing there, waiting. Or maybe I just didn't want another dead body to have to deal with. At any rate, the father hoisted the son onto his back, positioned the *naamlo* (carrying strap) across his forehead and under the son's seat, and carried his backbreaking, heartbreaking burden out of the hospital and onto the long two-day trail home. We returned to our work, our thoughts immediately refocusing on the many patients that remained to be seen, each one having brought his or her little world of sorrow and pain. Somehow, if we had reflected on it too deeply, I don't think we could have gone on. It was a greater load of grief than any of us could carry on our own.

One morning a month later, I'd just walked out of the operating room when two things happened simultaneously: I was arrested by the police (more on that later) and a man came up to me and said he wanted some vitamins for his son. Already having enough to preoccupy me, I curtly told the man to go and register at the clinic and see one of the other doctors.

"No, no," he said. "It's for my son. Vitamins."

"I don't have time now," I said. "Besides, you have to register and be seen in the clinic like anyone else. I can't do anything for you here." My impatience showed.

"You don't understand," he said softly, putting his hand on my arm. "It's for my son."

Then in a flash, I recognized him. He was the father of the young man with the thyroid.

"Vitamins!" I almost shouted, completely forgetting the police.

"Yes," the father nodded.

"What do you mean, vitamins?" I asked, incredulous. "Is your son alive?"

"Oh yes, he's alive. Only he's a little weak, so I've come to get vitamins."

Then the father told how his son had woken up halfway home and had been fine ever since. He was having no trouble breathing. They had taken the stitches out on their own. The father seemed to take it all as a matter of course, as if he had fully expected his son to recover from the beginning. I told him he must bring his son, that I wanted to see him. Hurried for time, I gave the father a small Christian booklet I had with me, but he said he couldn't read.

"Well, get your son to read it for you," I said.

"My son can't read either."

"Well, surely someone in your village can read; let him read it aloud for you."

As the father hesitantly took the pamphlet, I said, "Look, your son ought to be dead. It's not because of any doctor or operation that he's alive now. It's the living God alone who has saved him. You ought to thank him. You can learn about him from this booklet."

The father shook his head. "It was my son's karma [fate] not to die," was all he answered.

Four months later, father and son came one last time to see me. The son was no longer weak. He had no mass at all in his neck; the thyroid tumor, originally the size of a large potato, had simply melted away. In the center of the wound, however, was a tiny fistulous opening suggesting the possibility that cancerous tissue was still present. Some of our Christian staff took the two men aside and tried to open their understanding to what God had done for them so far. We haven't seen them for over a year. I can only hope that their failure to return means that the son has been completely healed.

One last example will suffice to round out this portrayal of the vicissitudes of surgical practice in Amp Pipal. One month before we were to leave on our second furlough, a woman in her sixth month of pregnancy was brought to the clinic by several male relatives. They said the fetus had stopped growing, that there had been no fetal movement for several weeks, and that the young woman was distressed in mind and body. They asked me to operate and remove the baby.

Both Cynthia and I examined the patient and found the uterus to be about the size of a six-month pregnancy. Neither of us could hear the fetal heartbeat, which suggested that either the baby was dead or that the swelling wasn't a baby at all. However, since almost all dead or defective fetuses are delivered naturally, I told the patient and her family that we wouldn't operate at that time, but that if in three weeks' time nothing had happened, she was to come back to see me. I told them three weeks because we were to leave on furlough shortly thereafter, and then Amp Pipal would be without a surgeon for two months because my replacement had been unexpectedly delayed.

The young woman returned in the middle of a hectic morning on my next-to-the-last day of work. Nothing had changed. Her uterus didn't seem any bigger, and again I heard no fetal heartbeat. I wondered if she could have a mole, but the absence of bleeding made that unlikely. She again begged me to operate, and since I'd already scheduled three surgical cases for my last day, I decided to squeeze in her operation that same afternoon. I went on with the rest of the morning's work and gave the matter no further thought.

By the time I came back from lunch, the patient had already been given the spinal anesthetic and was prepped and draped. I scrubbed my hands hurriedly, got on my gown and gloves, and made a routine midline incision in the lower abdomen. The swelling was indeed an enlarged uterus, but otherwise it appeared normal. I then opened the uterus and inside, as we had suspected, was a dead fetus. I could see no reason why it hadn't been expelled from below. I drew it out, clamped and cut the umbilical cord, and with my eyes primarily on the bleeding edges of the uterus, held out my arm to drop the fetus into a bucket on the floor. At that instant I heard a tiny cry. It was almost inaudible, but it went up my arm like an electric current. The baby was alive!

"You lied to me!" I turned to the patient angrily, putting the blame on her to ease my own embarrassment. "You knew very well this baby was alive all along. You have deliberately lied to me."

She said nothing, but set her lips tightly together and stared at the ceiling. It was not her husband's child, I learned later, and she and her family had wanted it removed.

I could do nothing but treat the matter as an ordinary Caesarean section. The baby was very premature and probably wouldn't survive anyway, but we were obliged to give it what care we could. Rigmor Hildershavn, our Norwegian nursing superintendent, who could spot trouble like a hawk spots its dinner, swooped into the operating room a few moments later, demanding to know what on earth I was up to.

"Why has this case not been through the maternity unit?" she asked indignantly. "What business do you have admitting this patient from the doctor's office? This is outrageous! I never thought I'd live to see such a thing here. I'm shocked!" Then out she flew, sparing me the need to formulate a response.

Later, to her credit, Rigmor apologized, saying she realized only afterward how bad I must have felt, even without her remarks. It was the one other occasion on which I wished one of my patients dead rather than alive. It is also an illustration of something that haunts every doctor: a missed diagnosis. It's not enough just to keep on our toes. We meet each patient with fear and trembling, rarely expressed, but always present. Our only recourse is to commit every day to God—and leave the failures and successes in His hands.

For Doctors Only

*T*HE STORY of medical practice in the Amp Pipal Hospital wouldn't be complete without a brief comment on the pathology that passes through its doors. Although some of this chapter may interest only medical professionals, it describes the variety of strange conditions we treat in the developing world.

Ninety percent of our patients, of course, have routine problems—though often far-advanced—commonly found in any developing country: intestinal parasites, leprosy, tuberculosis in all its forms, bacterial infections of many kinds, and the usual assortment of injuries—not to mention all the other miscellaneous ailments that fill doctors' offices everywhere.

Yet even conditions that would provoke much excitement in our Western hospitals are commonplace at Amp Pipal: month-old dislocated jaws, elbows, and hips; rotting teeth with huge abscesses of the face and neck; severe malnutrition; perforated typhoid ulcers; watermelon-sized ovarian cysts (from one wizened, hundred-pound woman I removed a cyst weighing fifty-five pounds—more than half her total body weight! She just about flew home); blindness in children, from lack of vitamin A; amoebic liver abscesses (one man's liver abscess not only had perforated upward through his diaphragm and lung, causing him to expectorate mouthfuls of pus, but also had penetrated downward through his abdomen, finally bursting out near his umbilicus—creating altogether a bronchopleuroperitoneocutaneous fistula, a long word even for a doctor); two- and three-month-old retained placentas (one was four years old); football-sized hydroceles—to name just a few. The common denominator of all these conditions: neglect.

Why do patients wait so long? Most of them have to walk a whole day or more to get to a doctor—if they *can* walk. A person in the States can drive from Boston to Baltimore in less time than it takes our average patient to walk to the hospital. And it's bad enough puffing up and down these trails when you're healthy—let alone when you're sick.

Many conditions that are common in Amp Pipal are no longer seen at all in the hospitals of the West. An entire generation of medical students is totally unacquainted with scores of tropical and infectious diseases that still ravage the populations of developing countries. Typhoid fever, for example, is endemic in Nepal and is a major cause of death, especially during epidemics. Tetanus and diphtheria, all but eliminated from Western nations through the widespread administration of vaccines, are frequently seen in Amp Pipal.

To help train Western medical students to diagnose and treat such conditions, we've invited small numbers of them to spend six to eight weeks at Amp Pipal during the elective period of their senior year. Thus they gain the opportunity to see "in the flesh" diseases they've seen only in pictures. One enthusiastic student from New Zealand kept a record of all the Amp Pipal patients who had conditions he'd never seen before, and within a couple of weeks he'd listed dozens—all of them everyday occurrences for us.

Of equal interest, however, were the cases he did *not* see at Amp Pipal: heart attacks; high blood pressure; cancer of the lung, breast, and colon—the three most common cancers in the West. Why are Nepalis free of heart attacks and high blood pressure? Because they eat less and exercise more—and maybe are spared some other hidden plague of Western civilization we don't yet know about. Why don't they get lung cancer? Because very few smoke, and those who do, don't smoke very much, though the habit is increasing. And why so little cancer of the breast? Because Nepali women breast-feed instead of bottle-feed their babies; they haven't succumbed to that peculiar idiocy (or commercial chicanery) of modern society that claims it can improve on God's provision for feeding infants. And cancer of the colon? We haven't seen one case in twelve years. It's something that Westerners eat (or don't eat) that accounts for it; of that there can be no question. It can't be explained away by saying that Nepalis don't live long enough to develop colon cancer or the other conditions mentioned above. Most Nepalis who survive infancy and childhood live well into their fifties and sixties. Nepalis have more than their share of diseases, but the major killers of the West are not among them.

Appearing frequently in our stream of routine cases are the truly novel and startling problems that serve either to tax our ingenuity or to demonstrate the lack of it. For example, we see many burn-contracture patients, most of whom have been burned in infancy (usually by rolling into the fireplace, which in Nepali homes is often just a shallow pit in the center of the floor) and who have then gone on to develop disabling deformities. Interspersed among the "routine" contractures, however, are some that are positively grotesque. Several patients have had an entire arm, right to the fingertips, tightly bound to their shoulder in one encasing mass of scar tissue. Other contractures have joined ear to shoulder or heel to buttock. Most of these patients can't stay for the multiple procedures necessary to correct their deformities, so we do as much as we can in one or, at most, two operations.

Or take surgical infections—that is, infections requiring surgery (not to be confused with *postoperative* infections). The abscesses we treat come in pints and quarts—that's routine. One man had five huge abscesses. We had to make eight, six-inch incisions to drain them, and when we were through, we had collected over two gallons of pus, not counting what ran onto the floor. These were *simple* abscesses. Once I encountered a kidney that contained three quarts of pus. On another occasion I opened a man with a one-gallon liver abscess; I'd thought it was a pancreatic pseudocyst, of which we've also had several.

Bone infections are in a class by themselves. More often than not, the patients arrive with far-advanced osteomyelitis, with the entire bone—usually the tibia, femur, or humerus—suspended from end to end in a sea of pus. All we do is drain the pus, put on a plaster cast, and send the patient home for two or three months until it smells so bad they can't stand it. The patients are invariably cured, usually with three to four changes of plaster; only a small percentage require a second operation later on to fish out the residual dead bone. Sometimes we've had to remove large sections of the skull that have become infected following deep burns of the scalp. On one occasion, probing a small draining sinus in the shoulder of a nine-year-old girl, I plucked out her entire collar bone with a pair of forceps; it's been sitting in my cupboard ever since.

Other surgical conditions come to us in extreme or unusual forms. In our first year in Amp Pipal, one moribund child with an intussusception (in which part of the bowel gets drawn into itself like a sleeve turned inside out) came to us with six inches of small intestine hanging out his rectum. I was strongly advised not to operate on such a hopeless case: The child would surely die and the surgery be blamed. But knowing how simple the operation was likely to be, I went ahead anyway, and the child became our first dramatic surgical cure. It impressed our Nepali staff in particular, who before that had been quietly urging patients to refuse the surgery I recommended. Many other cases of intussusception have followed. While none has been as bad as that first one, at least half have been double intussusceptions, in which the full thickness of the initial intussusception *itself* telescopes into the bowel ahead of it, creating a mass of intestine ten layers thick. Many times I've said during surgery for some condition we'd hoped would be simple, but wasn't: "Why don't we ever get a normal case in this place?"

Or we could talk about volvulus (twisting) of the intestines. Three quarters of our bowel obstructions (over forty cases) have been due to volvulus of all or part of the small intestine— anyone of which would have made surgical grand rounds in the States. We've also had half a dozen patients with cecal volvulus, as well as one bizarre case of complete volvulus of the stomach in a six-year-old girl. At the same time, however, we haven't seen a single case of sigmoid volvulus, so common in the West.

Although most of our patients have had primary volvulus, which results from an inadequate attachment of the intestines inside the abdominal cavity, we are frequently surprised by the presence of unusual contributing causes. One elderly woman came with a recently incarcerated femoral hernia, but the actual reason for her obstruction was not the hernia itself, as would almost always be the case, but volvulus of the entire midgut twisting on two points of fixation: one at the base of the mesentery, as usual; and the other at the hernial ring.

An identical mechanism was at work in another case in which an inflamed Meckel's diverticulum had attached itself to the lower abdomen wall, producing a similar result. In yet another patient a cecal volvulus was secondary to a ruptured appendix. But most memorable of all was the case of a prominent Nepali businessman who, during a trip to our district, was seized suddenly with a volvulus of his entire small intestine. The stress was so great that by the time he'd been carried to us, his peptic ulcer had perforated as well—causing no little bewilderment during the first few moments of surgery. He recovered, however, from both of these lethal conditions and walked out of the hospital a week later.

Nepal's wildlife contributes to the list of unusual conditions we encounter. Bears are the primary culprits. Less dangerous, though more common, are the injuries inflicted by the horns of bulls and water buffalos, the worst of which have occurred when an enraged animal has charged up behind a man or woman bending over in their rice paddies, gored them in the rectum or vagina, and then tossed them six to eight feet in the air. What a shock.

Snakes are another hazard. One day Tony, our usually phlegmatic British lab technician, was sitting complacently in his house reading a book when he noticed a large black snake, three inches in diameter, slither past his foot toward the far end of the room. Still absorbed in his book, Tony made a mental note that a large snake was heading toward the far end of the room, but it was only when the snake began to head back that Tony sprang to life and rushed out the door yelling "Snake! Snake!" as if he'd met Lucifer himself. Some friends came and helped kill it; it was only a medium-sized rat snake, eight feet long.

One day our x-ray technician accosted me, highly incensed "at the way things are around this hospital." (Because I was medical director, most of the complaints came to me.) He'd just been in the darkroom groping around in his solutions when he encountered a snake in one of his developing tanks. Unaccountably, I began to laugh when I heard it. The more I pictured our mincing, high-nosed x-ray technician there in the dark getting hold of that snake in his tank, the funnier it struck me. The technician didn't wait for an answer but stomped off, muttering to the office assistants as he went, "I don't think he cares what goes on around here."

I could laugh because most snakes in our area are nonpoisonous. But if snakebites are harmless, the usual village treatment is not. When someone is bitten, a tourniquet made of rope or strips of cloth is bound tightly and left for hours and days. The arm or leg, of course, becomes swollen and painful below the tourniquet. But in the mind of the patient, this is merely proof of the venom's potency. Often at this point a second tourniquet is applied. By the time the patient reaches the hospital, the limb is blue and blistered. It's a pernicious practice that is difficult to eradicate; the more ghastly the extremity looks, the more thankful the patient is that the tourniquet is there to limit the spread of the poison. We have had to amputate three arms and two legs because of these tourniquets, in addition to treating scores of lesser injuries. The snakebite itself almost never needs treatment.

Sometimes we have trouble diagnosing unusual cases. One six-year-old girl had two big stones in her bladder, which looked on the x-ray like a pair of flashlight batteries. The only trouble was that when we opened up her bladder and looked in, they weren't there. They had eroded through the bladder wall into the vagina! Wrong approach! I could have gotten them out from below without operating. (Who would have thought to look for bladder stones in the vagina of a six-year-old!) Red-faced, I pulled the stones out through the fistulous tract and sewed up my unnecessary incision. My embarrassment was overcome only by the child's eventual recovery—including the spontaneous closure of the fistula.

One day we were doing a Caesarean section for a woman whose labor hadn't been progressing satisfactorily. No wonder. We had no sooner entered the abdominal cavity than there was the baby—outside the uterus! I called in our other two doctors and some of our Nepali staff to see this very rare full-term abdominal pregnancy. Everyone was duly impressed until, on removing the baby (which was dead), we discovered a gaping hole in the lower segment of the uterus out of which the baby had come, placenta and all. So it was only (!) a ruptured uterus after all. We sutured up the hole and tied the tubes. The mother recovered well. The two strange aspects of the case were the absence of abdominal tenderness and the persistence of labor. Impossible? Not in Amp Pipal.

Some of our patients manage to make even ordinary problems memorable—like the eighty-year-old Gurung tribesman with an enlarged prostate, who had gotten along for years by having a friend blow air into his bladder through a hollow bamboo tube inserted in the tip of his penis. When enough air had gone in, the urine came out—until, one day, it didn't. He was a much happier old man after his prostate gland had been removed.

Another man with an overgrown prostate "solved" his problem by sticking hypodermic needles into his bladder to drain off the urine. This method had less to commend it than the "air" method. The needle holes leaked, of course, and when he finally reached the hospital he was in a sorry state, with a belly full of urine. Similar though less imaginative examples of self-treatment occur almost daily.

We could go on and on—intestinal duplications; huge blood-filled mesenteric cysts; imperforate anuses; two compound, dislocated elbows seen in one afternoon; even two young women with no uterus seen in one morning; and then those horrible cases of rabies—but we've gone on too long already. Do you feel as if you've been watching one of those dreadful television programs with a title like "Can You Top This?" Well, don't blame me. We said this chapter was for doctors only.

As we look back over the first twelve years of the Amp Pipal Hospital's existence, it's not the rare and stimulating cases—the "museum pieces"—that we most remember. And it's not the hardships and frustrations that linger in our minds. No, what stands out most of all is the fact that so many severely ill and injured patients got well—many more than we possibly could have expected, given the meager material resources at our disposal. I say this as a doctor and a scientist. And in the same capacity I offer what I'm convinced is the only possible reason: namely, that praying friends from all over the world have had an investment in this little hospital—and, therefore, so has God.

twelve

All in a Day's Work

WHATEVER our circumstances, most of us sooner or later fall into some sort of routine: I'm no exception. For me a routine serves the useful purpose of making the day's work at least *appear* manageable. I like to imagine also that my routine is shielding me from the unexpected, though I might as well expect a layer of soapsuds to shield me from a sky full of hailstones. Which is to say, if you're the only surgeon for half a million people, routines are made to be broken.

Nonetheless, I invite you to relive with me one routine day that occurred back in our early years at Amp Pipal. At the time, I thought the day was remarkable; since then, however, with the steady increase in our work load, many days have been as eventful, and some even more so.

This particular day started as usual, at 4:00 A.M. with an hour of prayer and Bible reading, followed by three hours of Nepali language study. I kept up this routine for our first five years in Nepal, after which the language time was given over to preparing sermons and Bible classes, as well as keeping abreast of the growing catalog of administrative details connected with running the Amp Pipal Hospital.

I can say, parenthetically, that if one aspect of missionary life is distinctly unglamorous, it surely is the time and energy put into learning the national language, especially if you're a slow learner. It cost me five thousand hours of slogging to learn Nepali. Cynthia spent one-tenth the time and speaks it better than I do. It makes me sick thinking about it. I'll never forget the day a bright, young Nepali schoolteacher came to visit me— we'd been five years in the country. He and I conversed for three solid hours on a variety of subjects—religion, politics, ecology, education—and by the time we were done, I was congratulating myself on my mastery of the language and my wide-ranging vocabulary. Just before leaving, my visitor stopped to say good-bye to Cynthia, whom he knew slightly. Cynthia smiled and told him she appreciated the good milk his mother brought to us. He looked at her with admiration and said, "Oh, it's nice to hear you talk. It's a pleasure to listen to someone who speaks good Nepali."

She'd spoken only one sentence. I could have kicked him down the steps.

If you wonder why we—that is, some of us—struggle so hard to learn the language, I can only say that we'd be lost without it, especially out here in the boondocks where there is scarcely a single Nepali who can speak English. If you can't talk with people, you obviously can't hope to relate to them in any but a most superficial way. Besides, try practicing medicine without understanding your patients, or they you. We'd be doing a lot worse than asking them if they had pain in their umbrellas.

But, getting back to the day in question, at 8:00 I was ready to leave for the hospital to begin the regular day's work. No traffic jams or commuter lines here; just a two-minute walk down the hillside. First there were rounds to be made on the hospitalized patients. On this particular day there were about twenty inpatients to see, presenting an ordinary assortment of medical and surgical problems. In the female ward in the first bed was a young girl with congestive heart failure secondary to hookworm anemia. Hookworm infestation is the most common cause of anemia in Nepal. The larvae of the worms burrow into the feet of their victims as they walk barefoot in the fields and pass up the bloodstream to the lungs. The worms are then coughed up and swallowed. Once in the intestine they grow into adult worms and attach themselves to the lining of the bowel and, like leeches, feed on their host's blood. They had bled this girl to the point of death: Her hemoglobin was 2 gm. percent, or about fifteen percent of normal.

In the next bed was a moribund typhoid-fever patient with a temperature of 105°F, and next to her was a woman, three months pregnant, whose bladder was obstructed. Then came a middle-aged woman with a plugged nasolacrimal duct (tear duct) for whom I had performed a dacrorhinocystostomy two days earlier—that is, I opened it up—an operation I'd never done or even seen before, but a good description of which I found in one of my surgical books. Finally, there was a postoperative cataract patient, and a teenage girl with a broken leg.

The male ward contained a case of spinal tuberculosis; a postoperative urethral-reconstruction patient, who had fallen from the top of a tree, crotch first, onto a lower branch, shattering his urethra and pelvis; a boy with a tuberculous hand the size of a cantaloupe; a young man with bilateral fractured femurs and a dislocated shoulder; a pneumonia patient; a case of encephalitis; an undiagnosed fever; and two postoperative cases, one a hydrocele, and the other an anal fistula.

My most celebrated male patient at the time, however, was a middle-aged farmer who had been occupying a bed in the corner for three weeks. He had met with a singular accident. He'd been happily minding his own business weeding his corn patch (located, like every other corn patch in our area, on a steeply terraced hillside) when a large water buffalo cavorting on the next terrace up suddenly lost its footing and tumbled down the eight-foot embankment, landing squarely on the back of the unsuspecting farmer as he knelt at his work. The impact of the buffalo's fall broke the man's neck. When the man arrived at the hospital, he was almost completely paralyzed from the neck down; however, the tiny trace of neurologic function I was able to elicit on my initial examination suggested at least some possibility of recovery. We bored two holes in his skull, into which we fastened a two-pronged gadget resembling an ice hook. To this device was attached a rope that led over a pulley to some sandbags tied to the other end. By this means we were able to apply twenty-five pounds of traction to the man's head, thereby straightening his neck and relieving the pressure on his spinal cord.

Upon finding himself transfixed in this fashion and thinking he was dead from the neck down, he ordered his family to release him at once and take him home where he could die in peace. Fortunately, we were able to persuade the family that the patient was best off in the hospital, and so they refused to give in to his demands.

To everyone's delight, the man soon began to improve. Perceiving some return of function in his extremities, he again started agitating to go home immediately, insisting that since he was getting well he no longer needed to be strung up in this preposterous contraption. When his demands went unheeded, he passed long hours castigating his doctor, upbraiding his family over their callous disregard for his wishes, and generally ventilating his grievances to anyone who would listen. He eventually recovered completely. Although we were unable to keep him in the hospital as long as we wanted, he departed on good terms with us, having become a grateful and happy patient in the meantime. Indeed, for years afterward he continued to visit me every few months, and each time he came he brought me two eggs. Exactly two eggs, neither more nor less.

Moving on to the children's ward, there were a couple of burn victims, some dysentery cases, a postoperative harelip, two youngsters with osteomyelitis, and two with marasmus (a severe form of malnutrition). Then, in one of the private rooms, a young man and his wife were both being treated for advanced gonorrhea. The husband's urethra had perforated, resulting in a fulminating infection that had necrosed (eaten away) most of his scrotum and already had spread halfway up his abdominal wall.

In the second private room was a wealthy young woman who had flown up from a city in the south of Nepal to have her gall bladder removed. She had been to doctors in Kathmandu and even in India, and none of them had diagnosed her problem. How she heard about us I can't remember, but from her standpoint, coming to a primitive, little, out-of-the-way hospital up in the mountains was surely a long shot. It paid off, though, for when she left the hospital, she was without pain for the first time in many years. We couldn't have foreseen it then, of course, but after she returned home and told her friends that she was now cured, other patients began coming to us from her part of Nepal. And they have been coming ever since in greater and greater numbers.

My last stop on rounds that day was the tuberculosis ward, a separate shelter where we kept the sicker TB patients who couldn't be treated at home. On the way, I walked past the special isolation room usually reserved for the most severely ill TB cases. Today it was empty.

For a whole month, right up until the previous evening, the isolation room had been occupied by the loveliest Gurung girl I'd ever seen. She was twenty-one years old, and her name was Phul Maya, which means "love flower." For many months she'd been under treatment for tuberculosis at home and had been on the verge of recovery. Her flesh had filled out, and she had regained her former charm and vivacity. But then, like so many of our TB patients, she stopped taking her medicine. She looked and felt fine, so she assumed she was cured. We didn't see her at all for several months.

But then one day Phul Maya began coughing up blood in large quantities: Her disease had recurred. She came at once to the hospital, frightened and ashamed; she remembered our repeated warnings not to stop treatment. Amazingly, she still looked robust and healthy, only a little pale. We restarted her treatment, but this time the drugs had no effect. We weren't surprised: TB recurring after a lapse of treatment is almost invariably resistant to the original drugs. It wouldn't have been so bad if there had been other cheap and readily available drugs that we could have substituted for the ones that were no longer effective, but such was not the case. There were indeed other drugs, the so-called second-line drugs, which probably could have cured her, but they cost thirty or forty times more than the standard, or first-line, drugs. Neither the patient nor our hospital could afford such treatment. Given a situation in which resources are severely limited, as in Nepal, treating one patient with second-line drugs means, in effect, depriving thirty other TB patients of treatment with the cheaper drugs. Even in the rare instances when we do give the more expensive drugs, we insist that their use be limited to those dependable patients who've never stopped treatment on their own, whose TB organisms, in other words, had been resistant to start with. Thus, we couldn't justify giving Phul Maya the second-line drugs that might have saved her. And so she continued to deteriorate, coughing up blood in larger and larger amounts and growing progressively weaker with each passing day. We did give her one or two blood transfusions in the faint hope that the old drugs might yet begin to work, if only we could keep her alive long enough. But there was nothing we could do to stop the bleeding itself. And only the night before she had suffered a massive hemorrhage into her lungs and had drowned in her own blood. I had watched her die, helpless to do anything but hold her hand and pray silently to a God who seemed that night to be somewhere else.

Today, the emptiness of the room cried out to me as I went past.

Such was my collection of inpatients on that particular day. I saw Dr. Helen as she was making her own rounds; she would have around twenty patients also, only none of them would be surgical. Cynthia had no inpatients in those early years; she was busy at home, raising two small boys.

At 9:00 I was scheduled to do a cataract extraction on an old woman whom I'd met on one of my village clinic trips a week earlier. One advantage of these trips was the occasion to meet potential patients who ordinarily never would have come to the hospital on their own. Such was the case with this blind woman. She hadn't been easy to convince. Only after my repeated assurances that she'd be able to see after the surgery did she finally agree to come to the hospital. Then, of course, I also had to persuade her family that it was worthwhile. They would have to arrange for her to be carried the two days' journey, and they would have to provide someone to stay with her for the required week in the hospital. The woman had been brought the day before by four porters and six family members, all of whom were now waiting around to see how the operation would turn out.

The operation got underway without difficulty. I infiltrated the tissues around the first eye with a local anesthetic and proceeded to remove the cataract. Then I began the second eye. I was nearing the critical stage of the operation, the point at which the eyeball is actually entered and the cataract removed, when my hitherto placid patient began to make curious noises in the back of her throat; she gagged, swallowed, and wagged her head. I asked her to stop moving and reminded her that this was a delicate operation, that her eye could be injured if she didn't lie still. Unfortunately she understood very little Nepali (she was a Gurung and spoke mainly her tribal language), and therefore, it wasn't easy to communicate with her. We finally realized that she was trying to tell us something, only she couldn't speak; air came, but no sound. I thought to myself, *Good grief, she's had a stroke!* A stroke could well have affected her larynx and pharynx in such a way that she wouldn't be able to swallow or talk. But, whatever the cause, the patient was getting more and more agitated, and so was I. It was all I could do to keep my instruments in their places, let alone go on with the operation.

Soon the patient was completely beside herself, writhing about, wretching, coughing, and choking. Four Nepali assistants tried to hold her down, shouting at her to be still, but to no avail. Since the operation would take only another few minutes, I was naturally reluctant to stop; but after half an hour it was clear that her stroke was getting worse, not better, and that it was hopeless to continue. She had become uncontrollable.

Worn out and discouraged, I gave up the operation. I thought for sure she'd be brain damaged the rest of her life, so it wouldn't make any difference whether or not she could see out of that second eye—or out of the first, for that matter.

While my assistants tidied things up, I went out and had a cup of tea, wondering what on earth I was going to say to all those relatives whom I had urged so vigorously to have her brought for surgery in the first place. I didn't have long to wonder. Returning momentarily to check my patient, I was just in time to see a large pink worm, about eight inches long and as fat as a Parker pen, slither out of her mouth and onto her chest. The patient at once sat up and asked for a drink of water. So that was the cause of her problem! In an instant she had completely recovered.

The worm evidently had crawled out of her stomach and up her esophagus into the back of her throat, where it had caused her to gag. Then it had crawled partway into her windpipe, rendering her speechless and sending her into paroxysms of coughing. Why that worm, having lived peacefully in her intestines for months, had decided to exit in the middle of an eye operation, I'll never know. In any event, it was a complication of cataract surgery I'd never encountered before, nor wish to again. I finished the second eye the next day.

Helen and I had about ninety patients to see in the outpatient clinic that day. So until lunch, I worked my way through patients with tuberculosis, abscesses, pneumonia, abscessed teeth, and fractured arms. I saw a new cataract patient (this one will get worm medicine before surgery) and our *pradhan panch's* son, who was very ill with typhoid fever. Then there was the usual run of TB and leprosy follow-up cases, as well as an assortment of dysenteries and other parasitic diseases. The last patient of the morning was a small child with a retino-blastoma, a malignant tumor of the eye, bulging like a large tomato out of its socket.

After the lunch break, during which I had scheduled a language lesson with a local teacher, I still had thirty patients to see. The first of these was a spry Brahmin woman who sniffed her way into my office like a ferret on the trail of a rat. She plopped herself down on the stool opposite mine, and laying her dirty umbrella on top of my desk, she peered at me down either side of her nose, snuffling continuously. We sat knee to knee, eyeing each other.

"What's your problem today?" I asked her, in an amiable, professional tone.

"Wait," she said. "I'll show you what's wrong."

She began to snuffle violently and make explosive noises in the back of her nose and throat. I was watching her nose ornament bob up and down, when before I knew it, she had leaned forward and spit a mouthful of yellow phlegm right between my knees onto the floor. It fell exactly between my heels, which were barely an inch apart. She was obviously practiced.

"That," she said, with satisfaction, "is my problem."

Chronic sinusitis with postnasal drip. I prescribed some medicine for her and said it would make her better. She didn't seem pleased, somehow, as if she were loathe to part with her "problem" so quickly. I suspected that her family had forced her to come to the hospital: They were likely more eager to get rid of her problem than she was.

The next patient was a man with a large cyst on his face. I alerted our operating-room staff that we'd be doing him at the end of the day. Then, in the middle of passing a filiform catheter into the bladder of a man with an obstructed urethra, I received word that our district representative to the National Assembly had brought his wife to the hospital. They had already been waiting much of the day, unbeknown to us, and so without further ado, covered with my usual composite layer of sweat, plaster, and blood, I stepped out and extended to them our official greetings in the midst of a corridor full of groaning and yelling patients and their relatives. After I had examined the representative's wife, we decided they should go up to our house for tea so that Cynthia could offer them at least some semblance of hospitality before they departed. It was inconvenient to have them for dinner that night because we'd already invited the local Nepali pastor and his wife and two nurses. But Cynthia invited them anyway, and they decided to stay. It would make a mixed group. In addition, two Nepali high-school teachers, whom we knew well, also dropped in at the last minute to round out the party.

I was running behind schedule now. My next patient was a sixty-year-old village man with phimosis, a congenital narrowing of the opening in the foreskin, beneath which had accumulated forty-two stones varying in size from a split pea to a brussels sprout. He had been carrying around that sackful of rocks at the end of his penis for two decades! With a quick slit I lightened his load, and he became the happiest circumcision patient I've ever seen. He just about danced out the door.

There were only a few patients left, and it was 4:30. Helen was down on the ward tied up with a bad delivery case. I notified the operating-room staff that we would begin the cyst removal promptly at 5:00, and if all went as expected, I'd be home just in time to greet the dinner guests. So I proceeded to hurry along, which is always a mistake, and at 4:50 I had only three patients to go—all of them young, giggly, teenaged girls, who had been brought by a fourth, slightly older girl.

Ah, I thought, *I'll be able to dispense with these girls in a couple of minutes.* Second mistake. Unfortunately, I didn't have my office assistant, who was down with hepatitis at the time, so I was alone. I asked the first girl what was the matter, and she was able to wind up her answer about five minutes later. The "matter" went from her head to her feet: her head ached, her eyes burned, her mouth tasted waxy, she was short of breath, she had palpitations and stomach cramps, her periods weren't right, her joints ached, the soles of her feet burned, and her stool was bad. When asked in what way her stool was bad, she gave the standard answer: *paheelo,* the Nepali word for "yellow." (There is nothing worse you can label your stool than *paheelo*— whatever is meant by it.) If that wasn't enough, she felt weak and dizzy, like myself.

Well, after that, I began my usual routine of going through the body systems one by one in an effort to sort out the story. I saw it was futile to hurry, though I kept trying.

"So you're short of breath, are you?" I asked. As I ran through the systems, the older girl, who was kind of shepherding the three younger ones about, kept rephrasing and clarifying each of my questions, and then doing the same with the girl's answers.

I might have appreciated her services except that after every complaint we discussed or even mentioned, the older girl would ask, "Now why is that, doctor?" I had to think fast to come up with the answers: her tongue tingled because she ate too many spices; her feet burned because her vitamins were low—"Now why is that, doctor?"—because the worms in her stomach were eating up the vitamins, etc. This went on for a dozen or more questions. She gave me no peace. Then I made the mistake of asking the patient what exactly was wrong with her periods. I always do this when some young girl has twenty-odd complaints, because that's usually the real reason she's come—no children, irregular periods, or some other female problem—but she is embarrassed to say so. I regretted asking this time. Her periods came every two months. Now why is that, doctor? I mumbled something about the chemicals being out of balance— now why is that, doctor? Another half-witted answer. How is her blood pressure, doctor? Fine. How can you be sure she has worms, doctor? I refrained from telling her I had a special power of discernment when it came to worms and ordered a stool test instead—mainly to placate her. I'd been hoping to avoid a lot of unnecessary laboratory tests on this perfectly healthy girl. Why do her knees ache, doctor? This was a question that was hard enough to answer in English, let alone in Nepali.

"Well," I ventured, "sometimes knees do that, you know."

"Why is that, doctor?"

"For no reason at all." Silence. It was the right answer.

At that opportune moment the stool report came back showing roundworms and hookworms, whereupon I grandly announced that all her problems were due to these little parasites living in her intestines and that she'd be well in a jiffy. There's nothing like a timely stool exam to get you out of a pickle.

Well, I finished with the first girl at 5:15—thoroughly disheartened, because I could see the other two sitting out in the corridor looking as if they had the same story. They did. The sequence was repeated with number two. This time her back hurt instead of her knees. "Why is that, doctor?" queried my volunteer office assistant. And her periods come every two weeks instead of every two months. "Why is that?" I didn't dare say not enough vitamins, because that was what I'd told girl number one with the opposite problem; and to say too many vitamins was an answer too ridiculous even for me at that point. I forgot what I said—it probably wasn't intelligible. You can guess I didn't ask the third girl how her periods were.

By this time forty minutes had elapsed, and the "why-is-that?" girl was pressing me to say why the third girl's shoulder ached. I launched into an explanation of arthritis, thinking it would be quicker and easier than trying to explain anxiety and tension (her major problems) in Nepali. I got deeper and deeper into the arthritis bit, bringing in the knees and the back of the first two girls to elucidate my argument. I was figuring that one final presentation of the subject would make further discussion unnecessary. Doctors become skilled at smothering their patients' questions under a cloud of erudition. It was a technique

I'd used before in similar situations with modest success. I concluded my speech with the helpful comment that her pain had no real cause in the first place—and then made a fatal mistake. I mentioned, as a superfluous afterthought, that there were indeed two types of pain that doctors were at a loss to explain, joint pain and headaches, and that all we could do was give aspirin. "Ah," said my friendly office assistant, "then you know about headaches too. Could I tell you about *my* headaches?"

She hadn't even registered as a patient. I was too unraveled to tell her what she could do with her headaches, one of which she had given to me, so for the next ten minutes I sat passively listening as she gave me her life history. Reluctantly I delivered my tension-and-neurosis lecture, and after badly garbling the middle section, I wound up by saying that her headaches were all in her head. When this didn't satisfy her, I told her she would have to look for the source of anxiety in her life. "How do I do that, doctor?" I replied that I hadn't the foggiest idea, and wonder of wonders, that ended the discussion. Just like that. If I had given that answer to her very first question an hour before, I could have been through in ten minutes. We live and learn.

Finally I got to the operating room, where the attendants and patient had been ready for an hour and a half. While I removed the man's cyst, a young man with a badly lacerated foot arrived; and while I fixed the foot, a man who had blown off part of his hand with a gun arrived. We operated until nine o'clock, the surgery not being made any easier by the incapacitation of our generator, which had been on the blink for two weeks. (It's as easy to get spare parts for the moon vehicle as it is for our generator.) So we operated by flashlight and kerosene lantern.

After repairing the shattered hand, I arrived home to find the company getting on superbly without me. Everyone was engaged in animated conversation, especially our distinguished and loquacious visitor, the National Assembly representative. Near the end of the evening Cynthia played a few piano pieces, to which the guests, as usual, responded with polite incomprehension.

Then unexpectedly, the Nepali pastor got up to speak. He had originally been the main guest, all the others having been added on subsequently. He was a plain and unpretentious man, little educated and of low caste, with a partially paralyzed right leg and a completely crippled right arm, both resulting from polio. In spite of this handicap—and in defiance of the law of the land—he spent most of his time as an itinerant evangelist, somehow limping up and down the hills of Nepal with a determination and vigor that left his traveling companions exhausted. Although he was indisputably a man of deep and abiding faith, he was not ordinarily noted for either dynamic leadership or eloquent speeches. Nevertheless, on this particular evening, after Cynthia had finished playing, he stood up and said simply that now he would read from God's Word. Taking the Bible in his one good hand, he read slowly from various passages in the New Testament, while his wife held a flashlight and helped turn the pages. Then he spoke for five minutes with unaffected authority about the essential meaning of the Christian Gospel, for himself, and for all people. And after he had prayed, he said quietly that it was time to be going—it was then about 10:30. We'd never seen the pastor rise to such an occasion before and handle it so effectively. With that, the evening came to an end.

The Seminar

*T*HE VERY NEXT DAY we were expecting the arrival of seven government-trained health assistants, who had been assigned to run the different government health posts located throughout our district. These young Nepali men had recently completed their two-year basic health-assistant course, and although they were undoubtedly well grounded in theory, they had had almost no practical experience in the diagnosis and treatment of patients.

So the staff at Amp Pipal had decided to offer these health assistants some in-service training in the form of a week-long seminar on the hospital premises. We next had taken our plan to the members of the Amp Pipal village *panchayat,* who gave it their support. Our politically ambitious *pradhan panch* said he would arrange everything if we would just do the teaching.

That was where it all began; where it ended was quite another matter. Our *pradhan panch* was as good as his word. He was an agreeable, outgoing person who was highly persuasive when it came to stirring up enthusiasm for local projects. He had gone first to the district capital, a six-hour walk to the east, and stirred up the Chief District Officer and several other district officials, all of whom agreed to attend the opening ceremonies that were to launch our seminar. He then invited the *pradhan panches* from the neighboring six or seven *panchayats,* as well as other interested *panchayat* representatives. He encouraged many more to attend—staff from the government hospital, district health workers, just about anyone, it seemed, with whom he talked. All of these people were in addition to the seven health assistants—for whom, of course, the whole affair had been organized.

The arrangements were shaping up nicely, and our *pradhan panch,* so far the guiding spirit behind everything, was off in the next district trying to get those officials to come also, when suddenly the health ministry in Kathmandu decided to get into the act. How they even heard about it, I'll never know. First, they elected to send their own representative to take charge of all the teaching and programming, thereby reducing our role to that of innocent bystanders. Second, they sent word to the Regional Medical Officer, the person in charge of all medical work in our entire central region of Nepal, comprising eleven districts, and instructed him to officiate at the week's activities. Then a day or two later, for reasons known to none but themselves, the health-ministry people announced that the week's proceedings were to commence one day earlier than originally planned. This in itself would have created no problem but for the fact that word of the change failed to reach over half of those who had been invited or instructed to come—conspicuously including our own *pradhan panch,* who was still off rounding up potential participants, and also, most infelicitously, the Regional Medical Officer, the main functionary of the entire event.

The other especially honored guest was our own recently appointed Chief District Officer (CDO). He was planning to come for the opening ceremonies, inspect the hospital, and generally familiarize himself with our part of the district—a laudable intention, and one particularly suited to the occasion, considering that so many neighboring *panchayat* leaders were also going to be present. (Unfortunately, most of them never found out that the ceremonies were to begin a day earlier; thus they missed seeing the CDO entirely.)

Dr. Helen and I were eager to speak with these district

government and health-ministry officials about the future of our medical work, since it had been rumored for some time that the central government was planning to take over the hospital. Our *pradhan panch,* who had likewise gotten wind of these rumors, was also interested in the future of the hospital, through which, among other considerations, his own importance could be enhanced, especially on occasions such as this. He got back home from his public-relations campaign on the eve of the opening day, and found to his surprise that half the expected assemblage had already arrived and were impatiently demanding the food and lodging that he had carefully arranged for the *following* evening.

On the grand day, our peaceful little village was the scene of unaccustomed excitement and commotion. By late morning much of the neighborhood had already congregated in the outer waiting area of the hospital in order to get good places from which to view the pageantry. In honor of the occasion, some of our Nepali hospital staff had erected a special archway of bamboo, banana leaves, and woven flowers, under which the party of distinguished guests and other officials were expected to pass on their way to their seats. A party of cows, however, chanced along first and ate half of it away before anyone noticed. There was no time to repair the damage. Since it was impossible for our visitors not to notice the archway's shredded condition, the best we could hope for was that they would be kindly disposed and take the thought for the deed. We received some consolation from the thought that this surely wasn't the first special archway to have been eaten by cows or goats.

The opening ceremonies, scheduled for 1:00, got underway promptly at 2:00. Our *pradhan panch* started things off by fastening flowers to the pictures of Nepal's king and queen, which were displayed prominently outside the hospital entrance. (We had hastily purchased the pictures only two days before-hand. They should have been there all along; it had been a serious oversight.) A trio of Nepali nurses sang a song to welcome the Regional Medical Officer (who had not yet arrived) and the CDO. Then the speeches began.

Everyone seemed to want to say something on such an auspicious occasion as this—*pradhan panches,* district officials, schoolteachers, shopkeepers, other prominent citizens—and all had their chance. A few gave more than one speech, including our own *pradhan panch,* who gave four. Important guests kept arriving during the speeches, having expected that things would begin the next day. In the midst of the ceremonies, the Regional Medical Officer arrived, disheveled and dripping with sweat, having just trekked fifteen miles up our mountain in the steaming heat—and was promptly asked to deliver a speech. Someone sent to fetch him a glass of water before he collapsed. He presented a striking figure. He was short and swarthy, with a sleek black moustache curled at the ends, and on his head he wore a large, straw sombrero. Indeed, as he strode over to take his place next to the picture of the king, his appearance and deportment would have made him a perfect stand-in for Pancho Villa.

His oration was surprisingly energetic. The first third of his speech consisted of hearty denunciations of the health ministry for having changed the date of the seminar at the last minute without having informed everyone—himself, in particular. The middle third of the speech dealt with the intense discomfort of the trail, its length, steepness, the dust, the heat, and then being asked to give an address the moment he arrived. Were they trying to kill him? The last third of his speech portrayed his genuine and total perplexity as to why on earth he'd been ordered to come to this God-forsaken spot in the first place. He hadn't a clue.

It was a wonderful speech. Everyone loved it. All the speeches were wonderful—all twenty of them. It was a gala opening. And when it was over, all the guests and participants had to decide what to do next—where to go and whether to go there, where to eat, who would feed them, whether to stay, and so forth. That took at least an hour, and in the end no one was completely sure what he had decided. I do not exaggerate. The CDO decided three times to go and three times to stay. On the fourth round the "goes" won. Much of his indecision was due to the rain that came twice and went once. And a lot depended, you see, on what the CDO did. And on a dozen other variables.

Somehow, all those who stayed got fed, bathed, and bedded down for the night; some of the more important guests came to our house, including Pancho Villa. From then on, events were carried along pretty much by their own momentum. There were late evening meetings on the future of the hospital, through which Dr. Helen slept soundly. There were early morning meetings on the future of the hospital, through which Pancho Villa slept soundly. Seminars were held in one place while participants arrived in another. Field trips were scheduled, on which no one went. The mission staff more or less stood in the wings, ready to help out here and there with a lecture, some tea, a meal, or some movies. Seppo, our Finnish builder, spent ten hours trying to get our projector fixed in time to show some health and agricultural films. The night of the showing, not one of those taking part in the seminar showed up. They had decided at the last minute to see the movies the following night. That was all right: a crowd of villagers came instead, so we ended up showing movies both nights.

For the final evening of the seminar Cynthia and I had invited to supper all the participants, both instructors and health assistants—plus some of our senior Nepali staff members from the hospital. We had twenty-one guests. The idea was to give our own staff a chance to meet all these government people, and also to give the government health workers an opportunity to ask questions and get to know us. Well, you wouldn't believe it—our staff lined up on one side of the room and the government people lined up on the other, and not a word passed between them the entire evening except what was drummed up by myself with colossal effort. You would have thought it was a meeting of Arabs and Israelis on the eve of the Yom Kippur War.

The next morning they all left, and the ordeal was over.

The Mystique of Surgery

*T*HERE'S A MYSTIQUE about surgery, I suppose, a mystique that surgeons make little effort to dispel. Some surgeons have been known to cultivate it. Standing at the bedside, surrounded by anxious relatives and awed nurses, the surgeon, laying a hand momentarily on the patient's abdomen, says in oracular tones: "We operate tonight." Faint gasps go around the bed. Even the referring physician wonders how the surgeon arrived at his decision. This is the mystique of surgery.

And then the patient is wheeled off up the corridor, through the swinging doors, into that unknown world of the operating room—or theatre, as the British call it, which hits it right on the nose.

Notice that the surgeon is a man of few words. This is more a matter of necessity than design: most surgeons are inarticulate, having spent the prime years of their lives with a mask over their mouths and an active vocabulary limited to "suck," "pull," and "cut."

One sure way to dispel the ethereal vapors of the surgical mystique is to trot your surgeon off to an unfamiliar hospital for a few months—preferably a mission hospital—and there you will see both him and his profession stripped bare, exposed for what they really are. For the surgeon, I might add, it's like being operated on without anesthesia.

I once was asked to help out at another mission hospital, to relieve a fellow surgeon who had fallen and broken her leg;

Cynthia came along, too, to help in the female medical clinic. This hospital was one of the mission's premier institutions, a 100-bed hospital serving as a referral center for the entire western half of Nepal. After humble little Amp Pipal, this was going to be like downtown. Cynthia and I approached our assignment with awe.

One of the first signs that this was a high-class hospital was getting new names. No longer would Dr. Tom and Dr. Cynthia do; it was last names here: Drs. Hale, T, and C. This quickly became Dr. Teal and Dr. Seal. We fared better, however, than Clara, the nursing superintendent: The Nepalis called her "Sister Cholera."

My first case at this new hospital was a man with a bladder stone, an easy enough operation to start with. The diagnosis hadn't been so easy, however; there had been no blood cells in the urine exam, which there must be when a stone is present. Only when the patient demanded an x-ray did the stone show up as big as life, the size of a golf ball and covered with spines. I later learned that the lab at this hospital didn't spin down urines, which is done everywhere else in the world as far as I know— though I could be out of touch—so they weren't going to find red cells in any bladder-stone cases I sent them. (This wouldn't be the lab's only quirk we had to get used to: we were even turning up men with positive pregnancy tests.)

I was assured that all the preoperative preparation was taken care of routinely here and that I needn't trouble myself about anything except just going to the Theatre and operating—that was my job. This was certainly going to be a lot easier than working at Amp Pipal!

I went to the Theatre a little early, which was a good thing. I found out I couldn't go inside without putting on some special rubber flip-flops, which were neatly laid out on a rack outside the swinging doors. They were sterilized each evening, I was told, in disinfectant solution. Sterile footwear! This was going to be some place. The only trouble was I didn't like wearing flip-flops, and I didn't like blood and pus and whatever else dripping onto my toes. But luckily I had a pair of brand-new sneakers up at the house, and they said I could wear those instead; so I went back to the house and fetched them.

I was shown the dressing room. Someone had just washed the floor (these must have been some of the cleanest floors anywhere in Nepal) and there were puddles here and there. As I bent over to take off my dirty sneakers, my notebook and glasses slid out of my pocket into a puddle. I wiped them off and stuck them in my pants pocket. Then I looked for some operating clothes that would fit me. The green theatre clothes were arranged in piles on three shelves of a cupboard, with labels for pants and shirts— small, medium, and large. They had been autoclaved, I was told; that was impressive too. Sterile floors, sterile footwear, sterile clothes. We never went to that much trouble in Amp Pipal. We never changed shoes, we wore street clothes under our operating room gowns, and we certainly never worried about the floors. And we never had infections either—well, almost never. Up in Amp Pipal our germs didn't jump; maybe they did here. But, anyway, it was reassuring to see all these precautions being taken, even if they weren't necessary.

I got down a pair of "medium" pants; they were a bit short, though they covered my kneecaps. I got down three more pairs: the same. I went through the whole cupboard and finally found some pants that fit in the section marked "small shirts." Then I looked for a shirt. After finding only small pants in the "large shirt" section, I searched through every pile before finding a shirt that reached to my waist. It was tight in the armpits, but I could put up with it for a short case like a bladder stone.

The caps were all for much bigger heads than mine, so I chose one at random, and by rolling up the edges I could keep it above my eyes. A mask completed my outfit, and I was ready to enter the lists.

I had sort of thought—given the amount of time I had spent in the dressing room—that the patient would be lying on the operating table, anesthetized and ready for surgery; but I found the patient had not yet arrived in the Theatre. Just then I heard some activity in the anteroom outside the swinging doors, and looking out, I saw my patient being transferred from one trolley onto another.

"Did the trolley break down?" I inquired innocently.

"We don't allow outside trolleys to come into the Theatre," a brisk young Nepali told me. "Everything in here has to be clean."

That's good, I thought. I was all for that. But why was the patient's catheter just lying open between his legs, dripping urine, not clamped, no drainage tube or bottle or anything?

"He'll get a new drainage tube and bottle in the Theatre," I was told. "We don't bring the old ones in here."

"But he had his catheter put in only half an hour ago; the drainage tubing and bottle are hardly very old."

That didn't matter. They had their procedures, they said.

I looked again and noticed the catheter was a size #16, whereas I had ordered a #22. I muttered something about its small size and was assured it was perfectly routine and that they never had any problem. Besides, there weren't any #22s.

The trolley rolled into the Theatre, and I went and sat down to wait for the spinal to be put in. The floor washer had left a puddle on the stool I chose; I discovered it only by hindsight. After a while I got up to see how things were progressing. The Nepali anesthetist was just washing the patient's back. I could see that his back hadn't been washed on the ward, for dirt was blackening each piece of cotton as it was wiped over the skin. Washing backs on the ward wasn't part of the routine, I gathered; nor, I was soon to discover, was washing the operative site: the patients were told to wash themselves, a dubious proposition under any circumstances, but especially so when the taps in this hospital were turned off all day to save water—even in the monsoon season.

Someone noticed there was no electricity. The hospital was supplied by a local on-again-off-again power company, and today was an off day. The hospital had two backup generators, but neither of them, it turned out, was working. Did I want to proceed? It meant no lights and no suction. The operating room was fairly bright with the outside daylight coming in through the windows, and taking out a bladder stone wasn't much of a procedure, so I said I'd go ahead. The operating-room staff produced a battery-run spotlight, but someone had neglected to recharge the battery, so it wasn't working either.

I began scrubbing my hands at the scrub sink. The faucet was much lower than I was used to, relative to the rim of the sink, and there was no way I could scrub in the usual manner, with elbows down and hands up. The Nepalis, I'm sure, were better at it, though I couldn't help noticing that they too were letting dirty water from their unwashed elbows run onto their hands. When I had finished scrubbing, I contaminated one of my hands on the faucet and had to start over again. This happened twice. The Nepali staff, no doubt, were wondering why I spent so long washing my hands.

When I got into the operating room, my assistant was prepping the abdomen. I was given a towel the size of a greeting card to dry my hands with. Then I was given a gown that could have been cut from the cast-off tent of a polar expedition. It was rigid and heavy and hot—and this was August in Nepal. The morning sun was streaming in the windows. The sweat was streaming down my back. And we hadn't even begun.

I was given some powder to dust on my hands. We usually dust our hands before the gown is put on so as not to get talcum on the sleeves, but that was not the routine at this hospital. It didn't matter really, because the talcum was not all powdery; it had solidified into crumbly chunks that did nothing to aid in slipping one's hands into the sterile gloves. The gloves for their part had not been dusted either, so we spent several minutes getting the sticky rubber up over all my fingers. Then, too, the sleeves of the polar tent splayed out at the end and refused to tuck themselves inside the gloves. I ripped two pairs trying to get them on, which was about par, I learned, since the gloves, designed for only one use, were now on their fifth or sixth run. Finally I was ready.

I asked the assistant to wipe the patient's belly button clean with a swab stick. The assistant looked at me as if I had asked for bacon and eggs. It took a few minutes for someone to locate a swab stick; this was not part of the routine. It may seem fussy to be worrying so about belly buttons, but you'd be surprised what turns up inside. We dug in with the swab stick and discovered coal. The floor was ten times cleaner than this patient's belly button.

We got the belly button cleaned out, though we had to send to the ward for more swab sticks. Then we laid on the drapes.

First to go on were the four small towels. One of them had big holes in it. I held it up and looked at it, and then looked around at the staff. They didn't seem bothered by the holes, only by my hesitation. Perhaps I didn't know what to do with the towel.

"I can't use this," I said. They looked hurt. Another was sent for. One of the other towels had holes in it too, but I used it anyway; its holes were smaller.

The patient's hand suddenly swooped down on the sterile field and was grabbed in the nick of time.

"Don't you restrain the patients here?" I asked.

No, they did not.

"Well, please restrain this patient," I said. I'd had more than one patient in the past reach into his wound. It's an unnerving sight seeing a bare hand creep into the operative field from under the drapes. It means almost certain infection.

It took a few minutes to get the hands restrained because the staff weren't used to doing it, and they couldn't decide where to tie the restraints. At this rate the spinal would be wearing off before we even began.

I asked the anesthetist if it was all right to begin; and he nodded his head. Just then the patient began clearing his throat. It was one of those long clearings, and I knew what was coming at the end of it. The anesthesia screen, which is supposed to separate the patient's face from the rest of the surgical field, wasn't in the right place; it was too low and too far down over the chest. The bolus of spit sailed over the screen like a missile, clearing the top with two inches to spare. However, it was wide of the mark and landed harmlessly on a shelf where IV bottles were stored. I breathed a sigh of relief; maybe he'd gotten it out of his system. I once had a patient who spit right in his wound—it was another bladder stone case, come to think of it. It was no laughing matter.

The rest of the procedure went fairly well, and when it was over, we moved the patient onto the special trolley for the trip to the recovery room. One of the staff picked up the drainage bottle and put it between the patient's legs, allowing the urine collected in the bottle to run back into the patient's bladder. Didn't they clamp the tubing when they moved a patient like this? No, they never did. Well, they'd better start, I told them, right with this patient. That necessitated a hunt for a clamp. While waiting for the clamp, I noticed the little glass connector between the catheter and the drainage tube. It was the size of an eyedropper. Didn't anyone around here know that flow in a pipe was proportional to the square of the diameter? I asked for another connector. Four other packs had to be opened before I found one the right size. It was big and wide, all right, made of thin glass too, and when I shoved it into the catheter, it broke into a hundred pieces. We spent the next five minutes clearing glass fragments out of the catheter and in the end gave up and changed the catheter. As the patient was being wheeled out of the theater, I thought to myself: *And this is only the first case.*

Following the bladder-stone operation, there was a dilation and curettage to do, otherwise known as a D&C, a procedure that few women in the West escape having done to them at some time or other. The D&C takes all of five minutes and is one of the simplest procedures in the doctor's repertoire. After the bladder-stone case, a D&C was just what the doctor ordered to restore my joggled confidence. For what can go wrong during a D&C?

What indeed? I was a veteran of over four hundred D&C's. I did them all under general anesthesia. Here at this hospital they were done under paracervical (local) block. The patient was already anesthetized in the next room and ready for me. After another encounter with the scrub sink, I was fitted into a gown so small it couldn't be tied in the rear and the sleeves of which didn't reach my gloves. I stepped up to the table and put in the weighted retractor. The drapes were already in place. All that remained was to grab the patient's cervix with a tenaculum (long clamp) and start dilating. As I passed the dilator into the patient's cervix, she lunged upwards. The weighted retractor came out and crashed to the floor, carrying with it half the drapes, while the patient's right foot, along with its stirrup, swung in before I could duck and caught me square in the temple.

It was some time before the patient and I were ready to begin again. With the aid of a flashlight and four people holding the poor woman down, we got through the business at last, though I was considerably hampered by the tiny curette they provided, which would have been more suited for doing a D & C on somebody's cat. At least with a curette that size, the cervix didn't require much dilating—which was the painful part—and that was no small advantage, all things considered.

On the operating list next day was an infant hernia and a

below-knee amputation. Everything was as I had found it the first day: the hot gown, the soggy talcum powder, the miniature towel, the drapes with holes in them. But at least today there was electricity; we wouldn't be operating in the dark.

I found the illumination delivered by the overhead operating lamp to be marginal at best, and that would be a charitable assessment. With the bright light from the windows shining in, I had to look twice to make sure the lamp was actually on. It wasn't much help in sorting through the delicate structures of an infant's inguinal canal, and the light from outside lit up everything else but the inside of the wound.

After rooting about in the shadows for a quarter of an hour, it suddenly occurred to me that by covering the windows with curtains, I'd be able to see better. And I was right. The staff obligingly put up black curtains, and as my pupils dilated, I began to pick up the light from the overhead lamp. I was just beginning to make some progress when the electricity went off. We all stood motionless in the pitch blackness. Only the child moved; it was waking up. We were giving it Ketamine by injection, and this had to be repeated every ten or fifteen minutes to keep the child asleep. The anesthetist fumbled among his bottles. One fell to the floor. The circulating nurse began feeling around for the flashlight, but no one could remember where it had been laid last. An IV bottle was raked off its shelf and fell with a crash. The child began to cry. Then it began to kick, and several instruments slid to the floor. Word was sent to turn on the emergency generator, but the generator man was slow to be found. Someone finally went to take the curtains down, contaminating the instrument table in the process. When light came, one might have thought the Furies had been operating there. I finished up in the daylight as best I could, and the child was wheeled out sleeping contentedly. We moved on to the next case.

Leg amputations are routine affairs. The light would be less of a problem too, for the structures are all easily visible. Literally anybody can cut off a leg, as battlefield surgeons have demonstrated for centuries. There is really only one thing that's needed—that's absolutely essential, one must say—and that is something to cut through the bone with. Without it, I don't care who you are, you won't be successful in amputating legs.

I got to the bone without any difficulty and then asked for the saw. You won't believe this, but after three minutes of sawing, I hadn't made a mark. I looked around helplessly at the eyes peering at me over their masks. I knew what they were thinking. Was it the saw, or was it the surgeon?

Someone said there was another saw, and after several minutes it was located. This saw worked better; after ten minutes of violent exertion I had made it a quarter of the way through the tibia. Sweat filled my gloves, not to mention what was going on inside my polar gown.

"Do you have a Gigli saw?" I asked between breaths. Blank stares from five sets of eyes. Somebody went out to ask.

I continued sawing. An assistant bounced in exclaiming cheerily, "A Gigli saw," and I was handed a little packet with a Gigli saw in it. I preferred Gigli saws, actually; they could slice through the bone in half a minute. They are clever little devices: just a wire, around which is coiled another studded wire that does the cutting. I slipped the saw under the bone, attached the two handles, and began sawing back and forth, pulling steadily upward. Nothing seemed to be happening. I might as well have been trying to cut through a bone with a kite string. More pressure upward, I thought. Then—you guessed it—the saw snapped and went flying off in opposite directions. Happily, the surgeon did not go flying off—though we shall say nothing of his inner mental state—but he held his ground and smashed his way through the rest of the bone with a hammer and chisel. Looking back, it's hard to believe I survived eight amputations in two months. More to the point, the eight patients survived too.

The next day produced my first emergency case, a man whose bowels had been blocked for a week. He was blown up like a balloon, his belly tense and tender. He was very sick; it wouldn't be easy pulling him through. I took a personal hand in the preoperative preparation, and when they took him to the operating room, his condition was reasonably stable.

Again I found puddles in the dressing room, something I would find almost every time I went in there, as if they were washing the floor just for me. I found some pants my size and put them on, but the drawstring was missing. I found another pair, but these had no drawstring either. After searching each shelf, I found no other pants my size. I finally settled for something smaller, which bound slightly but was bearable if tied loosely. Again I could find no shirt my size, so I emerged from the dressing room looking like the "other company" in a no-shrink fabric advertisement. There were no caps today; they got me a wet one from the laundry.

I tried to scrub up at the awkward sink but was delayed by the absence of soap. Soap was found, and my assistant and I scrubbed up.

The man's intestines had twisted on themselves and had perforated in one place. The operation went along well enough until it came time to close the abdominal wound. Somehow the muscle relaxant the anesthetist was using didn't work—it was old, he said, and new hadn't come—and we couldn't push the intestines back into the abdomen. We tried and tried, but it was no use.

"Let me show you a trick," I said to my assistant; and I began suturing the wound from top down, with half the intestines still hanging outside. The assistant looked skeptical, as did everyone else in the room.

"We just begin closing the wound," I went on, "and as it gets smaller we just push the bowels in bit by bit, and in the end, they're all in and the wound is closed. You watch."

It wasn't easy suturing the top part of the wound—even with half the bowels out. We hauled and pulled and struggled. The hospital didn't have any sutures I was used to, so finally I settled for nylon fishing line, which is good and strong. After half an hour, two-thirds of the wound was closed. It was time to get some of the bowel back in.

But the bowel wouldn't go back in, bit by bit, or any other way. I had closed too much of the wound. I couldn't bear to cut out the stitches I'd put in with such difficulty, so I merely extended the incision at the lower end. I was about to say it was another trick, but I thought better of it. It was a trick in a way, for an abdominal wound is always easier to close the farther down you get. But I was in no mood for humor; I was beginning to worry if we'd ever get the intestines back in. It's hard enough getting a wound closed in obstruction cases under the best of circumstances, let alone without muscle relaxant.

Well, we did it, and at the end of the case, the patient's condition was still surprisingly stable. In fact, my main concern was that his stomach tube wasn't draining; I had asked for a large tube to be put in preoperatively, but they had put in a small one, saying they had no big ones. So I took it out and put down a rectal tube, which was the only tube big enough to drain off the fecal matter that had backed up into his stomach. We tried to hook it up to the electric suction machine, but there was no connecter the right size. When I went to tape the rectal tube to the patient's nose, I was told there was no tape; the hospital was out. The main road to Kathmandu had washed out that week, and the mission truck hadn't been able to get through with supplies.

The patient was wheeled into the recovery room, and I went to write the postoperative orders. After I'd been writing a minute or so, I noticed people scurrying back and forth with unaccustomed speed between the operating room and the recovery room, dragging with them oxygen tanks, suction machines, respirator equipment, and other odds and ends. My curiosity aroused, I went into the recovery room to find my patient had aspirated the contents of his stomach and had then gone on and had a cardiac arrest as a result. We had left the endotracheal tube in place precisely to avoid such a thing; but the young nurse on recovery-room duty had not noticed that the clamp keeping the endotracheal-tube balloon inflated had somehow come off, thus allowing the patient's vomitus to run down into his lungs.

Well, if doing bladder stones and D&C's was a tricky business at this hospital, you can imagine what it was like resuscitating a patient. Somehow, in spite of ill-fitting connectors, leaky syringes, sticky valves, and a general absence of needed equipment—not to mention the lack of electricity at the height of the excitement—the man survived, which I can attribute only to an act of God. We cleaned out his lung, emptied his stomach, and reinflated the endotracheal balloon; and at the end of an hour he was doing fine. A little while later, to the delight of the surgeon and the distress of the nurses, the patient had a gigantic bowel movement in his bed and continued going nonstop for the next twenty-four hours.

That evening I had my first real exposure to life on the wards. I had ordered continuous nasogastric suction for my obstruction patient, but when I came around to see how he was doing, I found the hand-pumped suction machine all nicely hooked up but the valve turned off. When I asked the young nurse on duty why the valve was shut, she said it was to keep the pressure from running down. I was about to ask the nurse what in thunder she thought this suction machine was accomplishing with the valve shut off when, opening the valve myself, I was greeted by a loud hiss; in ten seconds all the pressure in the machine was gone. The connections between the machine and its drainage bottle didn't fit, and as a result, the thing was useless. I asked for another machine but was told it was out of order.

I dropped the matter and asked the nurse for a suction tube with which to suction the patient's lungs. She brought me a tiny, red rubber catheter.

"I won't be able to get anything out with this," I said. "Don't you have a regular suction tube for endotracheal suction?" She bustled about on the ward and came back to inform me that she couldn't find a suction tube. "No suction tube? That's impossible in a hospital this size, doing all this surgery. Please phone the ward supervisor on duty."

The ward supervisor was phoned. It was about 10:00 P.M. It was a while before she could be reached, and by the tone of her voice, it was clear she wasn't happy about the intrusion.

The nurse on the ward spoke with her. "We need a suction tube."

"A what?"

"A suction tube. For intertracheal suction."

"Endotracheal suction," I corrected.

"Intertracheal suction," repeated the nurse.

"What kind of suction?"

The discussion went on for a minute or so until the supervisor had some grasp of the problem. Then she said, "We have no suction tubes like that. Use one of your regular catheters. You shouldn't call me for something like this." And for the the next two minutes she berated the poor nurse until the girl had tears in her eyes.

"Let me speak with the supervisor," I said, in a voice loud enough to be picked up by the phone.

There was silence on the other end of the line. "Who wants the suction tube?" the supervisor asked.

"One of the doctors," the nurse replied. Another long silence.

"What doctor?" the supervisor asked.

fourteen

The nurse looked at me inquiringly; I was new and she didn't know me.

"Dr. Hale," I said.

"Dr. Hell."

"Dr. Hale," I repeated.

"Dr. Horle," said the nurse.

"Dr. who?" said the supervisor.

"No, Dr. Horle," said the nurse.

Another pause.

"Well, tell him there are no suction tubes of the kind he wants." And she hung up.

At that moment one of the assistant nurses on the ward came up and showed me a tube she had found; it was an endotracheal suction tube. I said thank you and went off to suction my patient, thereby warding off an almost certain lobar pneumonia.

Suction problems aside, my most lasting impressions of the wards of this hospital relate to the bedside curtains, the contribution of Western nurses who had worked here in earlier years. Nepalis rarely demand privacy; in fact, they delight in sharing their wounds and aches with their neighbors, and they have an insatiable curiosity about what is going on in the next bed. There were thirteen beds in each of the two surgical wards, male and female, and between the beds a network of wires had been strung up so that at the wave of a nurse's arm the patient could be instantly surrounded by curtains and shut off from friends, air, and light.

The curtains themselves hung innocuously along the walls between each bed, gathering dust and serving as handtowels and handkerchiefs for dirty hands and noses. I quickly learned it was the policy here that the doctor could only see his patients if they were enclosed in curtains. Even laying a hand on the abdomen required the full-curtain treatment. It took me a while to get used to the procedure. I'd reach for the abdomen and *whish, whish, whish,* three curtains would close in around me, dragging over my head, shutting out the light, and filling the air with dust.

It took the nurses about three days to learn that I didn't like curtains dragged over me and that I considered it useful to have light by which to examine my patients. I have seen nurses struggling behind curtains in the dark trying to put in a catheter, when all they had to do was open the curtains a peep and they could have seen what they were doing. But habits die hard, I guess, especially when they are inherited from the West.

Though I fought the curtains to a draw, I made no headway at all against the wires they ran on. The wires were strung at eye level, plus or minus an inch, an easy height for the nurses to reach. I calculated that to make my way through rounds on just thirteen patients in either the male or female surgical ward required ducking under curtain wires forty times, and even if I remembered to duck nineteen times out of twenty, it still meant getting twonged twice on each ward every day. I'd start each morning determined that no wire would get me, but then someone would ask me a question, I'd turn to answer, and *twong,* the whole network of wires would be set to vibrating and the nurses to tittering. I asked what other doctors did here who were taller than I, and they assured me, "Oh, they get used to it." Well, I never did.

One of the other things that struck me on rounds was the large number of fractured-femur patients lying about, all roped up in special contraptions with pulleys and weights, and pins through their tibias. I thought maybe I ought to introduce the "simplified" fractured-femur treatment we had used successfully at Amp Pipal in over three hundred cases. We hadn't had a single failure.

I had my chance a few days later when a young girl of eighteen was brought in with a fractured femur and a concussion. I showed the nurses how I wanted the traction set up and drew a diagram of the two accessories I needed: a sling for the calf and a little wooden support for the thigh. These would have to be made in the workshop.

It took a full week for the accessories to be made. Meanwhile the girl spent the time thrashing about, totally out of her head from the bang she had gotten, and by the time I finally had her set up and she settled down, a monstrous hematoma (collection of blood) had formed at the fracture site and a callus the size of a grapefruit was beginning to develop. It was not an auspicious debut for the "simplified" treatment.

I had two other chances to show off our technique, both of which, I should say, were total busts. One man had broken his leg while robbing a store. A few days later the store owner came to the hospital and recognized him. The patient, strung up in bed and fearful the police would nab him, got his cronies to carry him away. He'd been in traction only a week.

The second case had a worse ending: the patient died. But not of the simplified treatment; the patient had far-advanced tuberculosis.

I was pinning my hopes, then, on the girl with the grapefruit. At the end of two months, I pronounced her healed. She promptly got out of bed, fell, and rebroke her leg, which gained her six more weeks of simplified treatment. I doubt that the treatment caught on in the end—though the nurses are likely still talking about it.

One of the things I dreaded about being at this new hospital was obstetrics call. The amount of obstetrics I know (other than doing Caesarean sections) you couldn't cut in half with a scalpel. Luckily I had managed to avoid it all the years at Amp Pipal; Dr. Helen usually did it, and when she wasn't around, Cynthia pitched in. But here, on my very first week, I was put on obstetrics call.

Babies, as any doctor knows, are almost always born at night. So on about the fourth night, I was called for a patient whose labor was not progressing. The baby's head was just visible, but there it had stuck for two hours. The midwife on duty thought I should do something to pull the baby out.

I said, "Let's push on the belly"; and when I did so, out slid the baby as slick as could be. I smiled benevolently at the midwife and went back to bed.

The next night, would you believe it, the very same thing happened. In fact, this time when I pushed on the belly, the baby popped out so fast the nurse had no time to put on her gloves. Maybe obstetrics wasn't going to be so bad after all.

The third time, however, my luck ran out. I was going to have to "do something" to pull the baby out.

"What do you suggest?" I asked, wanting to make the nurses feel their opinions were valued.

"Maybe the vacuum extractor would work," said one of them.

"Yes, a fine idea," I said. "Help me set it up."

We—I mean, they—set it up and helped me apply the suction cup to the child's head. Then they pumped up the machine. I said, "Tell me when to pull."

"Pull," they said.

I pulled. I heard an explosive noise, which was followed by a shower of material. I thought the machine had exploded, but it hadn't. It was only the patient, who had evacuated her enema all over me. The nurses were doubled up against the wall, shrieking with laughter, and it was several minutes before they could get hold of themselves. Meanwhile, dripping wet, I delivered the baby. I then walked out, my dignity intact—and visible, doubtless, to no one but me.

After my initial experiences in the bowels of the hospital, I looked forward to my first day in the outpatient clinic. I was shown the two tiny rooms where I was to see all the surgical referrals and do the minor outpatient surgery. The place also served as the emergency room for the entire outpatient department. An area four times as big would still have been too small. Crowds coursed in and out. You'd be in the middle of examining a patient, and they'd lay a dysentery case on a stretcher right on the floor. There'd be no room to walk until someone started an IV and carted the newcomer off to the ward. It was altogether too small, too congested; and we were understaffed.

My biggest problem, though, was the stream of referrals that Cynthia—bless her heart—sent me from the female medical clinic. She, a pediatrician, wasn't practiced at feeling the uteri of adult women, so if she had any doubt, she referred them to me. We had many good laughs over the imaginative diagnoses she came up with in women who turned out to be pregnant or had nothing at all.

It's wonderful how laypeople are wont to lump doctors together. So, why can't a pediatrician cover the gynecology clinic? Well, there's a big difference between pediatricians and gynecologists, that's why. To say nothing of surgeons and shrinks, who are as different as butchers and belly-dancers, and you'd do best, by the way, to keep clear of them both.

I wouldn't have minded Cynthia sending me all those women to examine under ordinary circumstances, but in this surgery clinic, circumstances were far from ordinary. First of all, before doing someone's pelvic exam, the crowd that had herded in had to be herded out. Next, the examining table faced into the glare of the window, so down below one groped about in the darkness. We had one disposable, small plastic speculum that barely reached the cervix. We used it over and over until it cracked and began to pinch the patients. We had a two-foot-long "cervical" biopsy forceps designed for biting off polyps of the large intestine; but it had long since lost its bite for anything. The first time I bit down on a cervix and nothing happened, I asked the nurse what to do next. "Just pull," she said. I wept no tears a week later when the thing fell apart in my hand.

The minor surgical procedures were done in the tiny treat-ment-dressing-injection room in the surgical clinic, and competition for space was fierce. We usually saved the operative procedures for the end of the day when the crowd was less, but even then we were elbow to elbow. My recollections of struggling here are all a blur, but I do remember one little diversion we had: it was guessing the size of the hole in the eye towels we used for surgical drapes. There I would be, about to take off a wart on a man's nose, and they'd give me an eye towel you could slip his whole head through. Next would be an abscess the size of a melon, and I'd get an eye towel an egg wouldn't fit through. We made it a game, but I always seemed to lose. And if I complained too much, I was offered a sterile page from the *Rising Nepal* and told to cut my own hole.

Working here was indeed a form of warfare, a succession of skirmishes whose outcome was in no way predictable. It struck me this way most vividly back on my very first day in the clinic. I'd just finished elbowing my way through about eight surgical procedures, and had left the last patient sleeping off his anesthetic on the little operating table in the treatment room with a friend watching over him. I was outside examining the last of Cynthia's referrals when I heard one of those sickening thuds typically made by skulls striking concrete. Since all the staff had disappeared, I rushed into the treatment room and found the operating table tilted up at about 60° and the patient crumpled in a heap on the floor, still blotto from his anesthetic and still more blotto from having slid off the table onto his head. At the same moment I noticed the friend, pale as a ghost, tottering back and forth, but before I could reach him, he too had collapsed in a heap beside his fallen comrade. Come to discover, the table was equipped with a special lever, which at the slightest touch released whatever held it in the horizontal position, turning the table into an instant seesaw. The friend, in the course of fainting away, had inadvertently touched this lever and set his comrade in motion. Happily, in the end, neither patient nor friend were phased in the slightest, though I can't say the same for their doctor.

There's a memory of the clinic that lingers still, like the beat of a drum corps accompanying troops to battle. On the roof above the outpatient department stood an old pump that pumped water (when there was any) up to a storage tank nearby. The pump (when it was working) gave forth a triumphant *da-da-dum, da-da-dum, da-da-dum,* drowning out most of the groans, cries, scrapings, and scuffings of the clinic below. It was a relic of the British Raj, made in Bombay in the early forties, and resuscitated many times since by a succession of missionary maintenance men. I don't know how much water it pumped, but if you went by the sound, it should easily have emptied Lake Meade in a day. It's no wonder Cynthia couldn't tell if her patients were pregnant: she could never hear the fetal heartbeat through the sound of that pump.

Many evenings after work I used to stand outside, looking out across the valley, and watch the birds—hundreds of them—flap their way across the sky. The birds lived in the tall trees surrounding the temple in the nearby village. And every evening, when the temple bells were rung, the birds flew off in a great flock across the hospital to the hills beyond, to return as stragglers, one by one, throughout the night and early morning.

One evening toward the end of our stay, as I stood and watched the little black specks grow larger and larger in the golden-orange sky, the five-year-old son of one of the other doctors came up and stood by me.

"Look at all those crows," I said, thinking to expand the boy's appreciation of the natural world.

"Crows?" said the youngster. "Those aren't crows. Those are bats."

I looked again. "Ah, so they are." I'd taken them for crows all along, but bats they were. And perhaps, by this time, so was I.

Battling
on the Health Front

Community Health

C OMMUNITY HEALTH is a dull name for an important subject. Simply speaking, community health refers to health activities that take place out in the community rather than in a hospital. In most developing countries, hospitals are too few and too expensive to meet the health needs of more than a fraction of the population. In Nepal, two-thirds of the people live a full day's walk or more from the nearest hospital. It's readily apparent that if health care isn't brought to the people, most of the people will end up going without it.

Community health has been likened to a protective fence at the top of a cliff, whereas hospitals are the ambulances parked at the bottom. While there's nothing wrong with an ambulance (except for its cost), it's the fence that saves most lives. In the same way, it's community health work that is most important in raising the health standards of developing countries. The role of hospitals, though essential, is secondary.

Community health work has two main parts: first, the *treatment* of illness at the earliest possible stage, for the cheapest possible price, and at a location closest to the patient's home; and second, the *prevention* of illness by means of education and simple community-based public health measures.

Such a description of community health work, however, all too often evokes the image of a drowsy, scruffy worker passing out pills in a sleepy village and spraying mosquitoes from time to time to relieve the monotony. More appealing by far is the usual romantic concept of medical mission work: first you get expert training (so you can *really* contribute to the host country) and then you go out and build a clinic or hospital in some remote area where no medical care has been available at all and inundate yourself in the floods of grateful patients who come pouring through the doors. That's exciting. And relatively simple. You can just import your foreign training and technology (with a few adjustments) right into the developing country and set up shop. Presto—you have professional and personal satisfaction plus that inner assurance that you are honoring the Lord's name by giving the highest quality medical care.

Unfortunately, high-quality medical care is *not* what's needed most in developing countries. What's needed most is *basic,* affordable care for the majority of people, combined with simple preventive health measures. All over the world, missions have built and staffed excellent hospitals that have had little or no effect on the mortality rates, the life expectancy, and the general level of health of the populations they serve. Most of the people simply can't afford either the time or the money to come to such a facility. So all around these superb hospitals people continue to die of malnutrition, dysentery, and other easily treatable diseases, as if the hospital had never been built.

We know, because we happen to work in just such a hospital—way out in the foothills. We pride ourselves for having "gone out to the people where they are." But in fact we haven't. The people living on the surrounding hills and mountains look over at us sitting pretty on our mountain and in no way share the illusion that "we have come out to them." Perhaps 60 percent of the half million people we "serve" wouldn't think of coming to our hospital. We're miles away at the end of a hot, dusty trail named Expense & Inconvenience. This is brought home just by taking a little three- or four-hour excursion in any direction from the Amp Pipal Hospital, where one will find scores of sick and malnourished people who are essentially without medical care.

I recall only too well my farewell address to our home church as we were about to leave for Nepal the first time. "Only the very best medical care is worthy of our Lord," I pronounced to the enthusiastic applause of my listeners. Neither they nor I had a true understanding of what "best" really meant. I was repeating the old missionary dictum: "Since you can't treat them all, at least treat the few well." However, this isn't an appropriate philosophy for medical missions today—if, indeed, it ever was. With personnel, time, and money so severely limited, we ought rather to be concentrating our efforts and resources on the masses of people, especially the poor, who are not reached by the hospitals. And that is the focus of community health work.

Specifically, then, what does community health involve? First of all, it involves providing basic medical care right in the local community. (A hospital, for example, offers such care to people living in its immediate vicinity.) In developing countries, this kind of care is usually delivered not by doctors but by paramedics, nurses, and locally trained village health workers. Its emphasis is on early treatment, using simple, cheap, and readily available remedies.

Along with the treatment of disease, and more important in the long run, is the *prevention* of disease. This is the hard part of community health work. It's an easy matter to cure an acutely ill person and then greet the grateful family with a smile radiating Christian love. It's much more difficult, in the face of skepticism and hostility, to change patterns of behavior that lead to illness. And yet, this is ultimately what community health is all about.

Health education is therefore of paramount importance, and this means teaching health in the schools. Only when widespread and effective health education has been made available to the younger generation will there be any hope of seeing significant improvement in health standards. The older people, most of them uneducated, are generally resistant to new ways.

A comprehensive community health program involves other elements as well. One of them is training local health workers for each village. Another is doing home visits and following up tuberculosis and leprosy patients. Others include vaccinating children, providing clean water, improving nutrition, building latrines, killing flies, eradicating rats, and most crucial of all, encouraging family planning.

Community health work is not easy. It exacts a price from its workers in terms of bad food, sleepless nights, and long walks on steep trails. It requires getting down to the village level, understanding local problems and viewpoints, and motivating lethargic, fatalistic communities to look after their own health instead of looking only for a handout. Above all, it means living with frustration and discouragement, toiling long and patiently for few visible results—and all the while one's hospital-based colleague is attracting crowds of adulating patients.

It's tempting to disparage village work as being beneath one's professional dignity, as being unstimulating, unchallenging. But the fact is that removing a pituitary tumor or an aortic aneurysm is easy compared to getting rid of rats in your attic, or persuading people to use latrines, or training some local yokel who doesn't know a bacteria from a grasshopper to be a competent village health worker—to say nothing of motivating communities to start solving their own problems. The drama of bringing the benefits of modern medicine to the world's uncared for people will be played out under the name of Community Health, and it needs, therefore, to be the centerpiece of both government programs and Christian medical missions.

What kind of missionaries are needed to face this challenge? First, the main need is for nonspecialists with broad interests: doctors and nurses oriented to community health, general practitioners, nurse practitioners, nonformal educators, teachers, social workers, nutritionists—to name but a few. Second, medical personnel are needed who are *not* looking primarily, or even secondarily, for job satisfaction or professional fulfillment. People are needed who are willing to take a professional step "down" (sometimes two or three steps), to be learners as well as teachers, to forgo the satisfaction of seeing immediate results.

It's personally rewarding to be the ambulance driver (hospital worker) parked at the foot of a cliff and, when the victims fall off, to pick them up and race through town with sirens wailing. It's a lot harder to be the unnoticed person (community health worker) who builds a fence at the top of the cliff to keep the people from falling off. Fewer ambulance drivers are needed than fence builders, and fewer fence builders are needed than teachers of fence building. And, of course, for budget-strapped mission agencies (and Third-World governments as well) it's a lot cheaper to build a fence than to buy an ambulance.

My first exposure to the vicissitudes of running a community health program came shortly after arriving in Nepal, when I met with the director of United Mission's community health work, a Japanese physician named Dr. Iwamura. Dr. Iwamura was well qualified to head up this work. He had trekked through all of Nepal's seventy-five districts, gathering data on disease incidence and familiarizing himself with the medical needs of the entire country. He was now in charge of setting up community health programs in all the areas where the United Mission was working. Since we had just been assigned to the new Amp Pipal Hospital in Gorkha District, Dr. Iwamura was interested in helping us formulate a rural health program that would be suited to our particular area. So he had invited to his house both me and Val Collett, our project's chief public health nurse. And now after an ample meal of Nepali-Japanese food, we had settled down to discuss community health plans for our district.

We talked and planned with Dr. Iwamura for six hours. At midnight, after having finished up with a long and involved discussion of fly control, we were startled by a strange commotion out on the porch, punctuated by excited oriental accents and the clattering of some kind of hardware. After this prelude, the door swung open to admit a Japanese couple, both of them physicians with our mission, and a Japanese entomologist who was in Nepal on a short-term assignment. Trailing them were several other Japanese bearing five large platters heaped with steaming Japanese delicacies, including two enormous stuffed carp. These midnight visitors had just come from an elegant banquet hosted by the Japanese ambassador. Not knowing what to do with the leftovers, they had decided to share them with their friend Dr. Iwamura.

We had barely laid this unexpected treat out on the table when dozens of flies appeared from nowhere and alighted on the mountains of food, especially the carp, to which they seemed peculiarly attracted. The flies were decidedly lethargic—whether because of the late hour or the hypnotizing fragrance of the carp, I don't know. Having settled into the gravy and sauces of the various dishes, they remained stuck, unable or unwilling to extricate themselves. We tried every way of shooing them out of the gravy; we waved at them, we blew on them, we yelled at them. In the end we had to pick them out with our fingers.

Dr. Iwamura, our public health director, was naturally embarrassed at the sight of these flies swarming about in his sitting room, especially so, as the flies were increasing in number. Soon there were over two hundred, and for each fly picked out of the gravy, two more were getting stuck. Deciding, therefore, that a more aggressive approach was needed, Dr. Iwamura fetched a swatter and gave it to the Japanese entomologist. The entomologist, his latent energies awakened, took the "fry" swatter, as he called it, and began prancing about the room, swatting all the flies he could see. Plaster fell from the walls and ceiling under his merciless attack, and his shouting of Japanese battle cries would have intimidated tigers. But his efforts merely spurred on the flies. After ten minutes of vigorous combat, there seemed to be no fewer flies than when he'd begun.

I was witnessing my first battle on the public health front, Here we were—our chief public health nurse picking flies out of the carp as fast as she could; the entomologist charging here and there shouting, "this is not fry control, this is fry eradication"; and the community health director, in between large mouthfuls, giving new and incomprehensible instructions to his warrior. We left at 1:30, stuffed to the gills, having managed among us to consume all five platters.

That meeting at Dr. Iwamura's house was the beginning of the community health program in Gorkha District, and the plans that were drawn up then have survived, with modifications, down through the years—though the original document has been all but lost beneath the dozen "annual plans" that have succeeded it. Not long ago it was rediscovered by one of our recent Amp Pipal community health directors as she was cleaning out her files. She was amazed to find that almost everything they were currently planning had been mentioned back in that first document. Indeed, the meeting at Iwamura's had been a fruitful one, and the community health program that Val Collett initiated as a result of it has served as the basis for all that has gone on subsequently.

The Amp Pipal community health program, as it has evolved over the years, contains several major elements. The first is village clinics, which are run in cooperation with the government maternal and child health program. These clinics are primarily curative and serve children under the age of five, the group most vulnerable to illness. Because the village clinics are held only weekly or twice weekly, we've trained several villagers within each village to treat simple illnesses and handle emergencies whenever they occur.

The second element of our community health program is health education. In order to help people prevent illness, health workers teach health in some of the neighboring schools as well as in the hospital, where they instruct both inpatients and outpatients.

A third part of our community health program has been village water projects. The majority of life-threatening diseases we see in Nepal are waterborne (dysentery, amoebiasis, typhoid). Providing a village with an uncontaminated water supply can dramatically reduce the incidence of these conditions. Not only do villagers then have clean water to drink, but they also have more water for washing their hands and dishes.

Putting in a water supply involves first finding a water source—often many hundreds of yards from the village—then building a contamination-proof reservoir, and finally laying a plastic pipe to carry the water to a village storage tank, with a tap to control the usage. The villagers supply the labor, while the mission supplies the pipe, the cement, and the know-how.

Village water projects are an example of the kind of community development that is most needed in the world's undeveloped areas. These community development projects are inexpensive, involve the villagers themselves, and benefit everyone—and the benefits are substantial.

However, things often go wrong. Putting in and maintaining even a simple water system requires a sense of community responsibility, which often is lacking in Nepali villages. Sometimes we've completed a water project one day and gone back the next to discover that some man upstream has blithely cut the pipe and run the water into his own fields. He couldn't stand the thought of all that water running past his house and not getting any of it for himself. Or if the pipe hadn't been cut, we'd find that some village women had pried the cover off the reservoir and were washing their clothes in it. But these have been minor frustrations in a program that has benefited dozens of villages in our area and hundreds of others throughout the country. Water, in Nepal, is never taken for granted.

A fourth element of our community health program is agricultural work. Improved agricultural practices lead to improved nutrition, and good food is essential to good health. Failure to improve the people's nutrition, for example, will negate many of the benefits of their improved water supply. And, obviously, so will failure to improve sanitation.

Thus, a fifth part of our community health program has been sanitation and hygiene. Part of this concern has been directed to the promotion of latrines. I'm sorry to have let down the outhouse advocates, but latrines have been an almost total failure in our part of Nepal. We've had trouble enough just getting our community health staff to build their own latrines, so you can be sure we haven't sold the idea to too many others. And with good reason: latrines, if misused, are an absolute menace. One pregnant lady, about to deliver, went to her pit latrine to relieve herself, and the baby started coming out. It was a near catastrophe; just thinking about it gives me the willies. And latrines are filthy places; it's not surprising Nepalis won't use them—even when an effort is made to keep them clean.

At the hospital we decided to support the community health team's efforts by constructing a latrine near the main entrance, for the benefit of the crowds milling around outside. The staff were instructed to encourage patients to use the latrine, and a sweeper was sent out daily to clean it. Then one day Rigmor, our nursing superintendent, decided the grass around the latrine needed cutting, so she sent the caretaker out with his sickle. When Rigmor came later to inspect the job, there to her horror was the outhouse, prim and tidy, surrounded by a hundred little piles that before had been neatly hidden. Yes, latrines are a hazard to health, even if they are good for the grass.

Our community health team is engaged in other activities too, such as visiting and teaching in the homes, following up old TB and leprosy cases and looking for new ones, and working with village and *panchayat* officials to find ways of promoting health in general. The team supports the isolated, government health workers whose posts are scattered through the region. And finally, our community health people participate actively in the government's family planning program. In Nepal, no one's health will improve unless population growth is brought under control. But that's another chapter.

Most of the illnesses we see in Nepal fall within the scope of community health: that is, they are easily treated in the village in the early stages, and they are to a great extent preventable. Most result from either malnutrition or infection—and often both at once. Malnutrition predisposes people to many illnesses because it lowers resistance, but it's the infections that account for most of the diseases we see. And it's here that our community health program has had its greatest effect.

The most common affliction health workers encounter is worms: roundworms, hookworms, pinworms, whipworms, and every now and again, tapeworms. These worms are transmitted from person to person through the improper disposal of excrement. When the infestation is heavy, worms are debilitating and occasionally life-threatening. They cause their harm mainly by consuming what the host eats, or in the case of hookworms, by sucking the host's blood. In either case the worms make the victim weak and unable to work at full capacity. Most worms are small, but roundworms can be up to ten inches long. The incidence of roundworms in the population is so high that the community health team annually gives roundworm medicine to all the school children in several neighboring schools—and awards prizes to those who pass the most worms. The proud winners, some of them tiny first and second graders, often produce over a hundred!

The second most common condition health workers see is dysentery (severe diarrhea). As with worm infestation, dysentery results from improper stool disposal, which in turn contaminates the water supply. Dirty water and dirty hands constitute the common means of transmission. Except for the mildest cases, dysentery is dangerous and frequently fatal. Dysentery is the main killer of children under five; once a child reaches the age of five, he or she stands a reasonable chance of living to adulthood. It's natural selection at work: the weakest ones die off at an early age.

Yet dysentery cases and dysentery epidemics are not simply statistics: They are a series of individual tragedies that touch each family with sorrow and death. A dozen times I've struggled to start an IV or to put in a cutdown on a new dysentery patient with no pulse or blood pressure—but have been too late. We might be tempted to say the patient should have come sooner, but saying so never helps. Especially when, as is often the case, the family has hurriedly carried the patient several hours across hill and valley only to have the patient die within minutes of arrival. One father had lost two sons in two days, and on the third day he had brought his third and last son. The son died while I was putting in the cutdown. If only I'd been able to work faster . . .

A third category of illness health workers commonly see is pulmonary infection, especially pneumonia and tuberculosis (TB). Both diseases are communicated by coughing and spitting in the proximity of susceptible persons. Although pneumonia can be fatal, in most instances it responds quickly to treatment and thus never reaches epidemic proportions. TB, on the other hand, has been spreading out of control, in part because of resistant strains, and has now become the foremost public health problem in the country. And the combined efforts of both private and government agencies have made little headway against it.

Community health workers also see many cases of leprosy, which is spread through prolonged contact between family members and through nasal secretions. Government and mission agencies have launched ambitious, cooperative programs to combat this disease. Although we are optimistic, progress is slow.

And the list of diseases could go on—measles, whooping cough, diphtheria, and many more—all of which are the concern of any community health program.

How can a community health team of only one doctor, a few nurses, and a handful of Nepali assistants carry out an effective community health program for a region containing half a million people—and no roads? The answer is, of course, they can't. But that doesn't mean the situation is hopeless.

In the first place, a small team can start out in a limited geographic area. Before long, as the benefits of a concerted community health program become apparent, other communities will take note and adopt similar programs of their own.

In the second place, our community health team is not alone. The government has its program too—limited though it is at present—consisting of a dozen health posts located in key villages throughout the area. In countries like Nepal, mission organizations need to join hands with government and not try to "go it alone." Much more can be accomplished by pooling resources than by working independently.

More important than the government's resources, however, are the latent resources of the people themselves. Government and mission combined can't begin to meet the health needs of every community in Nepal; rather, communities must be enabled to meet their own needs. This is a cardinal principle of development: help people help themselves. In accordance with this principle, community health work in the developing world has acquired a new emphasis in recent years. Health is no longer considered to be the sole province of the professional—something to be handed down to the people from above. Instead, responsibility for health is gradually being handed over to the people themselves. Community health programs are becoming community-*based* health programs, that is, programs that are planned and managed by the community. It's amazing what people can do on their own with a minimum of outside help. For instance, three-quarters of all deaths in developing countries occur in children under five. Most of these deaths can be prevented by the mothers alone—with only the slightest amount of teaching. People *can* take responsibility for their own health, and the chief role of health professionals should be to encourage and to enable them to do so.

In the long run, then, the success of a community health program depends not only on the efforts of mission and government but equally on the response of the people themselves. It's their health that's at stake, and ultimately it's their responsibility to maintain it.

Traveling to Village Clinics

F OR HOSPITAL-BOUND doctors and nurses, the opportunity to attend a village clinic is always welcome. It
affords a refreshing break from the routine—or if not always
refreshing, at least it's a break.

In addition to the half-dozen "under-five" children's clinics
held in villages near the hospital, we have conducted general
clinics in areas like Lapsibot, a village fifteen miles to the north, a
journey of six to twelve hours, depending on how fast one
walks. Lapsibot lies in a fertile, terraced valley at the foot of
25,900-foot Himalchuli Peak; its elevation is 4,000 feet, the
same as Amp Pipal's. The trail certainly was not engineered
according to American tastes; there are fewer than a dozen
consecutive, level steps to be found the entire way. After
descending 2,000 feet from Amp Pipal and rising 2,500 feet
back up, the trail follows diabolically up and down for many
miles along an irregular ridge of peaks and saddles extending to
the snow line.

The traveler proceeds much after the fashion of an ant, who,
upon encountering a series of stones, goes over the top of each
one instead of around. The rewards, however, are commensurate
with the effort expended. The Himalayas rise above the clouds
in front and to either side. Flowering trees and brightly colored
birds greet the eye, and occasionally monkeys can be seen
frolicking along the trail. Glimpses of unspoiled rural life,
unchanged for centuries, glide by on either hand: white and

orange thatch-roofed houses, clustered together here and there between the fields of rice and corn; old women sitting on front porches, picking lice out of each other's hair; old men squatting in doorways and smoking large, clay water pipes; young women nursing babies, carrying water in big earthen jugs, grinding corn on ancient grindstones, and bathing at the numerous roadside springs; young men cursing, pleading, chattering with their oxen as they plow the narrow terraces; small children tending water buffalos and herds of goats or carrying baby brothers and sisters on their hips or collecting fodder to feed their animals.

Since footpaths in Nepal serve as economic lifelines, the traveler meets with a continual succession of porters: some carry foodstuffs to sell, such as rice, potatoes, and tangerines; others carry building materials, such as stone, bamboo, and wooden beams; others carry kerosene, cigarettes, and incense sticks to supply the tiny shops in the larger villages; and still others trudge along, almost invisible beneath enormous loads of hay or leaves. Most of these loads are carried by means of a strap called a *naamlo,* which passes across the forehead, the weight being borne in a straight line down the spine.

Sooner or later you meet just about everyone on the trail: large groups of schoolchildren tramping gaily to the nearest school an hour away; Gurkha soldiers coming home on leave or returning to their posts; festive wedding processions in which the teenage bride is escorted weeping and wailing to her new husband's home by his merrily singing and laughing relatives; rich Brahmins and government officials on their way to or from Kathmandu with their entourage of family and servants trailing behind; bands of Tibetans and other tribespeople coming down from the north to trade; and last, of course, all manner of sick and injured making their way to the hospital, accompanied by family and friends, some being carried bareback or in baskets or hammocks, while others slowly plod on foot.

Nepalis are wonderfully inquisitive and open people. They

will ask you where you come from, where you're going and why, how old you are, and how many children you have—all in the time it takes the average American just to acknowledge your presence. You are never long on the trail without someone to converse with, and it hardly seems to matter whether or not you speak their language, since they are happy to engage you at length in animated conversation without either of you understanding a word the other is saying.

There are some cautions to be observed on the trail. In addition to the numerous main paths, there are countless minor ones; every house has a trail leading to it. And there are no street signs. Furthermore, Nepalis are delightfully nonspecific about directions. They'll cheerfully tell you that the trail you're on will get you to Lapsibot without bothering to say it will take you two hours out of your way in the process. As in all gadgetless societies, rural Nepalis are inexact about everything; they haven't grown up with our preschool toys and puzzles designed to teach children distinctions of size, shape, color, and distance. And characteristically, Nepalis have little appreciation of our Western concept of time. The first thing a doctor learns on the trails of Nepal is not to make house calls if he expects to reach his destination on schedule. We were frequently asked to see a sick person who lives "just over there," a "minute" away. It took me only once to learn that the Nepali "minute" can mean anything up to three hours.

The clinic at Lapsibot was a far cry from the hospital outpatient department. Anyone needing a break from the hospital routine could be sure of getting it here. Usually a team of three or four nurses and assistant nurses preceded the doctor by a day or two in order to announce the clinic in person (Nepalis don't count on anyone showing up until they've seen the whites of his eyes), do some health teaching in the nearby schools, give inoculations, and begin to see patients.

Fortunately, the villagers made little distinction between doctors and nurses. Our nurses, even some of the assistant nurses, could treat most of the patients as competently as the doctor could. Thus in our village clinics the doctors and nurses worked side by side, diagnosing, prescribing, lancing boils, or pulling teeth. Much of the work was done before the doctor ever got there, his function being primarily that of consultant and teacher.

In Lapsibot the clinic was held in a small, two-story mud house. The top floor was used for our living quarters, while the bottom was divided equally between a windowless "dispensary" on one side and a cow stall on the other. The people of Lapsibot had often talked about providing a proper place for the health workers to work, but because the various *pradhan panches* in the area each wanted the new clinic located in his own *panchayat,* no action was ever taken. We could have built the clinic ourselves, of course, but we held to the principle that the community ought to participate in its own health care, at least by contributing the land and the clinic building.

We would ordinarily see about a hundred patients on one of these monthly clinic visits. Many people would get the word late and come on the last morning, just as we were hurrying to leave in order to get back to Amp Pipal before dark. The patients had the usual illnesses, though they were generally more mild than those encountered at the hospital. One distinctive feature we would see at the Lapsibot clinic, however, was the large number of Brahmin children suffering from severe protein deficiency, which resulted from their parents' religious strictures against eating meat and eggs. It was ironic that the most affluent and educated members of society should also be the most malnourished.

We examined the routine patients on a straw mat laid on the

mud floor, while crowds of curious and apprehensive villagers viewed the proceedings through the opening into the cow stall or from the doorway, effectively blocking off our only light source. We drained abscesses and pulled teeth outside in the sunlight, where we could see what we were doing. During such procedures the crowd would press around, watching in silent wonder. Then, when the pus burst forth or the bloody tooth appeared, they'd ooh and ah like spectators at a sideshow.

On one visit, the woman who owned the house we were using had a toothache. Naturally it was a difficult tooth, abscessed at the root. She was a difficult patient as well. When she wasn't hollering, she went stiff, as if she'd been electrocuted. Her screaming got on my nerves after a while; fortunately, I was able to silence her by stuffing her mouth with a cloth. But the onlookers took up where she left off. Each time I tugged or jerked my wrist, they groaned in unison. It was a happy moment for all of us when at last the tooth came free. The patient was profuse in her gratitude and offered to donate her house, rent-free, as a permanent clinic—as long as she could keep her cows downstairs.

It's uncommon at these once-a-month clinics to see acute injuries—they usually occur anytime *but* when the doctor's in town. One evening, however, I had just arrived from Amp Pipal when I was summoned to see a man who had fallen out of a tree that very day, fracturing his back and injuring his spinal cord. That house call was only forty-five minutes away in the dark.

The patient was completely paralyzed from the waist down and had almost no prospect of recovering. I advised the family against taking the injured man to Amp Pipal; we had had several similar patients in the hospital for months, but they always died as soon as they got home. There was no way to take care of a paraplegic in a Nepali village. Complications invariably developed—bedsores, pneumonia, and kidney infection—despite all efforts to prevent them. In this case the injured man's family seemed grateful to know the worst; they had no desire to spend a lot of time and money if the patient was only going to die in the end anyway. We told the family how to take care of the patient, how to catheterize him and how to delay the onset of bedsores. Then we prayed with the man and left.

Some weeks later we heard that the family had taken the patient to Kathmandu, bypassing Amp Pipal. Because the family was one of the wealthiest in Lapsibot, they could afford the trip. But it was no use. After months in Kathmandu and many more months at home, the patient died, his suffering prolonged by the efforts to save him.

When it came to mealtime on our clinic trips, we went "native," eating with our fingers from tin plates set on the mud floor. The floor was coated daily with a mixture of red clay and fresh buffalo manure. Hands wiped the floor "clean." Hands wiped the nose, handled the animals, and then were used to wipe the dishes. Even Val Collett, our community health director, had adapted to the local culture so thoroughly that I once caught her placing the freshly wiped cups upside down on the mud floor to keep the dirt out. It was rare that we returned from one of these trips with our gastrointestinal tracts in a state of equilibrium.

The same hands, of course, were used to prepare the food. But at least it was cooked. The cook was Dal Bahadur, our chief carrier, whose knowledge of hygiene and sanitation absorbed over six years of working with the community health team could have been served out with an eyedropper. Meals consisted of rice sprinkled with bits of lentils, fat, potato, and chicken bones—all flavored with fiery hot peppers that you'd have thought would kill every germ on the plate, but did nothing more than scald your intestines, not to mention your tongue.

Once we had eaten, we were ready to sleep. Between the various insects sharing our quarters and the landlady's cat, who spent much of the night overturning our pots and plates in search of leftovers, we'd rarely get much sleep. And should we have fallen asleep by chance, we could count on being awakened each morning at 4:00 by the rhythmic thudding of the landlady husking rice in the cow stall below us. It was always good to get back to Amp Pipal again; the routine of the hospital seemed much more welcome after a few days at the Lapsibot clinic.

Sometimes, however, instead of returning to Amp Pipal we traveled a day's walk north to Barpak. Barpak was another world altogether; once there, Lapsibot seemed less primitive and remote, and Amp Pipal seemed like the center of civilization.

Barpak has always held special significance for us. For one thing it's the home of many patients who've come to Amp Pipal hospital over the years. It's the largest and most important village in the northern part of our district. And it's home to a small congregation of Christians, who struggle against great odds to maintain their faith and fellowship.

Barpak, relatively isolated from its neighboring communities, is perched on the side of a steep ridge at an elevation of 6,500 feet, overlooking a narrow river valley 3,500 feet below. Barpak's northern location is evidenced by its bleak surroundings and its predominantly Tibetan and Buddhist culture, only slightly modified by the Hinduism of the south. The frequent storms that gather around the high Himalayan peaks take their toll on Barpak's fields and farm produce; savage hailstorms have been known to wipe out an entire crop in minutes. Barpak's inhabitants are tough and hardy, a characteristic shared by most of Nepal's tribespeople. And it is said that of Barpak's five thousand residents, seven hundred are, or have been, Gurkha soldiers, members of that elite corps whose reputation for valor and ferocity has been acclaimed the world over.

It's a source of no little amazement, then, that in a village so liberally endowed with ex-soldiers of the British Raj, scarcely any trace of modern civilization can be found anywhere. To set foot in Barpak is to step back a thousand years. The only discernible hints of twentieth-century life are cigarette wrappers, Secret Agent 007 belt buckles, and an occasional kerosene lamp. Whereas in most Nepali towns sewage flows in open gutters along the street, in Barpak there are no gutters. In a more jaundiced moment, the entire town could be likened to one great toilet for goats, pigs, chickens, cows, and humans; and your nose would not belie it.

Barpak's medieval-looking stone dwellings are jumbled closely together, divided here and there by foul, narrow alleys. The houses inside are virtually dark except for the light from the fire, the smoke from which adds to the general obscurity by coating everything—including the people—with a layer of soot. In fact, the smoke burns your eyes, preventing you from seeing at all— an advantage at mealtimes: you can usually eat with better appetite when you don't see what's on your plate.

Barpak has not escaped the population explosion. Far from it: the crisis of too many people has been felt more acutely in Barpak than in most parts of Nepal. There is absolutely no additional land around Barpak to settle and cultivate. The existing fields can support the population only in a bumper year, and famines are increasing in frequency and severity. Families have been forced to go south in search of food, leaving fields untended, thereby jeopardizing the next year's harvest. Men have to travel a full day's journey to cut firewood in the receding forests; they generally spend a couple of weeks and procure a whole year's supply at one time. They take their livestock up to a day away just to find fodder, and consequently, they spend a third to a half of their lives out in the fields with their animals. Short of fodder, short of fuel, short of food, with half the population youngsters running around getting ready to repro- duce in a few years—where will they go then? Amp Pipal? There's no spare land or food there either. India?

Much of the pervading social torpor and indifference to social progress that characterizes Barpak's residents can be attributed to their heavy consumption of the local brew. People need something to get them started in the morning and to fight off the chill of winter evenings. In addition, Barpak has suffered from its arbitrary division into two *panchayats,* each with its own *pradhan panch,* neither of whom has shown much inclination to cooperate with the other. On one of my last visits to Barpak, I was met by the younger of the *pradhan panches,* dressed in a dapper tweed vest, red-white-and-blue-striped pajamas, and dark glasses. He invited me to his house for the night and fed me, in the midst of a famine, a plate of rice so big I could barely manage a third of it. The rest was consumed by a huge fat dog, which appeared at my elbow the moment I was through eating.

Our reception by the villagers has always been cool at best. They regard any outsider with suspicion and hostility, partly as a consequence of their isolated location. I'm always surprised that a town this burdened with sickness and suffering isn't crying out for medical help and welcoming us with open arms. I'm afraid we medical types all too often wander through life with just that conscious and subconscious expectation; and it's with a jolt that we finally reach Barpak and have our self-importance shattered by the indifference of these desperately needy people. In their eyes we've merely come to take their money in exchange for some trifling medicine of untested worth, and very likely with an ulterior motive besides. It's a healthy thing for a doctor or nurse to encounter a reception like this because it reminds us how easy it is to be propelled and sustained by dramatic needs and tears of gratitude instead of by God. We need to remember that there's nothing intrinsically holy or good about the field of medicine that entitles us to be welcomed everywhere as heavenly angels of mercy. Barpak is the place to go when we begin to forget it.

Attacking Nepal's Population

O N ONE OF THE HOTTEST days of the year, I was on my way to a government-sponsored vasectomy camp in a place called Simjung—an easy half-day walk from Amp Pipal, I'd been assured. The government health promoters had been there a few weeks before, and finding great interest in family planning, had signed up twenty or so vasectomy "acceptors," more than enough to justify holding a camp.

At about 10:00 A.M., I arrived in the town of Jaubari, where I was to meet a government worker who would accompany me to Simjung. Having put four hours of trail behind me, including a 3,000-foot ascent over a high ridge and a corresponding descent on the other side, I figured it would take us only another hour to reach Simjung. The vasectomy camp was scheduled to begin at noon, and I planned to return to Amp Pipal the next morning.

I found the government worker well rested; he'd left Gorkha, the district capital, the day before, and having spent a comfortable night in Jaubari had been waiting around for me to turn up. We set out together in good spirits. The trail first descended to the bottom of a narrow river valley, which we proceeded to follow for some miles. Then we began to climb. I quickly found I had exhausted most of my store of energy just getting to Jaubari; now, with the midday sun glaring down on us out of a cloudless sky, I rapidly began to wilt, requiring more and more frequent rest stops and even more frequent infusions from my nearly empty canteen. Up, up we went, the miles lengthening;

soon we were 1,000 feet above the valley floor, then 2,000 feet, and still we went up. Twenty times I was told our destination was close at hand. My companion was not slack in encouraging me, gently at first, and then more harshly, as he began to fear I might not make it at all and that the waiting line of "acceptors" would be stood up and he be blamed. He refilled my canteen twice—from where I cared not, since I'd have gladly provided a home in my intestines for any number of typhoid bacilli or amoebae just for the chance to moisten my tongue.

It was 3:00 P.M. when we reached Simjung, and as I dragged into the village, I didn't feel capable of doing anything except stretching out somewhere in the shade. I murmured something to my friend about getting things ready, and that's all I remembered until I awoke with a start to find the afternoon gone and dusk fast approaching. I'd been left alone in the schoolhouse, where the vasectomies were to be performed, while the government worker had gone into the village to notify everyone that the doctor had arrived and the camp could begin. When I awoke, no one was around. I stumbled outside, rubbing my eyes, trying to recall where I was and what I had come for. As soon as I appeared, the government worker jumped up.

"What's going on?" I mumbled peevishly, seeing quite plainly that nothing at all was going on.

"There will be no vasectomies."

"What do you mean, no vasectomies? Have they all gone home?"

"No one came." The family-planning worker looked embarrassed, though he was as chagrined as I. He hadn't been part of the team motivating the men of Simjung to have their vasectomies done, so he didn't feel personally to blame.

"You mean not even one person came?" I dreaded the thought of returning to Amp Pipal the next day not even having done one vasectomy; it was too ridiculous. Not all my missionary colleagues were keen to have me leaving the hospital even for worthy endeavors: To return with my scalpel unbloodied would merely add fuel to their feelings. I recalled a letter I'd received some days earlier from a supporter in the U.S. questioning if it was right for me to be running all over the district doing vasectomies, and I must say I was wondering the same thing myself at that moment.

"They've all gone to their fields to get ready for rice planting," my friend explained. "They've started earlier than usual this year. They say we should've come sooner." It was an unlikely story. People gave dozens of excuses for backing out of vasectomies. In this case, to avoid the doctor the men of the village had simply up and scattered to their fields, inventing for one another's benefit some important work to be done in order to cover up their fear of being operated on.

Expressing some displeasure—to cover up my relief at not having to do any work—I went back in and lay down in order to think. Kneeling on a straw mat doing a dozen vasectomies that afternoon would have been murder. Two weeks earlier, on a similar expedition to another village, I had gotten unbearable cramps in my legs as I operated. Today would have been worse: my legs felt as tight as guitar strings.

I saw a few ordinary patients that evening—at least I could say I'd done that—and stayed the night in the house of a woman whom I had treated at the hospital some months earlier. The next day, as a final touch to the fiasco, I discovered a much shorter—and more level—route back to Amp Pipal. Coming, I had walked four hours out of my way.

That was the only vasectomy camp, however, in which I did no vasectomies. Usually I did anywhere from six to twenty operations, with a record-breaking number in Jaubari the year before: twenty-seven cases in four hours. That time I'd had the benefit of two wooden tables on which to lay the patients, so I could work standing up. I'd do one operation, while behind me a second patient was readied for his ordeal. I simply turned back and forth between the two tables, using a single set of instruments from a tin pie plate filled with disinfectant solution. It made no difference that the instruments weren't washed between cases: we never had an infection on these trips. The only problem on that day, in fact, was the low ceiling beam running lengthwise between the tables, on which I slammed my forehead each time I turned around. Low beams are a hazard in Nepal, and not just for your head. I remember one of our missionary science teachers giving a classroom demonstration of centrifugal force with a pail of water. The idea was to swing the pail up and around in a circle and see how the water stayed inside even when the pail was upside down. It would have worked fine except that the pail hit a low beam at the top of the swing—abruptly ending the demonstration, much to the delight of the class.

We maintained a cordial and fruitful association with the government family-planning team over many years. Only once was the relationship strained. A new government worker had been assigned to the team as a "motivator," and had been sent off to a village to stir up interest in family planning and line up vasectomy "acceptors." He came to me several days later and said that fifteen men had signed up for vasectomies and that I was to come in a week's time to operate on them. When I got to the village a week later, I discovered that the motivator hadn't lined up any vasectomies at all. In fact, he hadn't even visited the village. Only the day before had someone from the family-planning team gone to the village, and that was just to prepare for the camp. I was understandably disgusted. The day was partially redeemed when two men, passing through the village by chance, heard I was there and had their vasectomies done "on the run." Then at three o'clock I decided to leave, as I could still get back to Amp Pipal before dark.

Some time later the chief of the government family-planning team came to see me, saying how disappointed he was that I had seventeen

left the last camp "before it was over." He told me that eleven men had showed up for vasectomies, but I had gone off "in a huff," it was said, moments before they arrived. Word of my conduct had been quickly conveyed to the district capital by the new motivator, who had informed not only his own chief but also the district medical officer and other district officials as well. I was stunned—what if eleven persons had indeed come? I had no way of knowing for sure if the motivator's story was true or not. It was months before the matter was cleared up. The story of the eleven "stood up" vasectomy acceptors circulated so widely that it finally got back to the village in question, where it was promptly exposed as a lie. The guilty motivator, who had concocted the story to cover up his own negligence, was eventually discredited and dismissed. Not long after that the family planning program was reorganized, and my services were no longer needed. It was just as will: it was getting more and more difficult for me to be away from the hospital, even for a day at a time.

The chief complication of vasectomy is hematoma, the leakage of blood into the scrotum. Surrounding the vas deferens are many tiny blood vessels that are often torn, even by a careful surgeon. Occasionally the patient becomes aware of the bleeding only when the scrotum begins to swell and grow painful—usually in the middle of the night. The patient wakes up, feels down in his pants, discovers a big, tender tomato, and in a state of hysteria sends for the doctor.

During one of our monthly clinic visits to Lapsibot, we also did a vasectomy camp. We had done seven operations in the evening by kerosene lantern after the regular clinic had finished, and at 10:00 we had decided to call it a day. Utterly exhausted, we retired for the night, all of us—men and women—lined up like mackerel in our cramped sleeping quarters. Sure enough, in the middle of the night came a knock on the door, and up the log ladder climbed a relative of one of the evening's vasectomy patients.

"The patient is bleeding," he said, "and all swollen up. I've come to get the doctor." The room was completely dark; he was just a voice coming from the top of the ladder.

I tried for a moment pretending I wasn't there, but that didn't work. An acute case of amnesia would have helped, but I didn't feel one coming on.

"Where is the doctor?" said the man on the ladder, addressing the motionless bodies stretched out on the floor.

I felt an elbow in my ribs. It was Val Collett, our chief community health nurse, who happened to be lying next to me. "It's for you, Doc," she said, a bit more cheerfully than I thought necessary.

"I don't speak the language very well," I reminded her, falling back on the next best thing to amnesia. "What's he saying?" Valerie had been in the country for years and knew Nepali well; I'd been in Nepal only eight months.

"One of your vasectomy cases is bleeding. They've come to get you."

"Tell them to apply pressure," I said, rolling over.

That netted me another jab in the ribs. "Wake up, wake up," I heard Valerie saying. "You've got to do something." It was the first time surgery of any kind had been performed in the area, and Valerie didn't want to jeopardize the entire community health program by one unpleasant experience with a vasectomy.

I sat up and tried to gather my wits. The problem couldn't be serious, I knew, in spite of the fact the messenger claimed the patient was bleeding "like a fountain." No major blood vessels ran anywhere near the operative site. The incision was less than a quarter of an inch long—too small even to bother suturing. All that was needed was to apply gentle pressure to the incision for fifteen or twenty minutes, and the bleeding would stop. No harm could possibly come to the patient, other than the slight discomfort of a swollen scrotum, which would subside by itself after a few days.

Furthermore, the patient lived an hour away. It was no small matter spending the rest of the night trekking off to his house in the dark when I couldn't do a thing that the family couldn't do just as well. I didn't know enough Nepali to comfort the patient—"OK, OK, you get well quick, no worry" was about all I could manage—and I doubted my radiant presence would do much to elevate the patient's mood. Besides, how was I going to see forty or fifty patients the next morning and then walk the more than fifteen miles back to Amp Pipal—all on two hours' sleep?

Though Valerie had misgivings, she related my thinking to the relative on the ladder and persuaded him with difficulty that it wasn't necessary for the doctor to see the patient that night. If the patient was still having problems in the morning, he could come to see the doctor then. As I predicted, there was no problem by morning. But two weeks later the patient showed up at the hospital with his scrotum looking like an oversized eggplant and demanded to know when his body was going to return to normal. That one case set the cause of vasectomies in the Lapsibot area back five years.

Out of hundreds of subsequent vasectomies, I have had only one other hematoma of any consequence, and that was in a hemophiliac. The patient had come to the hospital for his vasectomy and had offered no history of a clotting deficiency. He was walking home after the operation when he noticed his pants were dripping with blood. He returned to the hospital in a state of some agitation, and I was called down to the ward to see him. I blandly assured him there was nothing to worry about, and showed him how to apply pressure to the wound. I left him lying in the treatment room and gave instructions to the evening nurse to let him go home when the bleeding had stopped. The man fell asleep, sadly, and bled for much of the night before anyone noticed and called me down to see him. I told the Nepali assistant nurse on duty (a male nurse, conveniently) to hold onto the patient's scrotum himself until the bleeding was under control. That took the rest of the night, and since the assistant nurse was alone on duty, he was hard put to render care to anyone else who might have needed it. Every time he left the vasectomy patient, the bleeding would start up again and the patient would yell out that he was bleeding to death and call the nurse back. By morning the bleeding had stopped, and the patient tottered pale and perspiring out of the hospital, leaving behind three pints of blood in payment for his night's lodging. The operation, as always, had been done for free.

There is no question that hematoma has given vasectomy a bad name in the minds of many Nepalis. We once took an extended trip to an adjacent district to conduct vasectomy camps—a district, incidentally, with over 150,000 people with not one doctor or nurse. We had expected a big turnout, but another doctor had been through the year before doing vasectomies and had left a trail of hematomas. The memory was still vivid—no one recalls, of course, the nine out of ten successful cases—we figured that our numbers were halved by that previous experience. Few things so focus a man's thoughts as a pint of blood in his scrotum.

Fear of hematoma is not the only reason men are hesitant to have a vasectomy. The imaginations of village Nepalis are agitated by all sorts of notions—all untrue—about how vasectomy will weaken them, take away their appetite, make them unable to carry loads or walk, cause their teeth to fall out, and do a host of other dreadful things. But the major reason Nepalis are reluctant to have the operation arises from the Hindu belief that sons are necessary to insure a man's salvation. Nepalis believe that unless the proper funeral rites are carried out by one's own son, a man's soul will not find rest. Thus every man tries to have at least two sons (in case one dies), and that means he'll average two daughters as well. As a result no one volunteers for sterilization until he has first gotten his two sons *and* they have grown past infancy and early childhood (the period of high mortality)—which usually allows for a couple more children in the meantime! Indeed, this need for a son remains the principal impetus for Nepal's high birth rate (currently 2.6 percent). It also places one more burden, perhaps the heaviest of all, on Nepal's women, who must bear these children. And, of course, if a wife fails to produce a male child, she is replaced.

Usually, then, the men who volunteer for a vasectomy already have seven or eight children, and thus the operation so far has made little headway in controlling Nepal's burgeoning population. What's needed is for men with only three or four children to be sterilized. Only then will the fertility rates begin to decline. The same can be said for women who are candidates for tube-tie. The less permanent methods of family planning have not been very effective in the hills of Nepal, though they remain useful for those with small families.

The main drawback to surgical sterilization—and it's a serious one—is the high mortality among Nepali children, especially those under five. One man for whom I had done a vasectomy two years previously came to me with the sad story that his two sons, ages six and eight, had just died of measles, and he wanted to know if I could put his vas back together so he could have more sons. I told him I could do the procedure, but I could guarantee him only a fifty percent chance of having more children. Happily in his case the procedure was successful, and he came back a year and a half later bringing with him a baby son and a pregnant wife.

It's important to be able to reassure people, especially those with young children, that a vasectomy can be reversed successfully. I've rejoined the vasa of six patients, and four have gone on to have more children. Naturally, we don't recommend surgical sterilization for parents who have fewer than three children or whose children are all under five. Considering the more than two thousand vasectomies that have been done in our area over the past decade, the fact that only six have returned to have their vasectomy reversed attests to the soundness of our selection criteria. And despite the aversion with which some people regard surgical sterilization, I believe that the introduction of a safe and simple vasectomy technique has been, in the long run, one of the most important surgical contributions we've made during our time in Nepal.

eighteen

The First Vasectomy Camp

O F ALL THE VASECTOMY CAMPS I've participated in, the very first camp was the best—or the worst—or, at least, the most memorable.

My introduction to the vasectomy business came shortly after we arrived in Amp Pipal. One day I was visited by a natty young Nepali attired in an olive-green sport coat, tight black pants, a pink shirt, and a black silk tie with a golden eagle on it. He wore thick, horn-rimmed glasses and sported a tidy goatee. Sneakers were his only concession to the exigencies of Nepal's trails. He introduced himself as Madhukar, the new government family-planning officer, recently transferred to our district from what I gathered to have been a somewhat softer post in the city. He had come to enlist my help in conducting vasectomy camps through-out the district. After impressing upon him the demands of the hospital for my time, we agreed that I would participate to a limited degree, perhaps by conducting a vasectomy camp once or twice a month in various nearby villages during the dry season.

The first trip, however, was to be a bit grander: a three-day campaign to the eastern edge of our district, not including the long day's walk both going and coming. I was to meet the family-planning team in a large market town situated on the banks of a major river. The year before, a huge landslide had dammed up the river slightly above the town, and the water had backed up for seventy-two hours. When it finally broke loose, it swept away the town's bridge, part of the embankment, and many of the buildings on the river side of the town's main thoroughfare.

On the day of our arrival, just as Val Collett and I were approaching the town, we were greeted by a tremendous explosion, the work of a construction crew dynamiting away the high bank in the middle of town to place the foundation for a new footbridge. We saw that the main road, running parallel to the river, had been blown away right to the very foundation of a big four-story house, which appeared for all the world as if it would fall any moment straight down into the river a hundred feet below. Its foundation had already begun to split and crack in several places.

As we walked across the wooden planks laid over the gaping chasm, we felt a little queasy and muttered to each other that we sure wouldn't want to spend any time in that house. It was all the more intriguing to learn shortly thereafter that the city fathers had thoughtfully reserved that very building for the performance of our vasectomies, on the top floor no less, with a stimulating view of the river below. You can be sure we hoped the house would collapse that same night to spare us the pleasure of working in it the next day; but it didn't.

We met Madhukar, the family-planning official, who had arrived an hour ahead of us, dressed in his same green coat, pink shirt, and black silk tie. He looked so spotless that he might as well have just stepped out of a downtown store window as have come a day's walk from the town of Gorkha. How these Nepalis avoided the sweat and dirt of the trail, I could never understand. I was about done in, especially since I had come down with a case of dysentery that morning. After a tolerably bad supper, I was ready for bed.

Just before retiring, however, we were aroused by a commotion outside our "hotel." It turned out to be relatives of a woman in obstructed labor, who, having heard that a doctor was in town to do vasectomies, had come from over two hours away to ask him to come to deliver the baby. Apparently one of the family-planning staff had already been sent to see the woman and had found the baby's arm presenting. The baby was already dead. Having pulled on the arm without result, in a fit of irrationality he had cut it off at the shoulder, a move not calculated to make the next person's job any easier.

The last thing we needed was an all-night walk to try to salvage a clearly hopeless obstetric case; and yet, if there was ever a time when we were on display as a Christian doctor and nurse in a town that had probably never seen a Christian, this was it. After a long discussion, we finally told the family to bring the woman to us. They said they couldn't possibly bring her; we must go to her. We pointed out that they seemed ready enough to let her die by *not* bringing her, yet they expected *us* to go there and be up all night, with little chance of our being able to do anything for her anyway. Madhukar jumped at this reasoning, and wanting me to have a good night's sleep for his program's sake, made them feel so guilty that in the end they agreed to have her carried to town. So at midnight, the family disappeared into the darkness to fetch the patient, while we retired to the house of a local Communist organizer to catch a few hours' sleep—at the foot of a wall-sized photo of Mao Tse-tung.

At 4:30 in the morning we were awakened abruptly: the obstetric case had arrived. The patient—a young woman, barely eighteen—had been placed on a rickety table in the unoccupied basement of an old school building, the dirt-caked rafters and crumbling walls of which were laced with spider webs and excavated everywhere by termites. There, by the dim light of a kerosene lamp, with twenty of her family and friends standing in the shadows, looking on with unflinching dispassion like the spectral crew of the Flying Dutchman, we tried in vain to deliver that baby. No anesthesia, no equipment—only a pair of gloves—and the woman beside herself with pain. We soon concluded that the uterus had ruptured, probably the day before, and that there was no hope.

One little wizened man among the spectators, obviously the leader of the group, acted as spokesman. We told him the woman had a very slight chance of surviving and then only if they took her immediately to the hospital at Amp Pipal. When he communicated this news to the family, they entered into heated deliberation for the better part of an hour, with the man continually officiating, advising, consoling. Finally they decided it was just too far to Amp Pipal; it would involve too great an expense and would disrupt the entire family—all for so slim a hope. Knowing well what the journey to Amp Pipal was like, I could appreciate their dilemma. They eventually settled on having a local practitioner cut the baby in segments and remove it piecemeal, in spite of our pronouncement that this would cause the patient needless suffering, as well as hasten her demise. And when the last of the relatives had filed away, carrying the woman in the midst of them, we turned, with a lingering sense of impotence, to the day's activities before us.

The family-planning team had come well prepared for this, our inaugural venture. They had lugged a heavy metal "operating table" a day's journey from the district capital, and a proper kerosene-fired autoclave as well—something we didn't have in Amp Pipal. Neither piece of equipment was necessary, of course; in subsequent camps we made do quite well with straw mats and disinfectant solution in pie plates. They had also brought a large quantity of rubber gloves for me to use, and they were distressed when I said I couldn't use them—gloves made a vasectomy much more difficult. Looking back, I must have been a great disappointment to them.

Most males, as we have seen, have a healthy regard for the real and imagined sequelae of vasectomy, especially in a superstitious country like Nepal, where one reckons to come out on the good end if he escapes without losing his virility and all of his hair. This was the first vasectomy camp in this village, and as with any other unfamiliar experience, it was a case of everyone standing back and graciously letting the other fellow go first. Therefore, we were much relieved when the first intrepid person to step forward to undergo the operation was none other than the new *pradhan panch* of the village, elected only the day before. *If he goes first,* we thought, *all the rest will follow.*

Well, I was somewhat new to the work at that time, and so were the family-planning people. And so, certainly, was the *pradhan panch.* Unfortunately, he was anything but intrepid. He couldn't stand pain, and he seemed immune to Novocain. On top of that, he had the smallest pair of vasa deferentia I've ever seen, before or since. We were at it forty-five minutes, and every time he groaned and hollered and said he was going to die, the fifteen men peering in through the doorway, waiting their turn, would begin to mutter and giggle, and the family-planning boys would burst into laughter as if it weren't anything and then say to me aside for heaven's sake to give him more Novocain before all the others were frightened away.

As the poor chap's groaning grew louder under my surgery, so did the laughter of the family-planning boys. Each time the *pradhan panch* voiced some new fear about what was happening to him, they would clap their hands and literally roar with glee. Perhaps they thought they were helping the patient—kidding him out of his troubles—but, if so, it was an odd method.

As for me, I wasn't in much better shape than the patient. And here I'd been preening myself with the thought that it was a fortunate thing for the success of this family-planning program that an actual American Board-qualified general surgeon should be doing these operations so as to assure that everything would go well and the operation wouldn't get a bad name!

The *pradhan panch's* agony didn't end with the operation. He sat down at the foot of the operating table with his head between his knees, tingling all over, numb, dizzy, nauseated, hot and cold by turns, saying he didn't have the strength to walk out of the room; and he continued to sit there moaning and groaning for the rest of the day, while all those others came right in and had their operation and stood around afterwards ribbing and teasing their *pradhan panch* in such a merciless manner that I suspect he began to wish he *had* died during the operation. Since the other cases went smoothly and quickly, he thought all the more that there must be something drastically wrong with him and that dreadful sequelae were sure to follow. Why the others hadn't left for the next county at the first scream of their *pradhan panch,* I'll never fathom. Only one changed his mind: He said he'd just gotten his wife pregnant and didn't need the operation now.

We ended up doing twenty-six vasectomies on that trip. It was the beginning of a happy association with the family planners, which would soon be taking me all over the district into areas where I wouldn't have ventured otherwise. But I'll never forget that first trip and how it taught me not to put too much stock in being an "actual American Board-qualified general surgeon." If a work is truly God's, it will prosper regardless of the human qualifications of the worker. The main question always remains: is this work God's or is it only ours?

Some time after that first vasectomy camp we held another interesting camp in an isolated Gurung tribal village, a hard six-hour walk to the north of Amp Pipal. It was a desolate spot on a narrow ridge, and the Gurungs, being unused to the concept of surgery and hence quite apprehensive, arrived for their operation in a state of moderate intoxication. Try to imagine doing a vasectomy on a drunk and struggling Gurung, being held down by four equally inebriated villagers on a straw mat in a filthy shed on a 7,000-foot ridge, with an icy wind howling through and a dozen giggling Gurung girls peering in to view the excitement, and you'll have an idea of the fun we had.

The thirteenth candidate turned out to be somewhat stronger than his predecessors and managed to break loose during the procedure, putting his elbow through the only kerosene lantern in the village—thus ending the operations. However, the two fellows that remained to be done were the most drunk of all, so we were spared further entertainment.

Meanwhile, I'd been providing entertainment of sorts on my own. I'd been troubled by recurring amoebic dysentery for some time and had suffered a mild exacerbation just the day before. Several months earlier I'd gotten hold of some new anti-amoeba medicine with the deceptively innocuous name of Falmonox. After extensive, or more aptly, exhaustive clinical trials on myself, I had concluded that this drug's mechanism of action was to asphyxiate the bugs with noxious vapors and then blow them out of the intestine altogether. This was made possible by the fact that each of these little pills, when swallowed, turned by some extraordinary process into a dozen liters of compressed gas.

On this particular occasion I decided that to have my full strength for the journey, I'd better start off with a loading dose, as it were; and since the daily dose was three tablets, I took all three the evening before the trip, calculating that I might even obtain a little propulsive effect from the pills to speed me along the trail. I also took a couple more in the morning, perhaps fancying I would turn into a balloon and not have to walk at all.

Unfortunately, my timing was just a bit off. The walk was uneventful. But I had no sooner arrived and knelt down to go to work on my inebriated patients than the pills began to take effect. It's bad enough, having hiked for six hours all morning, to kneel down on a straw mat and instantly begin to operate, without at the same time being afflicted with the effects of this dreadful medicine. It was like the soundtrack of the Battle of

Borodino. Everyone began to look around here and there, eyeing each other suspiciously and shifting from place to place with their noses to the draft. Fortunately, almost everyone was too intoxicated to identify the source of the commotion, and the wind howling through the shed was very welcome indeed.

The final episode in the day's entertainment came when I was called off to another part of town to see the sick niece of the local headman. While I was waiting there on the porch, he shouted some instructions to his wife inside to prepare what I presumed (erroneously) would be some tea. After I had finished examining the child, almost dead from amoebic dysentery, I was given some small, cooked potatoes covered with what looked like some sort of seasoning. Closer inspection disclosed it to be dirt. I wasn't hungry, but I started in on the potatoes, trying my best to fix a grateful expression on my face. On the third potato, in the midst of deliberating whether it would be better to chew it or swallow it whole, this same sick little girl appeared crawling out of the house with a potato just like mine in each hand, covering her potatoes as she came with dirt, spittle, chicken droppings, and a variety of other condiments from the porch floor. She squatted down opposite me, and try as I might not to look, I watched her take a large bite out of one of her potatoes. I hastily swallowed the rest of my own potatoes without chewing them, reflecting that even Falmonox would stand little chance against the hostile forces collected from that filthy porch.

Thus we have set about attacking the population problem. Dozens of these vasectomy camps later, we might well consider what on earth we have accomplished. Not knowing whether to laugh or weep, we face an awesome task with hopelessly inadequate means—too little, too late. If we were not doing it out of love for these people and out of a knowledge that an eternal God is going to redeem our labors, we would have signed out long ago—with a shrug and a few laughs.

In Defense of Family Planning

*I*N THE DEVELOPING world there is one paramount issue underlying the uncertainty and anxiety with which thoughtful men and women view the future: expanding population. In one way or another most of the Third World's material problems are in large part the result of too many people. Indeed, for most developing nations, including Nepal, the pressure of increasing population remains the overwhelming unsolved problem, as high birth rates continue to eat up every benefit that technology and development can provide, and more besides.

In Nepal, even after three decades of rapid economic development and massive infusions of foreign aid, there has been little or no improvement in the living standard of most of the people. The major area of progress has been in the health field, where Nepal has seen a moderate increase in average life expectancy. But in other areas there is little cause for cheer. Most ominous of all is the fact that per capita food production has been declining. The underlying reason is not hard to find: during this same thirty years, the population of Nepal has doubled.

Granted, the problems of the developing world are numerous and their causes complex and interlocking. Many of the problems have existed since the beginning of time: ignorance, fear, disease, poverty—each feeding on the other. While overpopulation may not be the primary cause of all these ills, it most certainly intensifies them all and makes their solution yet more remote. Nations can be likened to sailing vessels. There can be many reasons for a sailboat's lack of progress—poor design, insufficient canvas, incompetent sailors, interference from other boats—but the most important is an unfavorable wind. Population growth is such an ill wind, driving back the advances of developing nations with ever-increasing force.

Today, after more than two decades of government efforts to control population, Nepal's birth rate remains substantially unchanged. Many other developing countries report a similar experience. It's highly doubtful whether voluntary family-planning programs, as currently conducted, will prove adequate to the task. So far, they have not. For example, in our area of Nepal over the past decade, approximately 2,000 vasectomies have been performed; but in order to produce even a quiver in the statistics of our district alone, 20,000 such operations are needed. And Nepal requires more than a quiver. The fertility of her people must be reduced by fifty percent in the next twenty-five years just to maintain the present rate of population increase, to say nothing of the unattainable ideal of "zero population growth." It's no wonder that in some countries authorities have resorted to the institution of compulsory, government-enforced birth-control measures of a necessarily repugnant and radical nature. If that sounds bad, will not the consequences of failing to limit population be even worse? Ask people which they prefer, food or freedom, and they will choose food every time.

Having said this, however, we want to stress that neither we nor the United Mission to Nepal advocates abortion or any form of physically enforced sterilization as a means of reducing population growth. As Christians, we are opposed to such measures.

Although the impact of overpopulation extends to all areas of life, its most immediate and distressing consequence is hunger, together with its corollary, malnutrition. To focus our concerns, therefore, the comments that follow will deal primarily with overpopulation as a cause of hunger, a matter, surely, in which Christian missions should have a vital interest.

In recent years, regrettably, the problem of overpopulation has been de-emphasized in many circles. In its place people have begun to talk about inequitable structures (government trade and economic policies) and poor distribution as the primary causes of world hunger. If only the food surpluses of the rich nations could be shared with the world's poor, everyone would have enough—so the reasoning goes. Also included in this thinking is the belief that modern technology can bring about increases in food production sufficient to keep pace with increasing demand. This may be true for some countries for some time, but in Nepal per capita food production has in fact been decreasing in recent years. While no one denies the benefits of technology or the need to change inequitable structures, the main answer to world hunger does not lie here; it lies in controlling population growth. Clearly, population control must be the concern of anyone working to relieve suffering in the Third World. It is a legitimate and vital aspect of any community health program. And it is on this basis that the United Mission has welcomed opportunities to assist the government of Nepal in its efforts to promote family planning.

Unfortunately, this has provoked skepticism and even opposition among some of our friends at home. At the first mention of vasectomy, in particular, distress signals go up in the minds of many people who question what business a Christian doctor has going around mutilating people and tampering with God's creation. Aside from the fact that doctors are always "tampering" and that vasectomy is not mutilating, there are other positive considerations that compel Christian doctors to make family planning their business. What follows is an attempt to justify family planning from a biblical perspective and to show why Christians, of all people, should support efforts to limit population growth in developing countries.

Many people in America don't admit that overpopulation is a problem at all, claiming that overpopulation and famine have always existed in many parts of the world. What they are referring to, of course, is *relative* overpopulation in conjunction with an inadequate food supply. According to this definition, it can be said that North America was overpopulated by a few hundred thousand Indians before the European settlers arrived. The critical distinction is that in this chapter we are talking about *absolute* overpopulation, a condition in which even the potential food supply can't support the number of people in a given area. This condition has already occurred in the hills of Nepal and in much of the developing world. And now for the first time in history, the problem of famine can no longer be solved by migration, by technology, or by clearing more land. The increased yields brought about by the "green revolution" have largely peaked in many areas, and now both shortage of fertilizer and capricious rainfall are forcing many farmers to revert to their older and more reliable varieties of grain, which were less dependent on an abundance of inorganic fertilizer or ideal weather conditions.

An acre of land will yield only so much. God has created a finite earth and has given human beings rational minds with which to fill that earth intelligently. Today the hills of Nepal are already filled. But the real problem lies in the fact that the effect of current birth rates will continue into the next generation, even if from now on every Nepali family were to start having only two children. It is almost inescapable, short of widespread famine or other catastrophe, that Nepal's population will double within the next thirty years. Put plainly, this means that several generations of Nepalis are going to be chronically hungry and miserable, incapable of leading productive, happy lives.

The above considerations often evoke two responses among Christians: first, that God may be judging the developing countries by letting them starve; second, that He can, if He desires, provide a starving world with manna from heaven. Both of these responses might be valid in themselves, but they have no place in formulating our attitude toward the population problem. Concerning the first response, God has repeatedly forbidden us to judge others. Rather, He has commanded us to be compassionate and to become involved in other people's problems, both physical and spiritual. This surely is the example Christ gave us when He fed the multitudes and healed the sick. Furthermore, it flies in the face of reality to assert that only the "heathen" suffer, when Christians, too, are going hungry in the Third World today.

Concerning the second response, God can indeed do anything. But more often than not the Bible reveals a God who has done things through people. He has limited himself in order to make us responsible partakers in history and creation. Is it not more likely that God is gently telling us that instead of anticipating a supernatural increase in the supply of food, we ought rather to be reducing the demand? God no more determines how many children a family will have than He determines how many bushels of corn a farmer will raise; in both cases the outcome is in predictable accordance with the laws of nature He has established. And He has left the decision of "how many" in human hands. The Nepali people are not ants on an anthill that must propagate themselves to the point of starvation, without the ability to learn to conserve and to live in harmony with their environment. No more than God can be expected to miraculously reduce the weight of a person who persists in eating, can He be expected to provide the people of Nepal with manna from heaven. He *can* do it, but He can't be expected to. Rather, is God not grieved that the Nepali people have not only filled their land but also overfilled it?

Many people living in developed Western countries concede that expanding population is a problem, but they can't see how it relates to them. Most Americans, for example, are far removed from the reality of overpopulation and are understandably at a loss how to solve the problem, even if they felt constrained to try. Many predict that the problem will eventually be "solved" only through starvation, sickness, war, or the appearance of totalitarian governments that will limit families by force. However, we can hardly look with favor on these means, especially when the conditions resulting from overpopulation can be ameliorated to some degree by more constructive and compassionate methods. Even though it will be impossible to avert the tragedy that is now enveloping countries like Nepal, this doesn't eliminate our responsibility to try, at least, to minimize its impact, anymore than Jesus' statement about the poor being always with us eliminates our obligation to give to charity.

Christians have generally responded sympathetically to people in need, especially those in need of food. Clearly we should continue to employ all possible means to augment the supply of food. But it's futile to attempt to increase the food supply without limiting the mouths that will consume it, which is the heart of the problem and the ultimate key to its solution.

Some Christians will object and say that the Bible nowhere tells us to restrict procreation; instead, we are enjoined to multiply and count our offspring as blessings from God. Yet surely we must understand these Old Testament injunctions in the light of the circumstances to which they were addressed; to do this doesn't demean the authority of the Bible but rather provides the most reliable way by which we can interpret its meaning. God's original mandate to multiply and fill the earth was given in the context of a world that was *under*populated—certainly not the case in our world today. The Bible nowhere instructs us to overpopulate our world; on the contrary, it gives us a positive mandate for population control in the second great commandment: to love your neighbor as yourself.

It has taken these years of living in Nepal to make us fully appreciate the connection between loving our neighbors and helping them limit their families. At our hospital, we daily see families in which children are dying from lack of food; here the love of Christ clearly constrains us to teach these parents how to avoid having another baby, in this way sparing the children who are already born and preventing the birth of a child otherwise destined to misery. How often have we seen a first child die as a result of the birth of a second baby, simply because the mother had insufficient food or milk for both. Or, taking the mother's point of view, try to imagine what it would be like bearing your fifth or seventh or ninth child under conditions prevailing in Nepal, and picture the desperation on her face as she comes to you for help. To refuse to aid these families in limiting their children would not only undermine our effort to improve their health but also contradict our Christian calling. We need to begin where Christ began: with loving our neighbors.

We've also come to see the connection between loving our neighbor and limiting our own family. In the context of Nepal, it's easy to see that in a marginally subsistent community every child born is a threat to its neighbor's survival. In such a community, members are necessarily interdependent and mutually responsible one to another. As Christians, we too are called upon to be responsible to those around us. When our own "rights" conflict with our duty to our neighbor, we should put our neighbor first. Unless we are prepared ourselves to set an example of self-restraint, we will be in no position to exert moral leadership in such a threatened community, and we will necessarily be cast in the role of exhorting people to do what we say but not what we do.

Although in affluent, relatively underpopulated countries this reasoning holds less force, the principle still applies. We have no more right to plan our family in total disregard for our neighbors and our community than we have the right to construct a chemical factory in our suburban front yard.

Furthermore, it's time we began to consider the whole world as our community. Americans should recall that they produce eighty percent of the world's surplus food, upon which millions of people depend to avoid starvation. America no longer stands in isolation from Nepal; Christians, surely, should be sensitive to this fact. We must abandon the notion that having children is purely one's own private affair.

Lest Christians think that they'll soon die out if they are the only ones to heed these principles, we must remember that the spiritual laws governing the growth of the church are hardly contingent upon the physical laws governing reproduction. A Christian community that seeks before God to enter into the human predicament and to set an example of self-denial at all levels will never be in danger of extinction; rather, hungry and despairing men and women will increasingly look to it for leadership and inspiration and find through it the Christ who is the Bread of Life and the Hope of the World.

The Cost of
Discipleship

The Funeral

T HERE IS no telephone service in the mountainous regions of the kingdom of Nepal. So the missionary community at Amp Pipal installed a telephone system of its own—an anomalous wonder of modern technology, consisting of a dozen battery-powered, hand-cranked phones connected together in one self-contained party line, which links the mission houses with each other and with the hospital. The only other phone in the district sits in the police headquarters at Gorkha, a fifteen-mile walk to the east. From Gorkha one can place a direct call to one of two places: central police headquarters in Kathmandu (seventy miles further to the east) or zonal police headquarters in Pokhara (fifty miles to the west), Pokhara being the administrative center for the eleven districts in our region of Nepal.

All of our dozen phones ring simultaneously. So to distinguish one household from another, each has a Morse-code-like number, according to the number of rings cranked out: one long—one short or two longs or three long—one short, etc. The system is not perfect, of course. If one's batteries happen to be low (which is frequently the case), one's better off going outside and shouting to his neighbor rather than using the phone. A further difficulty is the interference produced by the hospital generator, whose wires run adjacent to the phone line in numerous places; with the generator running, talking on the phone is about as easy as carrying on a conversation with a jackhammer operator. All in all, however, the Amp Pipal telephone system probably removes more frustrations than it creates, and one gradually learns to live with its idiosyncrasies.

On the morning of March 17, 1981, a few minutes before 8:00, the Amp Pipal telephones were cranked into life by a vigorous one long—one short ring, Dr. Helen Huston's "number."

The voice on the other end was urgent: "Come quickly! She's serious." It was the assistant nurse calling from the hospital.

It's often difficult to interpret such calls from our inexperienced junior staff: how serious was the patient? Sometimes we've rushed down to find the patient in good shape but the relatives in an uproar. At other times the patient has been dead. On this present occasion it seemed more likely the former experience would be repeated: the patient was a thirty-eight-year-old woman who had been admitted the previous day with a relatively minor illness. There was no reason for her suddenly to have become "serious." But the urgency in the assistant nurse's voice precluded any delay; Helen paused only long enough to call us to let us know she might need help.

Cynthia and I left for the hospital at once. It was no ordinary patient we were hurrying to see; it was Moti Maya—a beloved Christian sister, a member of the governing committee of our local church and one of the first believers to be baptized in Amp Pipal. She was also one of the few local Christians who had obtained employment apart from the mission; she was the government family-planning worker for our area.

Moti Maya had suffered long and deeply for her faith. For many years she had been the object of derision and mockery from her Hindu neighbors. Her former husband had repeatedly abused and beaten her, in the end abandoning her and her two infant sons for another wife. Not content with that, he then had tried to have her arrested for being a Christian. After a prolonged and arduous court case involving dozens of trips to the district capital, six hour's walk away, she finally overturned her husband's case and won a divorce from him on the grounds of cruelty and neglect—a rare occurrence in this male-dominated Hindu society.

The past eight years had been relatively peaceful for her. She had seen both of her sons through the mission-built boys' boarding school in Pokhara. She had seen saw both of them baptized and growing in their faith. Amrit, the older son, was currently enrolled in the highly competitive government health-assistant course; and Jiwan, the younger son, was teaching at the boarding school, from which he had just graduated as president of his class. Beyond all this, Moti Maya had just moved into a large, recently completed house, which she had built with the savings accumulated over many years of work. Although she still owed several thousand rupees for its construction, she could now look forward to a future of well-earned comfort and security. She was a living example of the biblical promises come true.

All through these years, Moti Maya had been particularly close to Dr. Helen. It was through Helen that Moti Maya had come to know the Lord sixteen years before. Jiwan, then an infant, had been desperately sick, and after Helen had prayed for him, he had recovered. As a result of that experience, Moti Maya came to believe in the God who answers prayer. Helen, of course, had also been a principal support for Moti Maya during her long periods of difficulty and persecution. It was only natural, therefore, that in this present illness too, Helen should be her doctor.

When Cynthia and I reached Moti Maya's hospital room, we found her lying on the floor, surrounded by several Nepali staff in varying stages of confusion and dismay. Dr. Helen was kneeling over Moti Maya, listening to her heart. The resuscitation box already had been sent for, and an IV drip had been started.

"I can't hear a thing," said Helen as soon as she saw us at the door. "There's no heartbeat." She spoke uncertainly, as if unconvinced by the evidence of her stethoscope. Those gathered around stood or knelt in stunned silence. Helen listened intensely, as if by the sheer concentration of her will she could bring the heartbeat back.

Meanwhile, I hadn't even paused in the doorway. In cases of cardiac arrest, one's actions are swift and automatic. Stepping to Moti Maya's head, I selected an endotracheal tube from the resuscitation box and quickly intubated her; I then proceeded to ventilate her lungs by blowing into the tube. Helen began external cardiac massage, while Cynthia scurried around, helping the Nepali staff administer the various drugs required in such circumstances.

The efforts to resuscitate Moti Maya continued in silence for some minutes. I asked how long she had been unconscious before the doctors had arrived on the scene and was told it had been only moments. Periodically Helen or Cynthia would listen again to see if the heart had begun to beat, but each time the wordless resumption of cardiac massage gave sufficient answer that it had not. We continued for half an hour, trading off jobs as one or another got tired from blowing into the lungs or compressing the chest, all of us unwilling to give up hope or even to believe that Moti Maya could actually have died.

Finally I suggested that we stop. "No, no, we can't stop," Helen replied through her clenched teeth, pumping the chest with renewed determination.

But already the grim truth had become apparent to the Nepalis who stood around us. The Christians among them and others who had been close to Moti Maya had begun to weep openly and unashamedly long before we had ceased our futile efforts.

Unthinkable as it was, Moti Maya was dead. Helen broke down, and embracing the lifeless form, she buried her face in

Moti Maya's neck. Cynthia offered a long and fervent prayer, while others of us wondered with sadness and resignation what God had in mind by taking from our midst the most mature and fearless Nepali member of our tiny church.

We were never to learn the cause of death. Of our various speculations, not one was tenable; the case remained bizarre and mystifying.

A hastily arranged memorial service was conducted an hour later at the regular 10:00 prayer and tea time. The entire hospital staff and many outsiders, including the Amp Pipal *pradhan panch,* attended. Two Nepali Christians gave moving testimonies about Moti Maya's faith and about the Christian view of death. The service was openly evangelistic, and though many were attentive and sympathetic, others were later to raise a protest against using the hospital facilities to "advertise" the Gospel.

Even while the service proceeded, two members of the church, Prakash (our anesthetist) and Megh Nath (our purchasing officer), were already on their way to notify Moti Maya's two sons: Prakash to Pokhara, where Jiwan was teaching; and Megh Nath to Kathmandu, where Amrit was studying in the health-assistant course. The tentative plan was to hold a funeral service the following afternoon, Wednesday, by which time both sons should have arrived.

Our church had also instructed Megh Nath to invite Jacob Singh, the pastor of Kathmandu's largest congregation, to lead the service. This was supremely fitting because not only had Amrit been living with Pastor Jacob during his time in Kathmandu, but also it was Pastor Jacob himself who many years before had come to Amp Pipal and baptized Moti Maya. It must be said, however, that we entertained little hope that such a prominent and busy person would be able to drop everything and come out to Amp Pipal to conduct the funeral service of a simple village woman.

For the remainder of that first day, Moti Maya's body lay in a newly made plywood coffin in the hospital prayer room. She had specifically mentioned to some of her friends months before that when she died, whatever else might happen, she certainly didn't want to be put in the "dead house," the rat-proof hut where we placed all dead bodies until the families came to take them away. Members of the church, both Nepalis and missionaries, took turns staying with the body, passing the time singing and praying.

Prakash arrived back from Pokhara with Jiwan late that same night. Accompanying them was Attun, an older Nepali Christian who had in effect taken the place of Jiwan's father during his school years in Pokhara.

The next day there was much discussion about when and where the funeral service should be held, what kind of service it should be, and where the body should be buried. Permission was requested from the *panchayat* to bury Moti Maya's body on her own property, as she had requested, but a great outcry from a vocal segment of the Hindu community compelled the *pradhan panch* to turn down the request. The disposal of a corpse is a very sensitive matter in Nepal, and strict compliance with Hindu practice was expected. Nepali Hindus cremate bodies near a river and follow strict rituals for handling the corpse. We finally decided to bury Moti Maya out on the steep, forested slopes of Liglig Mountain, where we customarily buried the bodies of other patients who died in the hospital and whose relatives had abandoned them (to avoid paying the hospital bill) or could not afford to hire porters to carry the body three hours away to the nearest river to be cremated.

All day Wednesday, Christians from surrounding villages began gathering at the hospital. Moti Maya's older brother came from Gorkha, the district capital; although he was a Hindu, he'd always loved his sister and her sons. The Amp Pipal *pradhan panch* was in and out trying to head off an impending confrontation between the Christian and Hindu communities over the planned funeral and burial services. The *pradhan panch's* son, Bishnu, one of Amrit's closest friends, had also come to the hospital and had taken a decided stand in sympathy with the Christians. Other villagers showed up throughout the day, some to harass and plot against the Christians, others to enjoy the diversion the whole affair promised to provide.

Finally, Moti Maya's former husband arrived from Thadipokhari to claim the body and with it, implicitly, Moti Maya's new house. As this man's past history of evil and cruelty was well known to all of Moti Maya's friends, he was scornfully rebuffed and told he had no right to the body or anything else of Moti Maya's. However, he did not immediately give up hope. He had solicited the aid of some militant Hindu and Communist high-school students, whom he expected at any moment to appear in force. He had previously instructed these students to disrupt the proceedings, scatter the Christians, and make off with the body. He had also brought along a police officer to record testimony in his favor. As these plans became known, consternation spread among the Christians. It seemed as if they were on the verge of being engulfed by their enemies.

There was nothing left to be done but wait for Amrit, who was due to arrive with or without Pastor Jacob that same afternoon. At 4:30, Amrit's party was finally sighted on the path winding along the slopes of Liglig Mountain, and an audible wave of excitement swept through the waiting crowd. Accompanying Amrit and Megh Nath were Pastor Jacob and several other Christian friends from Kathmandu.

The impact of their arrival was decisive. The local Christians, who had been increasing in number throughout the day, were heartened and encouraged by the sight of this band of believers. The former husband, whom I'd never actually seen, sensed that the numerical and spiritual advantage had shifted against him and quietly left the scene together with the police officer. Others who had come to heckle and cause trouble either remained silent or drifted off in small groups.

At 5:00, close to two hundred people assembled in the hospital waiting area for the service, most of them believers, friends of Moti Maya, hospital staff, and patients. Pastor Jacob led the service and gave a stirring evangelistic message that moved many to tears. Amrit stood quietly by the pastor's side throughout the service. When the pastor had finished, Jiwan, by nature outspoken, gave a forceful testimony of his own, as if he were trying to encourage someone *else* who had just been orphaned by his mother's death.

After the service, with dusk fast approaching, the entire assembly—both foreign and Nepali Christians, as well as many non-Christian friends of Amrit and Jiwan—trooped together to the slopes of Liglig to bury the body. The coffin was carried at the head of the procession by twelve young men, including the *pradhan panch's* son and others who weren't Christians—a flagrant violation of local Hindu custom.

Midway in the half-hour journey we passed a group of twenty-five surly youths, the student contingent that had been called out by Moti Maya's former husband. The students had indeed come, but they had failed to gain the support they needed to carry out their plans. Since the procession numbered about seventy people, the students limited their opposition to silent scowls; and when we had passed, they dispersed to their homes and were not heard from again.

Night had fallen when, by the light of a kerosene lamp, the coffin was finally lowered into the ground not two hundred yards from the place where Pastor Jacob had baptized Moti Maya sixteen years before. Pastor Jacob again led in a short and simple burial service, which ended with singing and prayer. A nearly full moon had risen, casting its soft and eery light through the scattered treetops onto the narrow path as we silently and thoughtfully retraced our steps to the hospital and our homes.

twenty

The next day life would return to normal for most of us, but through the events of these past two days we had had a chance to reflect once more on the fact that we would all be called one day like Moti Maya, and not one of us knew either how or when.

The Arrest

*F*OR AMRIT and Jiwan life didn't immediately return to normal. Two days after the funeral, two Thadipokhari policemen arrived with a letter summoning the two brothers and me to the police station for "questioning." They gave us no reason, but we assumed it had something to do with the funeral—though I had no idea what they wanted with me, since I hadn't participated at all in the funeral arrangements. After a hurried consultation with members of the church, we left with the policemen at about 1:00 in the afternoon, expecting to return that same evening. The only other person to accompany us was Bishnu, the *pradhan panch's* son, who joined us out of loyalty to Amrit and—one had the feeling—out of loyalty to Jesus too.

After a two-hour downhill walk, we reached Thadipokhari and were ushered into the compound of the police station. No one in authority happened to be present when we arrived; the inspector and sub-inspector were both away, we were told, and the acting sub-inspector was out on business. Several of the ordinary police officers who were hanging around, however, began in a harsh and contemptuous manner to chastise Amrit and Jiwan for the disrespect shown to their father and for their disregard for the religion and customs of their country. A particularly unpleasant-looking policeman announced sourly that our case was one of the most serious they'd seen in a long time. Other similar comments led us to understand that our summons for questioning had, in effect, been a warrant for our arrest—on what charges, we still weren't sure.

While we were waiting for the acting sub-inspector, a group of a dozen or more men—some police, some villagers—entered the room where we were seated. Among them, as I soon learned, was the boys' father, Moti Maya's ex-husband. They sat down and eyed us coldly and silently, as if we were some curious and noxious species they'd never seen before. After an unnerving fifteen minutes of silence, the father turned aside to another man and, pointing at Amrit and Jiwan, said almost inaudibly, "Those are my sons."

Amrit sprang to his feet as if a 200-volt charge had been applied to his seat. Ordinarily soft-spoken, Amrit delivered for the next twenty minutes a passionate and withering denunciation of the man who called himself his father. He concluded: "You have no right to call us your sons—nor can we recognize you as our father. You have beaten our mother, you have treated us like dogs, you have fed us on excrement, and for sixteen years you've not even looked at us—and now you try to call us your sons? Never! We are not your sons!"

"What then, did you grow from a tree?" sneered the father, a nervous, unkempt, dissolute-looking man, who sat looking from one onlooker to another, as if seeking their approbation.

The malevolent grin faded from his face as Jiwan, built like a prizefighter, rose to his feet. With suppressed vehemence, Jiwan transfixed the amazed attention of his listeners, while with biting sarcasm he effectively demolished his father's every claim to self-respect and left him, abashed and silenced, staring at the floor.

As I was pondering whether the filial respect due fathers according to the fifth commandment could legitimately be rendered to this man, the arrival of the acting sub-inspector was announced, and I was called into his office. He was a young man of not more than twenty-five, dressed casually in civilian clothes, with a stubbly beard and shifty eyes. Whenever he addressed me, he averted his gaze or looked at someone else, making it difficult to tell when to respond. He asked some questions about my religion, about whether we preached at the hospital, and finally about why I hadn't given Moti Maya's body to the husband. As I was about to answer, I noticed the husband had also come into the office. Realizing suddenly that it was he who had prodded his cronies at the police station to instigate this case, I coldly fixed my eyes on the ex-husband and said to the acting sub-inspector, "I've never seen this man before today. I had nothing to do with the disposal of the body. But I can tell you this: he has no right to the body or to anything else connected with Moti Maya. He's been legally divorced and is simply trying to cause trouble out of spite and envy."

The acting sub-inspector made a face like a man who has just cracked his tooth on a stone in his rice, and mumbling something to a subordinate, he made a gesture to dismiss me. As I walked out, Amrit came in; we had just enough time to exchange winks.

While the officials questioned Amrit, I coached Jiwan in giving respectful answers that wouldn't provoke the officials' anger. He promised me he'd do his best to be polite.

Soon it was Jiwan's turn, and when he emerged from the office ten minutes later, we were informed that a "verdict" would be forthcoming. As we waited, we compared notes on our separate interviews. But even pooling our information, we could form no definite idea of what we were being charged with. After half an hour the unpleasant-looking officer came out of the office and informed us that we were to be taken the very next morning to Gorkha, the district capital, six to seven hours' walk to the east. "The case is too big to handle here," he added with exaggerated grimness. "It has to be referred to district headquarters."

This announcement was unexpected and a bit irritating, especially since the next day was Saturday, the weekly day off, and nothing would happen in Gorkha until the offices opened at 10:00 on Sunday morning. We huffily demanded to see the official written order transferring us to Gorkha, claiming that our case was being handled in an irregular and illegal manner. However the acting sub-inspector had again gone out, and the ordinary officers said they couldn't do anything about our demands. It was surely just as well; further criticism of the police at that point was hardly going to advance our prospects. So, of necessity, prudence gained the upper hand, and we resigned ourselves to following whatever course our case might take.

Late in the afternoon we sent Bishnu back up the mountain to give news to the church. We requested that Prakash and Megh Nath proceed directly to Gorkha early the next morning, figuring they'd arrive there at about the same time we would. We also suggested that Attun return promptly to Pokhara and notify Amrit and Jiwan's great uncle, who happened to be the chief police inspector of that district. Amrit wrote a simple letter outlining the difficulties he and his brother had fallen into and asking for whatever help their great uncle could give. The boys had never been close to him; years ago he had been the chief inspector of the Thadipokhari police station (where we were now), but he had long since been promoted to Pokhara, where he had gradually drifted out of touch with his niece and her two sons. It seemed unlikely that he would be either able or willing to influence the outcome of Amrit and Jiwan's case.

With Bishnu gone and dusk fast approaching, Jiwan began to think of his stomach. He straightway asked about the arrangements for the evening meal and was brusquely told that we'd have to make our own. Jiwan responded bluntly and accurately that it was the station's responsibility to feed us. When it became clear that the rich American doctor was not going to pick up the tab, the police reluctantly agreed to arrange for our supper. When it eventually came at 9:00, I began to wonder if the satisfaction of making the police provide for our supper fully made up for the unpleasantness of eating it.

As we waited for our meal, the three of us went out and sat on a grassy field within the police compound. Jiwan had brought his Bible, so we asked Amrit to read aloud from Acts chapter 4. As he read verse 3, "They seized Peter and John, and because it was evening, they put them in jail until the next day," Jiwan slapped his thigh in amazement and said: "Wow, that's us!" We sang some Nepali hymns and then each of us prayed. The full moon was rising over Liglig, its pale white gradually overcoming the fading pink of the sunset. It was a scene of exceptional beauty. Our hearts were filled with a great wonder and joy in anticipation of what the morrow would bring. The boys talked almost eagerly about the privilege of going to jail for Jesus and of their intention to fight the case right up to the supreme court in order to give the widest possible hearing to the Gospel.

Fortified with such visions, we endured the evening meal of soggy, partially cooked rice admixed with bits of sand and gravel, and went to bed. Since the Thadipokhari police station had no prison cells, we were given bunks in the large common room that served as the police barracks. Amrit and Jiwan immediately fell into a sound sleep.

I tried to sleep but was kept awake by a card game in the bunk next to mine. It was an animated game, punctuated by frequent oaths, jeers, and shouts of triumph from the men, several of whom were using my bunk as a seat. The game got progressively more heated as the night wore on, helped along by a large bottle that was periodically passed around the group. At about 11:30 the acting sub-inspector showed up, thoroughly drunk, and joined the game. His arrival was greatly appreciated since it was accompanied by the appearance of a second bottle. The players continued with undiminished enthusiasm for another two-and-a-half hours, most of the time being spent in arguments over who had won or lost, nobody evidently being quite sure but having strong opinions all the same.

The two boys slept peacefully through the whole ordeal. I, of course, did not. When the policemen finally quieted down, the fleas in the blanket I'd been given took over and played games of their own.

At 5:00 everyone began stirring, those few that had gone early to bed exhorting the others to get up and share in the exhilaration of the new day. When the boys and I went out to the field again to pray, their first thought was to thank God for the refreshing night's sleep He had given them. We had a brief but inspirational time together reading from John chapter 14, which was abruptly terminated by two of the previous night's contestants, now groggily in uniform, ordering us to get ready promptly as we were to leave for Gorkha without further delay. We asked once more to see the official letter, but it was now sealed in an official envelope, which could be opened only by the acting sub-inspector. That official being in a state of profound repose and likely to remain so, we judiciously decided to drop the matter of the letter. Our two groggy officers, who had been selected to escort us somewhat against their will, expended valuable energy grumbling in the general direction of their sleeping superior. They appeared far less eager to go to Gorkha than we.

When we were ready to leave, Amrit asked if we could stop to see a Christian friend who lived at the outskirts of Thadipokhari. Since it involved only a five-minute detour, the policemen agreed. After a brief meeting with the friend, we resumed our journey and were walking along a little back alley leading to the main path when, to our amazement, we encountered Attun, who was on his way back to Pokhara to notify the boys' great uncle of their arrest. Attun had prayed that morning that he might see the boys one last time before returning to Pokhara. He had gotten quite lost in the maze of trails around Thadipokhari and had wandered fully twenty minutes out of his way. The particular connecting path on which we met wasn't a hundred yards long, and if the timing had been two minutes off, we never would have seen Attun at all. Attun expressed no surprise at meeting up with us on such an unlikely path. He nonchalantly asked one of our police escorts to turn down the volume of the radio he was carrying so that we could talk with our God. The officer turned off his radio and edged closer as if to listen for God's voice. After we had prayed, the officer said skeptically, "I didn't hear your God say anything."

"That's because you are taking His children to jail," returned Attun without hesitation. "He doesn't want to speak with you."

The second policeman, much to the irritation of his colleague with the radio, readily concurred with Attun's explanation. He seemed awed by the fact that our God had arranged the meeting with Attun in such a remarkable way. Amrit and Jiwan, for their part, were greatly heartened by this clear sign that God was taking care to order every detail of their journey.

The meeting with Attun had aroused the policemen's interest in our religion, so Amrit and Jiwan each paired off with an officer and began to tell him about Christianity. The officer with the radio remained quite antagonistic, but the other officer kept saying over and over that he'd adopt this new religion on the spot if it wasn't for the fact he'd lose his job.

At each little village along the way people came out of their homes to watch us pass. Word of the funeral and our arrest had preceded us. We could hear the eagerly murmured speculations about how long the jail terms would be and about whether the hospital would be shut down. They were excited over the prospect of other arrests, of collecting together all the remaining Christians and packing them off to jail also. We thought of our Nepali brothers and sisters back in Amp Pipal, who even then, we knew, were fearing that they would be next.

Halfway on our journey to Gorkha we arrived at the Daraundi River and crossed over by a high, narrow suspension bridge. Because the rest of the trip would be a long, uphill climb to Gorkha in the heat of the day, the policemen elected to pause and have lunch in the town of Chepetar, situated just across the river. We were a little chagrined at this, because we knew our friends Megh Nath and Prakash were traveling by a slightly shorter and more direct route between Amp Pipal and Gorkha.

We were afraid that they might arrive in Gorkha ahead of us, not find us there, and return to Amp Pipal.

But there seemed no way to shorten our stay in Chepetar. The police were determined to rest and eat, so Amrit, Jiwan, and I decided that we might as well do likewise. So we sat down to wait for our meal in a corner of a teashop, each of us thinking of Megh Nath and Prakash getting closer and closer to Gorkha and wondering what they would do when they didn't find us.

As we waited, the three-year-old daughter of the proprietress overturned a basket of fresh buffalo manure just outside the entry into the tiny open cooking area. This was promptly tracked into the kitchen by her two-year-old brother, who then proceeded to play among the pots and pans and vegetables strewn about the dirty floor. As usual, the establishment was thick with flies swarming down on the plates and glasses, not as random stragglers but in squadrons, wave after wave.

When the food finally came, I had lost my appetite. But the boys and policemen ate heartily, mushing up the rice, lentils, and spicy vegetables together into a large mound in the middle of their plates and then thrusting great handfuls into their mouths without leaving so much as a kernel of rice on their chins or shirtfronts. Then, when the meal was over and we had just gotten up to leave, who should suddenly appear but Megh Nath and Prakash! They had taken the long way to Gorkha with the intention of meeting up with us right there in Chepetar. We all sat down again for one more round of refreshments, marveling at this further indication of the Lord's hand in our affairs. Half an hour later we were finally on our way, the policemen now getting a double earful of Christianity for the remaining three hours of our journey.

In the District Police Headquarters

*W*E *ARRIVED* in Gorkha at 3:30 in the afternoon. I told our policemen that I wanted to see the Chief District Officer (the governor) and the police inspector that very day, even if I had to go to their homes. I was not going to delay our business just because it was Saturday and all the offices were closed. I thought of the surgical patients who would be coming to the hospital the next day, and here I was tied up for an unknown period in the district capital. However, the police were less than enthusiastic about my demand and suggested that it wouldn't be prudent or even possible. Besides, they were only junior officers from a local station, and they were under orders to turn us directly over to the district police headquarters. They also advised Megh Nath and Prakash to make themselves scarce lest they too end up in jail. But our friends decided to linger discreetly in the general vicinity of the police station in case we had any urgent need of them.

After ostensibly parting company with Megh Nath and Prakash, we approached the large, four-story building that housed the jail, the police department, and the office of the Chief District Officer (CDO). We entered the building through a side door, fully expecting to be put into a little room with a couple of bunks and told we had to wait until the next day for the offices to open. We had no sooner walked in the door, however, when an officious-looking man recognized me (I think I had once operated on a member of his family) and motioned to me and the boys. Without so much as a moment's pause, he ushered us into a large, well-furnished office lined with couches and chairs. At one end of the room stood an imposing paper-strewn desk, on one corner of which sat a little calendar proclaiming the day's date to be *Chait* 8, 2037 (March 21, 1981). Two large, colored photographs of the King and Queen dressed in regal splendor gazed serenely down on us from one wall.

Two men were sitting at the far end of the office. To my astonishment, one of them was the Chief District Officer himself, whom I had met eight months earlier in Amp Pipal. I had no way of signaling to the boys that this was indeed the CDO; they probably assumed him to be some minor official hanging around a big office on a Saturday afternoon. The CDO's appearance and manner did nothing to suggest other-wise; he was short, slight, and a little stooped. As we exchanged the usual pleasantries, he spoke in a soft voice, both gracious and unpretentious. No one would have suspected that he was actually the highest official in the district.

The other man in the office couldn't have been more than thirty. I took him to be a junior clerk or assistant to the CDO. He was a chubby, pleasant-appearing fellow, with bright round eyes, and an open honest face that often broke into a good-natured smile. One of our two police escorts handed this man the sealed letter from the Thadipokhari police station and then withdrew, leaving us alone with the CDO and his jolly young colleague. The young man opened the envelope, and after reading the letter, passed it on to the CDO. As the CDO read it, his expression became somber. When he had finished he turned to me, as if I were the boys' guardian, and said with a tone of grave concern, "*Dharmik pariwartan* [religious conversion]."

So that was the charge against Amrit and Jiwan: they'd been born Nepalis and by law, therefore, they were Hindus. Now that they professed Christianity, there must have been some point at which they had *changed* their religion—and that was their crime.

From the outset it was clear that the CDO was not eager to press the full penalty of the law, which was a year's jail sentence. Speaking like a kind uncle, he tried to persuade Amrit and Jiwan to be reasonable, to renounce their Christian faith and thus avoid bringing unnecessary trouble upon themselves—and, of course, upon himself and the other officials who would have to prosecute them.

"What's wrong with our Hindu religion," he asked, "that you have to go following after some foreign religion?"

We had agreed among ourselves that Amrit should be our spokesman. Jiwan still chafed under this stricture, even though he knew that any impetuous outburst could land us all in a hotter kettle than we were already in. I had determined to say as little as possible so that I would in no way appear to be sponsoring or protecting the young brothers. This was their day, and it was important they stand on their own.

It was Amrit, therefore, who answered the CDO's opening question. "I don't want to criticize Hinduism, but I have met Jesus Christ, and through him I have received eternal life and forgiveness of my sins. Christ has also given me a peace so real that even now, having been brought to this police headquarters, I have no anxiety or fear; I know God is with me." Amrit spoke easily and naturally; perhaps it was an advantage not to know whom he was addressing. He went on to add that he really had known nothing but Christianity from his childhood up, so that it wasn't a question of his having deliberately rejected Hinduism anyway.

The CDO sat silently for some moments and then spoke earnestly but gently. "I don't see why you make so much of this religion. All religions are basically the same. They all point to one God. Religions are merely different paths to the same end. The only difference between Christianity and Hinduism is that in Christianity the path is easy, whereas in Hinduism the path is difficult, and great diligence and effort are required to reach its end." The CDO had indeed struck upon one of the fundamental differences between the two religions.

How Amrit would have replied we'll never know, for at that moment the doors of the office swung open and in strode a tall, thin, immaculately dressed gentleman, quite out of breath, but projecting an air of dignity and self-importance. Shooting knowing glances at the boys, he walked across the room and lowered himself onto the couch next to the CDO, carefully arranging his long limbs in a comfortable position. He sat for some moments taking us all in one by one, his head swiveling loosely about at the end of a remarkably elongated neck, which seemed to have more than the usual allotment of cervical vertebrae. He was dressed in the customary Nepali fashion: for trousers he wore a *suruwal*, a distinctive garment baggy in the seat and skintight from the knees down; on top he wore an undershirt; then a *daura*, a thick outer shirt tied snugly about the neck and extending halfway down the thighs; then a thicker vest; and finally, a heavy tweed sport coat—altogether an admirable outfit for a January stroll in the Scottish highlands but a trifle confining for that subtropical office, where the temperature was well above eighty degrees.

The CDO handed the tall gentleman the letter, which he read carefully, from time to time looking up and peering at us intently through his horn-rimmed glasses. As soon as he had put the letter down, he drew himself up, and without any preamble, launched into an impassioned speech about the virtues of Nepal, its constitution, and its religion. He lamented over the young people of today, who questioned the old traditions and rebeled against their elders. He explained how one born a Nepali was necessarily born a Hindu—that it was impossible legally for a Nepali to be a Christian—it was simply not recognized by the constitution. He finally wound up by saying, "Look at these two lovely boys! They shouldn't be here; they don't need to be here. Why should they go to jail for being something that it's impossible for them to be anyway?" As no one offered to answer his question, the tall gentleman ended his discourse and sat looking about him with a perplexed expression.

After a short silence I asked the gentleman what his position was. He replied that he was the government attorney for Gorkha District and was responsible for prosecuting our case. He then introduced the CDO, explaining to us that he was the highest official in the district. He then pointed to the pleasant, rosy-cheeked man and said, "This is the chief police inspector for the district. He is responsible for filing the formal charges in this case and will have custody of these boys until they are brought to trial."

The boys' mouths dropped open when they heard these introductions. It would have been hard enough to have arranged a meeting with just one of these men on a regular working day, let alone all three together on a Saturday afternoon—without so much as waiting ten seconds. Neither could these men have known we were coming on that particular day; there was no telephone communication between Thadipokhari and Gorkha. We never learned what the three officials were doing in the government office building on that Saturday afternoon. But one thing we knew: it was God who had arranged this meeting for His children. As Amrit said later: "From that moment on we knew beyond doubt that the Lord was in charge, whatever the outcome."

It was now the police inspector's turn to speak. He started out by reviewing the provisions of the constitution, a copy of which was located and passed around for us all to examine. It clearly stated in the religious section that no person born a Nepali could legally change religions; this was a crime against the state, punishable by one year in jail. If at the end of that time the offender should still profess his or her new religion, that person could be sentenced to an additional year in jail, and thus on and on indefinitely. The police inspector finished by urging the boys not to persist in their determination to be Christians—at least not openly. He didn't want to put them in jail—two such nice-looking boys. They could have been his own brothers the way he pleaded with them.

Amrit, who had been thumbing through the copy of the constitution that had been passed around, suddenly pointed out that this was the *old* constitution, not the revised constitution that had gone into effect four months earlier and had been heralded throughout the country as a compassionate and liberal document, free of the restrictive and archaic laws of the past. The prosecutor was clearly embarrassed by this disclosure; he fidgeted nervously and rearranged himself on the couch. The revised constitution was searched for. It was not in the office. It was not to be found in the entire building. The CDO muttered that the religious section hadn't changed anyway, so it didn't matter whether we found it or not. They decided to search again in the morning but in the meantime to proceed on the basis of the old constitution.

I then asked how a person brought up from childhood as a Christian by a Christian mother could be said to have "changed" religions by becoming a Christian. The inspector readily answered this objection by saying, "It's impossible for the mother to have been a Christian, so therefore the children can't have been born Christians either. There is no such thing as a Christian Nepali. Period."

Jiwan asked in a flash, "Why, then, in the 1980 census published in the *Gorkhapatra* [the national newspaper] are Christians listed as making up .04 percent of Nepal's population?"

The inspector and the prosecutor, evidently familiar with the census figures, each offered conflicting explanations for Jiwan's statistic, neither of which was acceptable to the other. Their dispute was finally terminated by the CDO who, impatiently waving his hand, said curtly, "You are both wrong. Those Christians aren't Nepalis; they are foreigners who have taken Nepali citizenship."

That answer was the least likely yet. There couldn't have been more than fifty foreign Christians (mostly Indian) who had taken Nepali citizenship, let alone 6,000—which was .04 percent of Nepal's population. I glared at Jiwan, fearing lest he tell the CDO to his face that his explanation was ridiculous.

The prosecutor by this time had recharged his rhetorical batteries and embarked on another dissertation on the wisdom of the constitution and the corresponding evil of deviating from that high standard by adopting another religion. He became increasingly agitated as he drew near the end of his speech. "To renounce Hinduism," he concluded, "is to betray the motherland, to trample on the honor of our forefathers. The evil, the shame, the—the—why, it will mean the whole undoing of our fabric of life, of Nepali civilization!"

Allowing a moment for the prosecutor to recover his composure, Amrit earnestly assured the three officials that he loved Nepal and had no desire to undermine its way of life. But he had known nothing but Christianity from his earliest memory. His mother had raised him as a Christian; she had sent him to Christian schools. There had been little chance even to learn about the Hindu religion; so that now if he were to profess Hinduism, *that* would be changing his religion and thus disobeying the constitution. "How is it possible for me to be anything other than a Christian? What could I have done differently? What have I done wrong?"

"Don't always talk about your mother," said the inspector. "You have a father, don't you? You've gone against him."

Amrit quickly produced the official paper, signed and stamped in that very building years before, granting to his mother a divorce on the grounds of cruelty and neglect. Amrit then movingly recounted in vivid detail the sufferings that his mother had endured at the hands of his father. He explained how he had never even known who his father was until a year before, when he had been introduced to him for the first time.

The inspector, obviously touched by the boys' predicament, said sympathetically, "Look, I understand your situation. But let's not make a big thing of it. We don't want to put you in jail. We can forget about your father. But we're stuck with this constitution. If you insist on saying you are Christians, we can't help but do as the law demands. Let's write out a little statement saying that you are not Christians and will not preach the Christian religion. Then you sign the statement, and the whole thing will be finished. How about it?"

Amrit said, "I'm sorry, but I can't do that. It would be a lie. It would be a sin against God. It would dishonor the memory of my mother and bring to naught her prayers for me all these years."

Jiwan said simply, "I won't sign any such paper."

The inspector shook his head in perplexity. "Do you know what you're saying? It's not just the year in jail, but it's the stigma that will remain for the rest of your lives. Your lives will be ruined. You won't be able to get a job anywhere; you'll be outcasts. Already you have no mother or father. You'll have no future either. You won't be allowed to continue your studies. Is your religion really that important to you?"

Both the CDO and the prosecutor chimed in with pleas for the boys to consider what they were throwing away. They encouraged the boys to sign the paper and the whole case would be dropped. Over and over they reiterated how they hated the thought of putting such lovely, sweet boys in jail.

Jiwan looked anything but sweet. "If the prospect of putting us in jail is so unpleasant to you," he said, "why have you brought charges against us in the first place?"

I broke the tense silence by asking who had filed the charges.

The inspector indicated that the police had filed the charges. "It's a police case, arising from the great commotion occasioned by their mother's funeral service. We received many complaints from the community, and we had to investigate. It's our duty to do so, whether or not the case is personally appealing to us."

It was a reasonable answer, so I said nothing more. It wasn't reasonable to Jiwan, however, who asked why Christians in Gorkha District should be so harassed when in Kathmandu they were free to gather by the hundreds in numerous congregations, to profess their faith openly, to hold public meetings, to start a Bible school, to set up a Christian printing press—all without persecution. "Why, even on Radio Nepal it was announced recently that Jesus Christ was the Light of the World."

The inspector replied testily that this was Gorkha District and not Kathmandu and that he was not to mention Kathmandu again.

"What's this," Jiwan shot back. "Do we have two laws, two constitutions? One for Kathmandu and one for Gorkha?"

Amrit and I glared fiercely at Jiwan, who having won his point was content to be silent.

The CDO, managing to remain patient and fatherly, made one final attempt to persuade the boys to sign a statement denying they were Christians. He was clearly seeking to escape the predicament of having to enforce the law under such circumstances. Perhaps he feared the adverse publicity that would surely result if the boys were prosecuted. After the CDO had spoken, Amrit and Jiwan politely repeated that they could not sign such a statement. With that, the CDO excused himself from the meeting, saying to the prosecutor on his way out: "Keep trying. The constitution has left us in a mess. We can't prosecute them, and we can't not prosecute them. Why is the thing worded that way, anyway?"

Try, the prosecutor did. Rotating his head back and forth on his long neck as if he were winding himself up, he settled his gaze on each one of us in turn and proceeded to deliver a long and impassioned speech, surpassing even his previous efforts. He went on and on about the pity, the futility of these boys bringing this unnecessary trouble upon themselves. "For what? If in life you meet a concrete blockade, you don't go through it—you go around it. You compromise. Principles are fine—in their place. Their place is in one's heart—not necessarily in one's actions."

This line of reasoning was seasoned with many Hindu parables and proverbs, which provided an interesting glimpse of Hindu belief and practice in Nepal. The prosecutor's performance was forever building to a climax, like an unending theme from a Wagner opera. He would rise from his seat, flourish his arms, and then sit down again, only to rise once more for the next aria. At the end, he sank down onto the couch and said, "Well, are you ready to sign a statement?"

Amrit looked the prosecutor in the face and replied, "We can't sign. It would be agreeing to a lie. We can't go against our conscience."

This answer, though spoken softly and meekly, incensed the prosecutor. He bounced up like a coiled spring and said in a voice filled with anger, "Are you so holy that you cannot lie? Are you so great and good? Who do you think you are, anyway? Gods? I'm just an inferior sort of person compared to you, I see. I lie whenever I please—my principles are phony, I suppose. Our Hindu customs are too low for you, you holy people."

Here he abruptly stopped and looked at me, as if suddenly recalling that I was there. His manner changed, and he began to wring his hands and lament the predicament the boys were putting him in, how unfair, how unreasonable they were being. Then, struck by a new idea, he said to me, "You've got to persuade them. They'll listen to you. You don't want to see them go to jail. Do something—anything—to convince them. Help us out!"

I was not disposed to be helpful. I said, "I don't believe they can be persuaded to sign. Jesus said, 'Whoever acknowledges me before men, I will also acknowledge him before my Father in heaven. But whoever disowns me before men, I will disown him before my Father in heaven.' These boys would rather go to jail than disown their Lord."

The prosecutor turned to the police inspector with a grimace of despair. "This doctor is ruining everything. Why did he have to be here?" A question, indeed, I had pondered myself.

The police inspector now spoke up. He allowed that Christianity was an excellent religion and described how in his youth he had attended some Christian meetings in Kathmandu and had been impressed and intrigued by what he heard. He could understand how one could be attracted to this religion—he felt attracted to it himself. He complained of the unreasonable wording of the constitution that seemed to provide no avenue of escape, either for the boys or for himself. But he concluded with the thought that Christianity was a Western religion, that it was foreign to Nepal and that Nepalis had an obligation to at least outwardly practice their own national religion. That had been his own experience, and he didn't see why it couldn't be the same for Amrit and Jiwan.

Amrit replied that Christianity was not a Western religion but had started in Asia. Furthermore, he and his brother had not changed to a foreign religion; they had never known anything but Christianity from their childhood up. Amrit repeated how he had gone only to mission schools, so that as he grew older, Christianity, instead of decreasing in influence over him, had actually increased its hold on him. "What can I do?" he said. "To me, it is Hinduism that is the foreign religion."

The prosecutor's testiness was exacerbated by Amrit's mention of mission schools, and my presence did nothing to inhibit the resulting outburst directed against the United Mission to Nepal. "Here's a perfect example for you," he began, pointing his long finger at me. "The mission has been subverting our culture and religion from the beginning. They have come in the guise of 'serving the people,' but what do they serve but their own ends? 'Oh, we'll just run schools and hospitals,' they say; but instead, they secretly make Christians. It was a terrible mistake to let them into the country in the first place. Look at all the trouble we've been having. Christians are rising up everywhere."

The decidedly nasty tone of his denunciation impelled me, wisely or not, to attempt to set the record straight concerning the United Mission. First of all, I explained, the mission had started work in Nepal at the invitation of the government. "We've never disguised the fact that we are a Christian mission. Our own constitution states clearly that our purpose is to minister to the people of Nepal in the name and spirit of Jesus Christ and to witness to him in both word and life. The government was told from the beginning that wherever a Christian mission works, Christians will rise up. It is inevitable." I went on to say that it wasn't missionaries or missions that created Christians or "subverted" Nepali culture and religion; it was the work of God's Spirit, and no person could either produce that result or, for that matter, prevent it. "The only restriction we have agreed to," I said, "is that we won't preach publicly or entice people to become Christians by the offer of material benefits. But a vital part of the practice of our religion is witnessing personally to our faith, to what God has done for us, to who Jesus is and why we serve him. We have received eternal life and the forgiveness of sins, and any man or woman who puts faith in Christ can receive the same. If I have found such a wonderful blessing, am I not obligated to share it with others? Why should I withhold from you the opportunity of obtaining peace with God and eternal life with him in heaven?"

There was a long silence. Then Amrit felt led to say, "You see, we know Jesus personally, in the Spirit. He is real to us. He is alive. He isn't just some principle we believe in, or some idea or philosophy. He is God's own Son, who is living now, and who lives in us."

"Bah!" exclaimed the prosecutor. "What's all this talk about spirits? Who is Jesus? Why, there are spirits everywhere, all kinds of them—here—there. Now one's here; now it's there. Where is your Jesus? What kind of stuff are you telling us? Do you suppose we don't know all about spirits? Where's your Jesus anyway?"

"He's here in this room," I said.

The prosecutor shot a hard, disbelieving look at me but said nothing. After about a minute, he turned aside to the inspector and muttered, "I told you we shouldn't have had this doctor here. He's messed up everything."

Jiwan broke the silence with a question addressed to me. "If you have agreed not to preach, Doctor, why have you come to Nepal?"

The prosecutor and the inspector looked at me expectantly and with obvious curiosity, as if a mystery that had long puzzled them was about to be solved. My answer came effortlessly, as had most of our conversation during the past twenty-four hours. I started with what Jesus had done in my own life, how he had called me to go to Nepal as a doctor. I told them about the two great commandments, about what it means to love God with one's whole heart and soul and mind, and to love one's neighbor as oneself. I said that the people of Nepal were our neighbors. I explained that it was God's love that motivated us to work in Nepal and that when people saw that love, they were naturally attracted to such a God. It wasn't even necessary to preach. I finished by saying that, in fact, all the members of the United Mission had come to Nepal for the same basic reason: to demonstrate God's love.

Amrit said, "We have understood the teachings of Christianity from their lives; they would not have had to say a word."

"That's right," Jiwan added. "Actions are more important

than words. What we are on the inside has got to show on the outside. Christians do good works. Running hospitals and healing sickness you agree are good things. To help educate our people and develop our country you say is a good thing. To show love is a good thing. Then how can people that do such things be harmful for our country? How can their religion be so bad if it leads them to do what you agree is good?"

The police inspector quickly asserted that they had nothing to say against Christianity or Christians and that if it hadn't been for the wording of the constitution they wouldn't be in the position of having to prosecute them.

The prosecutor puckered up his face in disgust, as if he considered the inspector's remarks far too conciliatory. Then in a final effort to reverse the unfavorable turn in the conversation and put an end to the silly and idealistic notions to which the boys were so stubbornly clinging, he rose to his feet once more and began to restate and summarize the government's case in a manner both dramatic and compelling. It wasn't for nothing that he had gotten his job. He presented to the boys' imagination in the most vivid terms the consequences of their going to jail. He unblinkingly described the distressing conditions in Nepal's prisons. He contrasted the boys' present, bright prospects as educated Nepalis with the gloom and despair that awaited them after their imprisonment—the shattered hopes and dreams, the rejection of friends, the contempt of society. They'd be outcasts, jobless, and destitute. Who would care for them then? Why, even now they were orphans. And then, if that were not enough to bring them to their senses, what were they going to do after the year's sentence was up—would they then renounce their Christ, or did they plan to spend an endless succession of years in prison?

With a grim smile of triumph, the prosecutor ended his speech and resettled himself in his seat. Then, squinting at the boys through his thick glasses, he said sharply: "This is your last chance to save yourselves from ruin. What is your answer? Will you sign a statement or not?"

Several minutes passed in silence. Amrit and Jiwan continued staring without expression at the floor in front of them. The inspector and the prosecutor watched them quietly and waited.

Finally Amrit looked up at me and said, "What do you advise, Doctor?"

"Oh, don't ask him!" snapped the prosecutor. "This is your matter, not his. Make up your own mind."

Amrit kept looking at me as if expecting some response or signal. I said, "It's best I don't tell you what to do. The Holy Spirit will show you; listen to him."

Jiwan had bowed his head; I thought he was praying. I did the same. After what seemed like an age, I heard Amrit's soft but steady voice: "We will not sign. We will go to jail."

There followed a brief conversation between the inspector and the prosecutor about how they should proceed. The prosecutor complained that it was hopeless to get anywhere with the doctor present, and if he could only be dismissed they might then be able to intimidate the brothers into signing the statement. The prosecutor asked, "Why did the doctor have to come anyway? Has he been charged with something?"

The inspector called to an assistant to find the charges against me, which had apparently arrived in a separate document. This was duly produced and handed to the prosecutor. Upon reading it, his aspect abruptly changed, and in an apologetic tone he exclaimed, "This is terrible. These charges are without substance."

"What are the charges?" I asked with interest.

"First, that you refused to give the body of Moti Maya to the former husband, and second, that you arranged for a Christian funeral service at the hospital."

The charges were indeed untrue. I explained that I hadn't even been at the hospital when the husband had come and I had taken no part in the planning of the funeral.

"Exactly," said the prosecutor. "This is terribly embarrassing." Turning to the inspector with a look of reproach, he said, "Imagine, calling the doctor himself and making him go to Thadipokhari and then come all the way over here. We have been persecuting him. It's disgraceful." Then, turning back to me, he said with evident sincerity, "We are very, very sorry. Please forgive us. This is awful. There was no senior or responsible official at Thadipokhari; that's the reason. If someone responsible had been there, this would never have happened."

Then the prosecutor called for his scribe, a young man who appeared somewhat new to his job. As soon as the scribe had readied himself, the prosecutor proceeded to dictate a long, flowery statement about my involvement in the case. The scribe had some difficulty in the beginning over the spelling of my name, but this was minor compared to his struggles over my address—Loudonville, New York. After several false starts and as many new sheets of paper, the prosecutor launched into the body of the statement. He used a large number of obscure and complicated legal terms over which the young scribe repeatedly stumbled, provoking the prosecutor to inquire irritably if they were going to be writing this thing all night. I didn't help to speed up the process, as I felt obliged myself to understand what I would have to sign in the end; and this necessitated my asking the meanings of numerous expressions and disputing several points with which I could not agree. Finally to the relief of all, I signed in the three or four indicated places, thus ending our five-hour session and my role in the affair.

As we all got up to go, the prosecutor resumed his apologies and thanked me for so graciously overlooking their shortcomings. I assured him that I felt in no way discomfited and that I considered it a privilege to have been able to take part in this case.

As we were about to leave, Megh Nath and Prakash, who had been waiting outside, suddenly came into the office. I was momentarily anxious lest they say anything imprudent and become entangled themselves in the religious provisions of the constitution. However, they no sooner entered the room than all restraint seemed to vanish, and we were emboldened to announce to those present that we were going to pray aloud to our God. I can't recall who prayed what, but together we called upon God to put forth his hand on this place and reveal His mighty power, to cause justice to be done, and to cause His name and the names of His children to be honored in this district. We claimed the sovereignty of God over all the authorities of Gorkha District and committed Amrit and Jiwan into the hands of the Righteous Judge who would vindicate the innocent and make His enemies to tremble. And then, to the stunned silence of those looking on, we walked euphorically out of the office, as if the prayer had already been answered. Accompanied by two policemen, Amrit and Jiwan went to a hotel, while Megh Nath, Prakash, and I went to the house of Moti Maya's brother, where we were to spend the night.

Just before breaking up, however, we made the following plan for the morning: I was to leave at daybreak for Amp Pipal, as surgical emergencies might have arrived during my unexpected absence; Megh Nath, as soon as the final verdict was known, was to go immediately to Kathmandu to inform the officers of the Nepal Christian Fellowship responsible for looking after the concerns of Christians who landed in jail; and at the same time, Prakash was to return to Amp Pipal with news of what had happened. One other important matter for the morning was to locate a copy of the revised constitution, to see if by any chance a loophole could be found through which the boys might escape imprisonment.

That evening we were guests of honor at the house of Moti Maya's brother, a prosperous former Gurkha soldier. The meal was lavishly seasoned for the occasion by Nepal's finest and hottest spices, whose effect on my tongue was still present next morning. I left for Amp Pipal before dawn, arriving at the hospital at midday in the midst of the usual busy Sunday clinic. Fortunately no surgical emergencies had arisen, and no one had suffered from my absence.

I had been back about an hour when I received word that a delegation of local community leaders, reinforced by a larger delegation of high-school students, was coming to question me about our religious activities at the hospital, especially in connection with Moti Maya's funeral. Word that I was back had quickly spread, and since it appeared that the police had dropped their case against me, the community had decided to take matters into their own hands in an effort to put a stop to our "Christian activities."

A very earnest but generally amicable meeting was held in the hospital prayer room, amidst tables and shelves piled with tracts, hymn books, and other literature. The group consisted of the headmaster of the Amp Pipal High School, several other teachers, and a number of prominent local citizens. We also invited the leader of the student union to attend the meeting, thereby mollifying his restless cohorts, who agreed to wait quietly outside the hospital until the outcome of the meeting should be known.

The group was concerned that young people were becoming Christians, families were being split up, sons were refusing to perform Hindu funeral rites for their fathers, and old beliefs and values were being eroded by this foreign religion. They were chiefly disturbed by the many Nepalis who, in their estimation, only pretended to be Christians in order to get jobs with the mission. In contrast, they expressed great admiration for Amrit and Jiwan, whom they considered to be true Christians, as evidenced by their willingness to go to jail for their beliefs.

They wanted to know how many of our hospital staff had been enticed to change their religion by the prospect of material gain. I told them that we had never enticed anyone to change religions, and that we were even more desirous than they that there be no false Christians. "In fact," I said, "if someone starts coming to church or to a Bible study, we are immediately wary lest it only be to get a job; and should such a person ask for work, he or she would never get it."

They seemed relieved to hear this, but they again insisted on knowing who on the hospital staff were Christians. "I won't give you their names," I said. "You know who they are. They don't hide anything. Our meetings are open, and anyone is welcome. Come yourselves and listen to what goes on and see who is there. As for the false Christians you talk about, I'm afraid I don't know who they are; and if I did, I'd have nothing to do with them."

They wanted to know if we preached at the hospital. I said we didn't, except for a couple of times a year when we might put on a special service. "We hold daily prayers in this room." I added, "because it is through prayer to the living God that this hospital keeps running and patients keep getting well."

They wanted to know if we talked to patients about Christianity. I said we did, that it was part of the treatment of many kinds of illness. If we knew the source of spiritual peace and wholeness, were we not obliged to share this with our patients? My answer didn't satisfy them completely, as they felt that Hinduism offered the same advantages; but they didn't pursue the matter further.

Basically, the community wanted our good works without our religion. I told them that that wasn't possible—that our good works resulted from our religion, and it was impossible to separate them. I said that this was a Christian hospital, that those running it were Christians, and that many patients who came to the hospital would inevitably hear about Jesus Christ and be attracted to him. If the community didn't want that, then perhaps we'd better pack up and go.

Oh, no, that wasn't what they were after. They wanted us very much to stay. They asked only that we not use the hospital to preach to captive audiences and to pressure dependent and impressionable patients into accepting Christianity. I assured them that that was neither our practice nor our desire.

The meeting broke up with the headmaster thanking me for being sensitive to their concerns and saying that most of the critical issues had been answered satisfactorily. When the leader of the student union rejoined his impatiently waiting comrades, he said to them simply: "The doctor answered all their questions, and no one had anything to say in reply. The matter is finished." The students, finding themselves without a cause to champion, drifted slowly off. Today, it is worth adding, that student leader is a Christian himself.

Only after the meeting was over did I have a chance to relate to members of the church what had taken place in Gorkha the day before. Helen and Cynthia were still trying to get through the busy clinic, so I first looked up Chandra Bahadur, the paraplegic who served as the chairman of our church committee. After I'd finished giving a complete account of the meeting with the CDO, the inspector, and the prosecutor, concluding on the pessimistic note that I saw no chance of the brothers escaping a jail sentence, Chandra looked at me and said, as if he hadn't listened to a word I'd been saying, "They'll be back tonight. I know it. I have complete faith they'll arrive tonight."

"Who will arrive?"

"All of them."

"Amrit and Jiwan too?" I asked. "Do you mean you think they'll sign that paper?"

"Oh, no. I don't think that. But they'll be here tonight. You wait and see."

I shrugged my shoulders and said something about God getting glory whether or not they were released. But Chandra shook his head. "No," he said, "God will get more glory from their release."

Right after supper I phoned Helen to tell her about our recent adventures. Just as I was telling her that the boys most likely would be spending a year in jail, someone else picked up a phone and tried to interrupt our conversation. Helen told the person to please call back later, but the intruder persisted. It was Else, the German schoolteacher, who lived up on top of the ridge near the Amp Pipal High School. She said, "They've all just gotten back. They'll be down at the hospital in twenty minutes."

"Who's gotten back?" asked Helen and I in one breath.

"All four of them. Amrit, Jiwan, Megh Nath, and Prakash."

"Are they free?"

"Yes, of course they're free. Prakash says to tell his wife to put on some supper for them."

Word was quickly passed on to the members of the church that a meeting for praise and thanksgiving would be held at Prakash's house as soon as people could get there. I had the supreme pleasure of going down to tell the news to Chandra in his room at the hospital. He had been plagued for weeks with tuberculous iritis, amoebic hepatitis, and repeated urinary tract infections, as if being paralyzed from the waist down were not enough of a thorn in the flesh. The medications had left him almost constantly nauseated, and he had been losing weight steadily. I had hardly seen him smile in weeks. But when I told him that all four boys were back, the room couldn't contain the joy he expressed. Without delay, we arranged for him to be carried to Prakash's house, where a very joyful meeting was soon under way.

Singing, prayer, and praise to God for what he had done were interspersed with accounts from Amrit and Jiwan. They related how that morning the inspector and the prosecutor had resumed their efforts to persuade them to sign a statement denying their faith. The two officials seemed more eager than ever to find a way to avoid the unpleasant consequences of a trial and jail sentence. They had found a copy of the new constitution, but the wording of the religious section was found to be unchanged.

After two or three hours of getting nowhere, Amrit repeated, for perhaps the tenth time, that he hadn't changed his religion. Then, in a flash, he added, "I'll sign a statement saying that much."

"You will?" asked the prosecutor.

"Sure," replied Amrit.

"So will I," said Jiwan.

"Ah-ha!" cried the prosecutor. "That's it!"

"What are you talking about?" asked the inspector.

"That's it," repeated the prosecutor jumping up. "That's all we need. If there has been no change in their religion, then technically there has been no violation of the constitution. We don't have to specify what their religion is. The law only recognizes Hindu Nepalis. There is no such thing as a Christian Nepali. Therefore, all they have to do is sign a statement saying they haven't changed their religion, and the constitution is satisfied, we are satisfied, and they are satisfied."

The inspector assented at once and called for the young scribe. This time his task was simpler; the statement said only: "We have not changed our religion." Amrit and Jiwan both signed and were free.

But not quite. Suddenly the inspector thought of an additional technicality. He was eager to cover himself lest later on someone accuse him of excessive leniency or even of bypassing the law and thwarting justice. "There must be a *jamanat* for each of them," he declared, "someone willing to stand responsible for their behavior and, if need be, to go to jail in their place if further charges are brought against them and they can't be found."

Jiwan immediately said, "We have two friends who would be happy to take responsibility for us. They are waiting outside."

"Go and call them," said the inspector.

Megh Nath and Prakash had indeed been waiting just outside the office all morning, but when Jiwan went out to call them, they were nowhere to be seen. Jiwan came back in to say he couldn't find them. After a few minutes of discussion between the inspector and the prosecutor, the inspector finally said, "Well, never mind. It probably isn't necessary anyway. Just go on now. You are free. Only don't go around preaching and get us all into trouble again."

The boys nodded their heads, said good-bye, and walked out of the office into the arms of Megh Nath and Prakash, who had just returned after a momentary absence. Within minutes they were out of town and on the trail back to Amp Pipal, stopping only long enough to give the good news to the boys' uncle, at whose house Megh Nath, Prakash, and I had spent the night.

The release of Amrit and Jiwan created a sensation throughout the whole community. Those who had been raising their voices against the church were silenced. The Christians, for their part, were encouraged and emboldened. Several young men, previously secretly interested in the Gospel, began coming openly to meetings.

Chandra had been right. He said to me several days afterwards: "I told you God would get more glory if Amrit and Jiwan were set free."

A week later Amrit received a letter from Attun in Pokhara. It described how Attun, after the remarkable meeting early Saturday morning on the little side trail near Thadipokhari, had hurried on to Pokhara, reaching his home that same evening. On Sunday he had gone to the police headquarters to look for Amrit and Jiwan's great uncle, who was the police inspector for the Pokhara region. Finding him in his office, Attun recounted, to the old man's surprise and dismay, the circumstances surrounding the sudden death of his niece and the subsequent arrest of her sons. At 2:00 P.M., the great uncle was able to make direct phone contact with the Gorkha police inspector, who informed him that Amrit and Jiwan had just been released. This news was passed on to Attun, who immediately informed the many members of the Pokhara church who had been praying earnestly for the boys ever since Attun's arrival the evening before. As Amrit finished reading us the letter, he said, shaking his head in wonder, "So the Pokhara Christians fifty miles away found out what happened hours before the Amp Pipal Church did. The telephone is really an amazing invention."

AFTERWORD

WHEN I REFLECT on the lives of Amrit and Jiwan, I am awed by the extent of their commitment to Christ, by the extent to which they were willing to sacrifice themselves for Him. Communist young people sacrifice themselves in hope of creating a better life on earth; Muslim young people sacrifice themselves to find a better life in heaven. But Amrit and Jiwan were ready to sacrifice themselves because of their love for a Person—Jesus Christ.

In a way, it's pointless to ask oneself, "What would I have done if I'd been in their place?" We cannot know. God's grace would have been sufficient, but would we have availed ourselves of it?

Yet, even though our circumstances are so different, we find ourselves inspired and challenged by the lives of Amrit and Jiwan. The distant and long-dead heroes of the faith may inspire us still, but in our experience our contemporaries—especially those who are our juniors—inspire us even more. Amrit and Jiwan knew Jesus intimately; I could see it. Did I know Him as well? Did I love Him as deeply?

Friends tell us: "What a great sacrifice you have made going to Nepal." And, I suppose, from their perspective we have. We have had to give up some things that they deem valuable. Yet, in fact, we've made no sacrifice; it's no sacrifice to give up things you do not value. Instead, in Nepal we have gone from blessing to blessing (albeit, with a few downward blips along the way). We have received infinitely more than we have given up. We've never even had the chance to really suffer for Christ.

Yet Amrit and Jiwan were given that chance; they were given the chance to prove their love for Him. They are modern-day examples of those early New Testament Christians who rejoiced "because they had been counted worthy of suffering disgrace for the Name" (Acts 5:41). We are thankful to God for the example of Amrit and Jiwan. We pray that when our time to sacrifice for Jesus comes, we will have the grace to follow in their steps.

There is a danger, however, in regarding Amrit and Jiwan as exceptions. All Christians are called to love their Lord and sacrifice their lives for Him. There are thousands of other Christians in Nepal, and hundreds of thousands around the world, who are daily sacrificing their lives for Christ. For them, sacrifice is not the exception but the rule.

And yet, when the sacrifice is made, it doesn't seem like a sacrifice at all. David Livingstone, the famous missionary explorer of Africa, was once asked how he could make such a great sacrifice—that of spending his entire life in the jungles of Africa. He said, "Sacrifice? I never made a sacrifice. It is no sacrifice to serve the Lord Jesus Christ. Rather, it is the highest privilege any man or woman could ever ask for."

May that be true for each of us.